AF798969

Using R for Trade Policy Analysis

Massimiliano Porto

Using R for Trade Policy Analysis

R Codes for the UNCTAD and WTO Practical Guide

Second Edition

Springer

Massimiliano Porto
Ritsumeikan Asia Pacific University
Beppu, Japan

ISBN 978-3-031-35043-6 ISBN 978-3-031-35044-3 (eBook)
https://doi.org/10.1007/978-3-031-35044-3

© The Editor(s) (if applicable) and The Author(s), under exclusive license to Springer Nature Switzerland AG 2020, 2023
This work is subject to copyright. All rights are solely and exclusively licensed by the Publisher, whether the whole or part of the material is concerned, specifically the rights of translation, reprinting, reuse of illustrations, recitation, broadcasting, reproduction on microfilms or in any other physical way, and transmission or information storage and retrieval, electronic adaptation, computer software, or by similar or dissimilar methodology now known or hereafter developed.
The use of general descriptive names, registered names, trademarks, service marks, etc. in this publication does not imply, even in the absence of a specific statement, that such names are exempt from the relevant protective laws and regulations and therefore free for general use.
The publisher, the authors, and the editors are safe to assume that the advice and information in this book are believed to be true and accurate at the date of publication. Neither the publisher nor the authors or the editors give a warranty, expressed or implied, with respect to the material contained herein or for any errors or omissions that may have been made. The publisher remains neutral with regard to jurisdictional claims in published maps and institutional affiliations.

This Springer imprint is published by the registered company Springer Nature Switzerland AG
The registered company address is: Gewerbestrasse 11, 6330 Cham, Switzerland

Preface to the Second Edition

When we first approach empirical analysis and we are about to estimate our first model, we may think that the toughest part is the estimation. Actually, that is not the case unless we decide to program the econometric model from scratch. But again this is not the case for most of us because, regardless the software or programming language we use, we just end up passing the names of variables to a ready-to-use function. Therefore, I may say that from an estimation point of view, the challenge is theoretical, i.e., it concerns the specification of the model and the interpretation of the results.

The real tough part, in my opinion, consists in building those variables that we want to pass to the model. We will have data from different sources that come with different formats and shapes that we want to put together. Then, we may want to generate additional variables for our analysis. These are kinds of operations that we cannot fully automatize yet. Furthermore, data building is key for our analysis because the model can be theoretically well specified, but if we pass wrong data, the results will be simply incorrect.

In this context, I want to mention the book by the UNCTAD & WTO, *A Practical Guide to Trade Policy Analysis* that is at the base of this book.[1] The book by the UNCTAD & WTO is a perfect combination of theory, econometric analysis, and practice to analyze trade policies. Even though there are now several books dealing with theory and analysis with a programming language, I still think that this book is unique in this genre of books because the UNCTAD & WTO's team provide raw data files and best practices for building the database for the analysis from scratch in Stata.

As I immediately realized the value of the UNCTAD & WTO's book, I thought that the same approach with the **R** programming language would be useful for students and professionals. I take this opportunity to thank the WTO for granting me permission to use some of their data sets to produce this book.

[1] Visit https://www.wto.org/english/res_e/publications_e/practical_guide12_e.htm to download the book.

This book is a second edition. The reasons for publishing a second edition are mainly two. First, the WTO has changed the location of the files to download that are used in this book. Therefore, the link to the data files in the first edition is not working anymore. Second, some **R** functions used in the first edition are deprecated functions. Therefore, it was necessary to replace the link to the data and those deprecated functions.

However, these are not the only two changes I have made to this second edition. While reading again the first edition, I was thinking how I could provide more value to a reader who is approaching **R** for the first time.

Even though I placed an appendix in the first edition with some basic information regarding **R**, I realize that that information is not enough for a beginner given that the book immediately starts with some advanced operations. Therefore, the first main modification is that I replaced the appendix in the first edition with the current Chap. 1. Chapter 1 is mainly based on the corresponding chapter of my previous book *Introduction to Mathematics for Economics with R*.[2] However, some modifications were made. A few modifications were necessary because of the different project (e.g., the working directory, the packages used) and purpose of the book (the introduction to the `apply()` family functions was moved from the exercise section in that book to Sect. 1.6.6). Then, I provide more detail about *vectorization* in Sect. 1.6.6. On the other hand, Sects. 1.7.2 and 1.8 are completely new. Section 1.7.2 is about data management operations. I show alternatives to accomplish a same task in **R** that mainly use base **R** functions, functions from the `tidyr` and `dplyr` packages, and functions from the `data.table` package. You may choose the functions you are more comfortable with to replicate the chapters in the book. Section 1.8 shows how to download, unzip, create directories, and copy files by using solely **R**. Note that to follow along, you have to set up the **R** project as shown in Sect. 1.3.1.

In Chaps. 2, 3, and 4, some modifications consist in code simplification, removal of typos, and a correction of code. Main modifications concern data visualization in Chaps. 2 and 3. Figure 2.3 now shows in the second panel how to zoom-in in a plot with `ggplot2` while Fig. 2.8 has been turned dynamic (in the book it is printed the static version). Chapter 3 is where I divert more from the original Stata script and from the first edition of this book in terms of plotting. I may be wrong but I think that econometricians fail to data scientists in presenting the output. That is, econometricians mainly present static output while data scientists build app and dashboard where the user can interact with the results. By using **R**, we can easily go beyond static output. Therefore, in Chap. 3, we will learn how to make interactive plots. Additionally, we will build an interactive dashboard with **R Shiny** to present some of the results from Sect. 3.1. However, since **R Shiny** requires a bit of a different mindset with respect to the standard **R** code, we will build it in Appendix A.

[2] Porto (2022). https://link.springer.com/book/10.1007/978-3-031-05202-6.

Finally, the code is printed with a new colored style to make it more pleasant and easy to read.

Ad maiora

Beppu, Japan Massimiliano Porto

Contents

List of Figures

List of Tables

Chapter 1
Introduction to R

This chapter introduces the reader to **R** (R Core Team, 2020) and **RStudio** (RStudio Team, 2020). The **R** version used in this book is 4.0.2. You can retrieve the version info by typing `sessionInfo()` in the console pane (Sect. 1.3). Following I print the first lines of the output of `sessionInfo()` in my console pane[1]

```
> sessionInfo()
R version 4.0.2 (2020-06-22)
Platform: x86_64-w64-mingw32/x64 (64-bit)
Running under: Windows 10 x64 (build 19042)
```

The **RStudio** version used in this book is 1.3.1056. You can retrieve this info by typing the following command in the console pane

```
> rstudioapi::versionInfo()$version
[1] '1.3.1056'
```

Note that even though you use a different version of **R** and **RStudio**, you can still run the code in this book. However, you may observe slight differences in the output. In Sect. 1.6.5, I will discuss a main difference if you use an **R** version before 4.0.0.

1.1 Installing R

R can be installed on different operating system such as Windows, Mac and Linux. The reader is referred to the Comprehensive R Archive Network (CRAN) (http://cran.r-project.org) for the instructions to install **R**.

If you have Windows, you may refer to:
https://cran.r-project.org/bin/windows/base/

[1] Do not write > because it is not part of the code—we will return to > in Sect. 1.5.1.

© The Author(s), under exclusive license to Springer Nature Switzerland AG 2023

M. Porto, *Using R for Trade Policy Analysis*,
https://doi.org/10.1007/978-3-031-35044-3_1

If you have Mac, you may refer to:
https://cran.r-project.org/bin/macosx/

1.2 Installing RStudio

RStudio is an integrated development environment (IDE) that makes easier to work with **R**. You can download **RStudio Desktop** from the following website:
https://posit.co/download/rstudio-desktop/

1.3 Introduction to RStudio

Figure 1.1 shows the interface of **RStudio**. It is divided in 4 panes:

1. **Console pane**: the console pane (1 in Fig. 1.1) is where you write your code, called **command** in **R language**.
2. **Environment/History pane**: in the environment/history pane (2 in Fig. 1.1) you can see all the objects you create in **R** and the history of your commands.
3. **Files, plots, packages,.. pane**: the pane number 3 in Fig. 1.1 is where you find your files, the packages you can install to improve the capabilities of **R**, where you can visualize the plots you create etc.
4. **Source pane**: the source pane (4 in Fig. 1.1) provides you different ways to write and save your code.

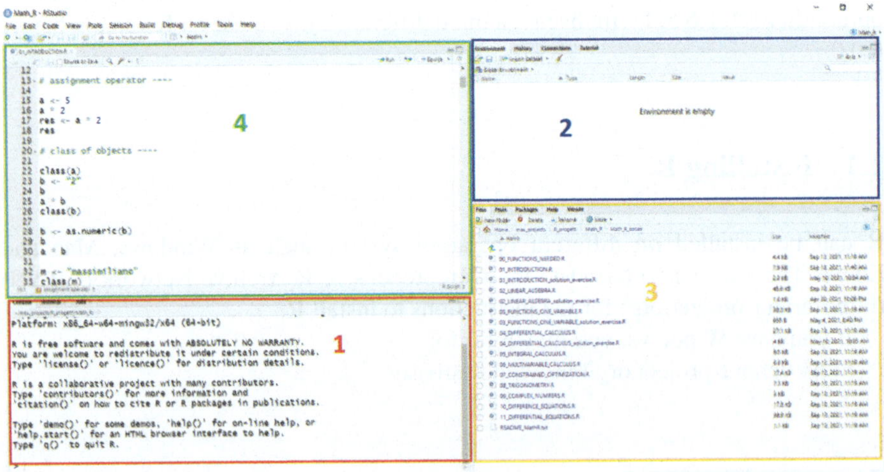

Fig. 1.1 RStudio interface

1.3.1 Launching a New Project

A project is a place to store your work on a particular topic (or project). To create a project follow the procedure as in Figs. 1.2, 1.3, and 1.4.

Click on the **R** symbol in the top hand right corner, click **New Directory** > **New Project** and then write the directory name (`WTO_R` for this book) and click **Create project**.[2]

I strongly recommend creating projects whenever you start what you consider a new project, not related to previous projects. For example, observe Fig. 1.5. This figure tells us that currently I am in the working directory `WTO_R`. You can see that I have other projects—for example a project about Econometrics in **R**, a project about creating interactive dashboards in **R** with Shiny and so on. Those projects are not related. Therefore, for each of them I created a project. For example, if I wanted to switch to the project regarding Econometrics, I would just click on `ModellingEconometrics`. This operation closes the current project and opens the project `ModellingEconometrics`. This means that my working directory would become `ModellingEconometrics`. Note also that the **R** session starts again when you switch between projects.

Now let's suppose that you start working without creating a project. In this case you can check your working directory by typing `getwd()` in the command pane. For example, my current working directory is

```
> getwd()
[1] "C:/Users/porto/OneDrive/Documenti/R_progetti/WTO_R"
```

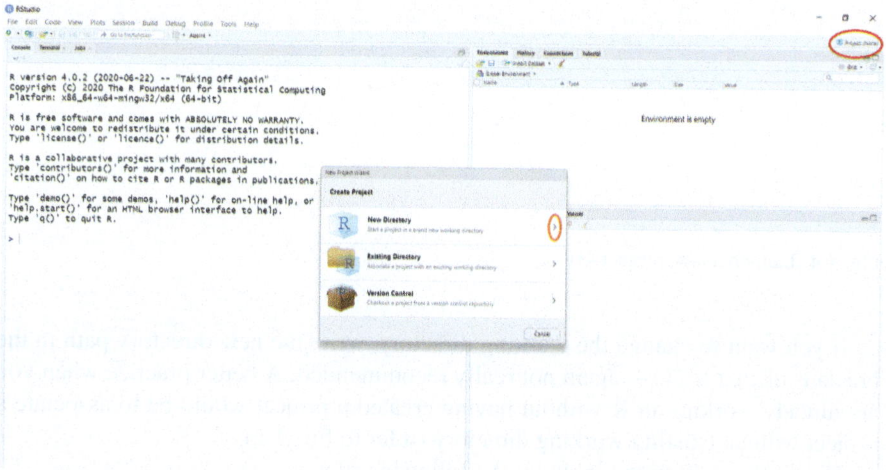

Fig. 1.2 Launch a new project (1)

[2] If you have already created a directory, you can click **Existing Directory**.

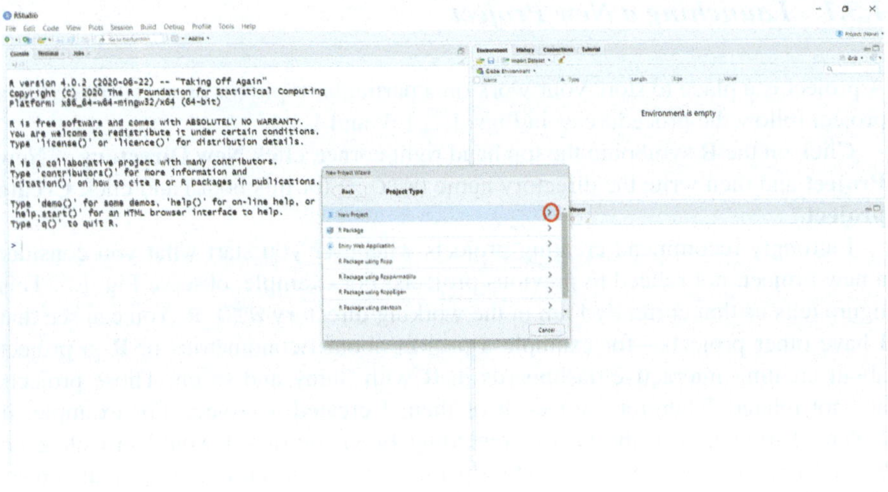

Fig. 1.3 Launch a new project (2)

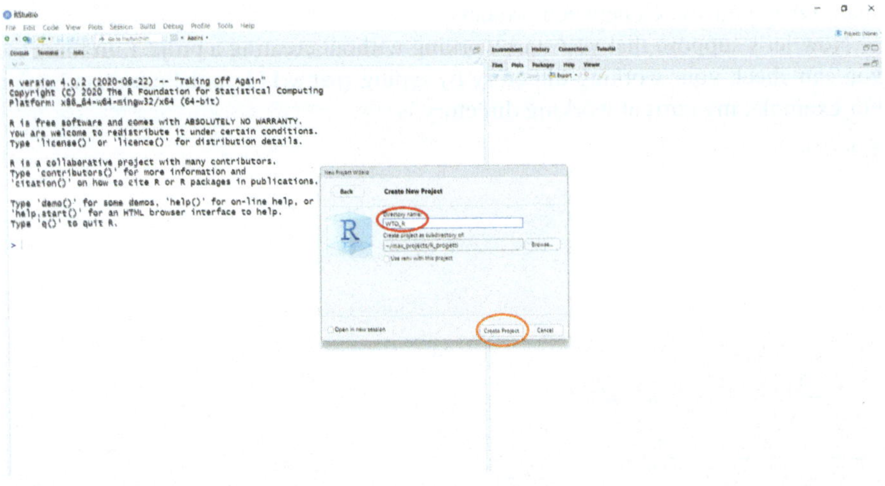

Fig. 1.4 Launch a new project (3)

If you want to change the working directory, write the new directory path in the brackets of `setwd()`—again not really recommended. A better practice when you are already working in **R** without having created a project would be to associate a project with an existing working directory (refer to Fig. 1.2).

The working directory includes the following files:

- **.RData**: Holds the objects etc. in your environment;
- **.RHistory**: Holds the history of what you typed in the console;

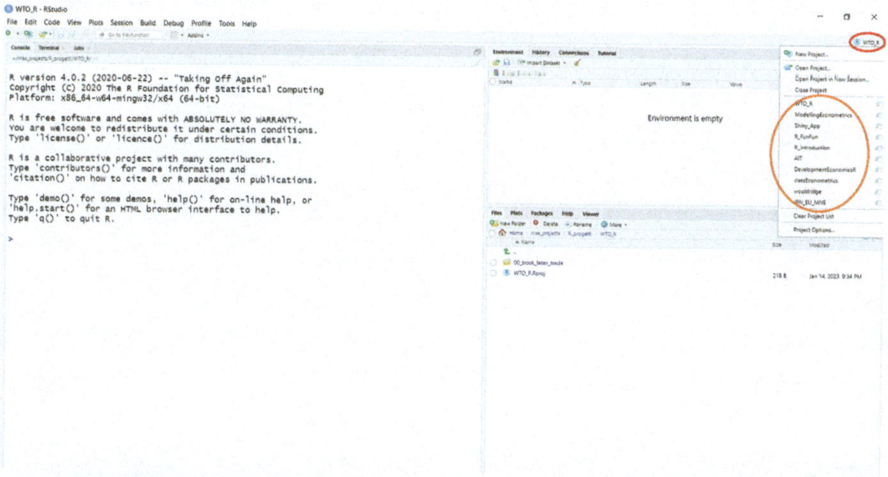

Fig. 1.5 Navigate through projects

- **.RProfile**: Holds specific setup information for the working directory you are in. For example, if you want to disable the scientific notation in **R** and set the number of digits at 4 for your output, you can write `options("scipen"=9999, digits=4)` in **.RProfile** (I did not set it for this project). In this way, this option will be loaded when you open your project.
  - To check if you created the **.RProfile**, write `file.exists("~/.Rprofile")` in the console pane. If you did not, **R** will return the value `FALSE`.
  - By typing `file.edit("~/.Rprofile")` in the console pane you can create the **.RProfile**.

Before continuing, let's create a folder in our working directory called `images`. This folder will contain all the figures that we will create in this book. For this task write `dir.create("images")` in the console pane after creating the `WTO_R` project (from now on I assume that you are in the working directory `WTO_R`)

```
> dir.create("images")
```

1.3.2 Opening an R Script

We open an **R Script** file in **RStudio** as shown in Fig. 1.6. Before starting working, it is good practice to save it (Fig. 1.7).

To run a code in the **R Script**, for a single line of code place the mouse pointer before the code, for a block of lines select it, and then click the `Run` button (Fig. 1.8), or press `Ctrl + Enter` on a Windows system.

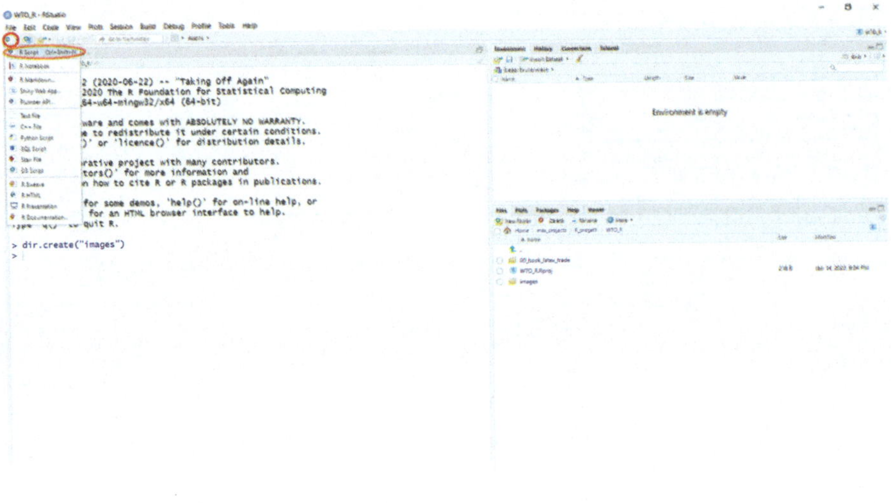

Fig. 1.6 Open an R Script

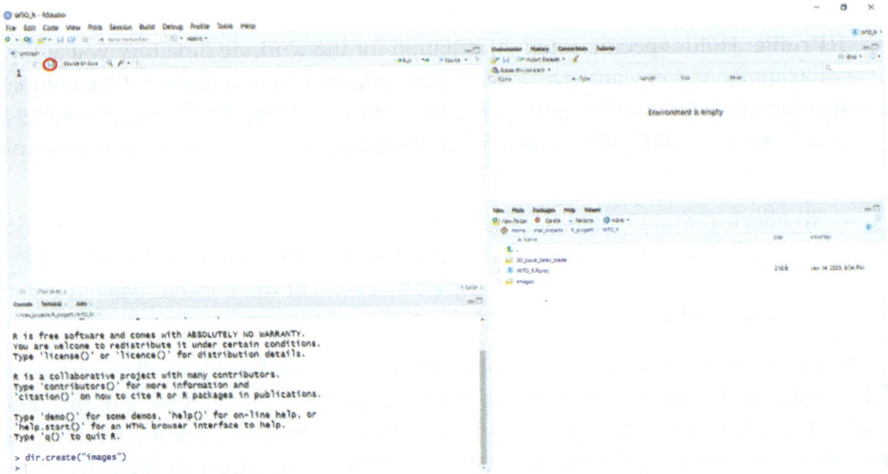

Fig. 1.7 Save an R Script

1.4 Packages to Install

Packages extend the capability of **R**.

To reproduce step by step the code in this book, you need to install the following packages:

- `lmtest` (Zeileis & Hothorn, 2002) (version 0.9.38)
- `sandwich` (Zeileis, 2004) (version 3.0.0)
- `zoo` (Zeileis & Grothendieck, 2005) (version 1.8.8)

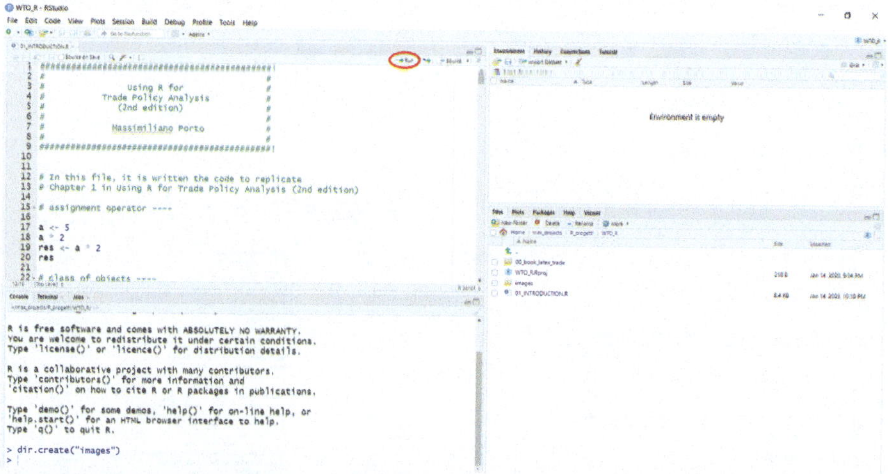

Fig. 1.8 Run button in RStudio

- `plm` (Croissant & Millo, 2008) (version 2.2.5)
- `ggplot2` (Wickham, 2009) (version 3.3.2)
- `png` (Urbanek, 2013) (version 0.1.7)
- `data.table` (Dowle & Srinivasan, 2017) (version 1.13.2)
- `gifski` (Ooms, 2018) (version 0.8.6)
- `scales` (Wickham, 2018) (version 1.1.1)
- `stargazer` (Hlavac, 2018) (version 5.2.2)
- `stringr` (Wickham, 2019b) (version 1.4.0)
- `dplyr` (Wickham et al., 2019) (version 1.0.2)
- `ggpubr` (Kassambara, 2019) (version 0.4.0)
- `tidyr` (Wickham & Henry, 2019) (version 1.1.2)
- `gganimate` (Pedersen & Robinson, 2020) (version 1.0.7)
- `haven` (Wickham & Miller, 2020) (version 2.3.1)
- `plotly` (Sievert, 2020) (version 4.9.3)
- `stringi` (Gagolewski, 2020) (version 1.5.3)
- `estimatr` (Blair et al., 2021) (version 0.30.4)
- `shiny` (Chang et al., 2021) (version 1.6.0)
- `shinyFeedback` (Merlino & Howard, 2021) (version 0.4.0)
- `Hmisc` (Harrell Jr et al., 2021) (version 4.5-0)
- `doBy` (Højsgaard & Halekoh, 2023) (version 4.6.16)

We will refer to these packages when we use functions from them.[3]

[3] In parenthesis the package version used in this book. To retrieve the package version of `ggplot2`, for example, after you installed it: `packageVersion("ggplot2")`. Again, it should be fine to replicate this code even though you have a different version.

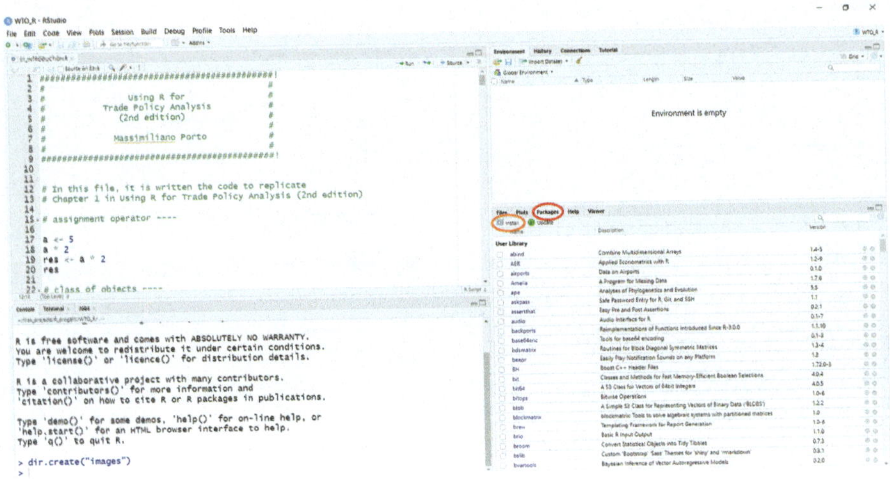

Fig. 1.9 Packages in RStudio

1.4.1 *How to Install a Package*

You can install a package in **R** with the function `install.packages()`. Write the name of the package you want to install in quotation marks. For example,

```
> install.packages("ggplot2")
```

You install the package once. If a new version is released, you can update the package by using the function `update.packages()`.

An alternative way—that I prefer—is to install packages in **RStudio** as shown in Figs. 1.9 and 1.10

1.4.2 *How to Load a Package*

After you installed the package, you need to load the package in **R** with the `library()` function to use it. For example,

```
> library("ggplot2")
```

You need to load the package you want to use anytime you start a new **R** session.

1.5 Good Practice and Notation

Before starting to replicate the code in this book, make sure you are in the working directory `WTO_R`.

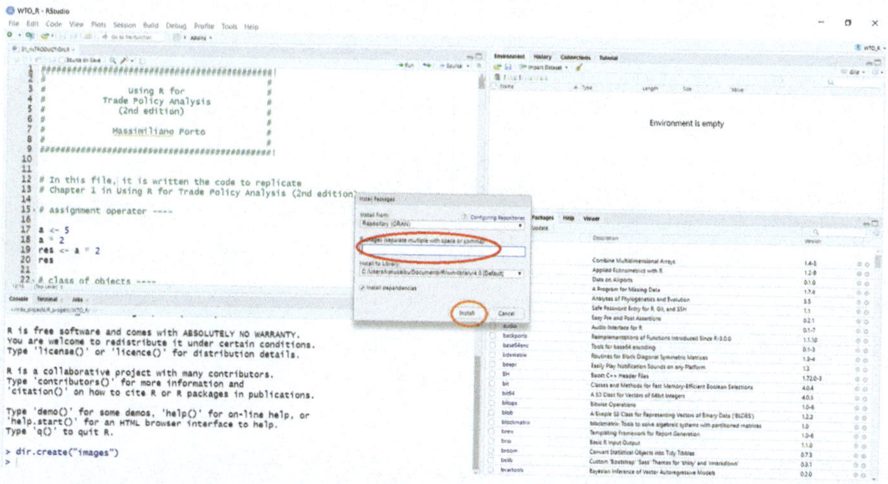

Fig. 1.10 Install packages in RStudio

Next step is to open an **R Script**. Even though we could write the code directly in the console pane, as we did when we created the folder `images`, it is better to write the code in an **R Script** when we have to write more than one line of code. The commands in an **R Script** can be easily traced back, modified and shared with colleagues. In an **R Script**, it is possible to add comments using #. Everything that follows # will be considered as comment and, consequently, will be not run by **R**. If you want to write multiple lines of comments you may want to use `#'`. Additionally, it is possible to set up a table of contents in an **R Script** file by typing at least four trailing dashes (-), equal signs (=), or pound signs (#). This allows to navigate easily through the script file. For an example refer to Fig. 1.11. Again, this is also useful if you share the file with a colleague. Therefore, we can say that it is convenient to work in an **R Script**.

At the beginning of any **R Script**, it is good practice to type the packages needed to implement the code in the file. After writing the code to load the package with the `library()` function, you may add, as comment, a keyword to remind about the use of the package. This would help us to remember the content of the file and make clear to a third person what will be needed to implement the code in the **R Script**.

It is also good practice to describe the project and write short comments in the body of the functions we create. Again this is useful for the author of the script and for a third person who will read the code.

Finally, a last remark before starting working: to avoid confusion in the text of this book, we will use the following `font` for all the words related to the **R** code we will write. Additionally, all the functions will be written with parenthesis. For example, `sum()` is the base **R** function for summation while `mtable()` is a function that we will write to compute multiplication tables. This notation is adopted

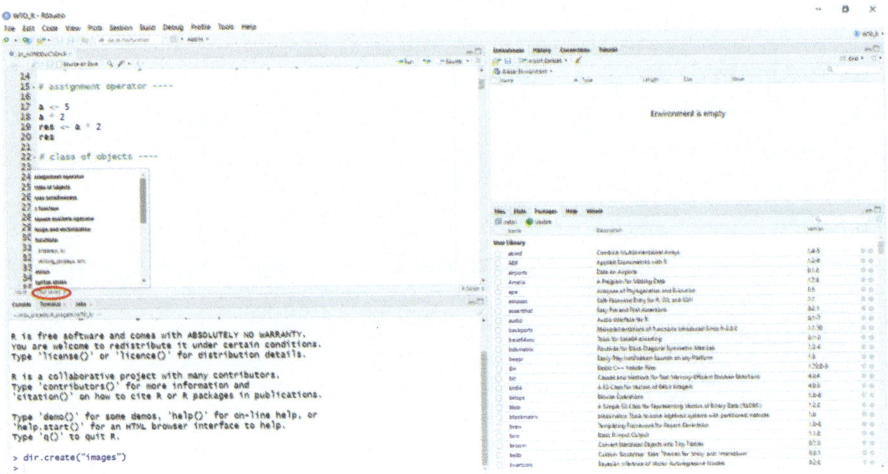

Fig. 1.11 Table of contents in an R Script file

to distinguish functions from other type of objects that will be written without parentheses.

1.5.1 How to Read the Code

In this book, you will see the code printed out in two different ways. A colored code and a black code. The colored code means that I am running the code from the **R Script** file while the black code is used to illustrate the code and its outcome that is printed out in the console pane. In this last case, the code is preceded by >, the prompt symbol. > is not part of the code written in the **R Script** file. It signals that **R** is ready to operate. However, keep in mind that I run the code from the **R Script** file. And I suggest you do the same to replicate the code in this book. Let's have a look to see how the two codes look like.

An example of just one line of code in **R Script**

```
x <- seq(-10, 10, 0.1)
```

and the same code printed in the console pane

```
> x <- seq(-10, 10, 0.1)
```

For one line of code it may seem that the difference is not so relevant.

Here, an example with two lines of code in **R Script**

```
x <- seq(-10, 10,
         0.1)
```

and the same code printed out in the console pane

```
> x <- seq(-10, 10,
+          0.1)
```

Now, note that in the code in the console pane there is a + that is missing in the code in the **R Script** file. Basically, this + is not part of the code. It means that the code is continuing on the following line. It is not needed in the **R Script**.

Let's see another example. The following example is a plot from Sect. 1.7.1 generated by using the `ggplot()` function (do not write it now).

This is how the code looks like in the **R Script**

```
ggplot(results_test_def, aes(x= Students, y = Total_Score,
                              fill = 'PASS/FAIL')) +
    geom_bar(position = "dodge", stat="identity") +
    ylab("Total Score") + theme_classic() +
    ggtitle("Total Score for a 50 question test") +
    theme(legend.position = "bottom")
```

and the same code printed in the console pane

```
> ggplot(results_test_def, aes(x= Students, y = Total_Score,
+                               fill = 'PASS/FAIL')) +
+     geom_bar(position = "dodge", stat="identity") +
+     ylab("Total Score") + theme_classic() +
+     ggtitle("Total Score for a 50 question test") +
+     theme(legend.position = "bottom")
```

Note that in this case we have one + from the **R Script** file and two + from the console pane. The + in the **R Script** file is part of the code. This is a feature of the `ggplot()` code. On the other hand, the second +, directly below the prompt symbol, >, is not part of our code and it just means that the code continues on the next line. When **R** has finished to run the code, the prompt symbol, >, will appear again meaning that **R** is ready to take a new command.

1.6 8 Key-Points Regarding R

Is **R** hard to learn? If we surf the net to find an answer to this question, it seems that **R** is hard to learn. In this section, I would like to share my own experience in learning **R** with the reader.

R is not the first statistical software I learnt. When I was a PhD student I moved from a property software to **R** to work with two professors of mine who used it. And yes, at the beginning it has been very hard. I was getting errors after errors. I was spending more time to clean the errors than to accomplish my tasks. However, the more errors I solved (mainly thanks to the community of Stack Overflow) the more I started to appreciate **R**. When I got used to the **R** language, I figured out what made it difficult for me at the beginning. Following I list the 8 key-points regarding **R**—with examples—that I think every beginner should grasp when working with **R**.

Let's check these points while coding. Open an **R Script** and save it as `01_INTRODUCTION.R`.[4] Again, I assume that you are in the working directory `WTO_R`.

[4] Note that you do not need to type `.R`.

1.6.1 The Assignment Operator

The assignment operator, `<-`, is used to assign values to objects we create in **R**.

For example, we store 5 in an object, `a`. We can compute operations with `a` as we were dealing directly with 5

```
> a <- 5
> a * 2
[1] 10
```

We can store the result of this multiplication in another object, `res`. In this case, we do not see the result of the operation, that is stored in `res`, unless we run the object

```
> res <- a * 2
> res
[1] 10
```

We can store different kinds of objects, such as functions and plots with `ggplot()`.

1.6.2 The Class of Objects

In **R**, we work with different types of objects. We check the type of object with the `class()` function. For example, the object we generated earlier is `numeric`.

```
> class(a)
[1] "numeric"
```

Now, let's generate an object, `b`, that stores 2. Note that we add quotation marks.

```
> b <- "2"
> b
[1] "2"
```

Let's multiply `a` times `b`. We should get 10 but

```
> a * b
Error in a * b : non-numeric argument to binary operator
```

We get an error. The error says `non-numeric argument to binary operator`. We already know that `a` is `numeric`. What about `b`?

```
> class(b)
[1] "character"
```

As we can see, although `b` stores 2, it stores it as `character` and not as `numeric` because we enclosed it in quotation marks. In the **R** language we cannot multiply a numeric value by a character value and consequently we get the error.[5]

[5] We need to specify that this operation does not work in the **R** language. In fact, if you are a Python user you are aware that in Python this is a legit operation that replicates the string many times as determined by the numeric value.

Now it is clear what caused the error. We should have stored 2 as numeric value. Currently, `b` stores something that is very close to a numeric 2. Basically, we need to remove the quotation marks. We have the opportunity to introduce a group of functions that starts with `as.` such as `as.numeric()`, `as.integer()`, `as.character()`, `as.data.frame()`, an so on. These functions coerce a class of an object to another class. In our case, we use the `as.numeric()` function.

```
> class(b)
[1] "character"
> b <- as.numeric(b)
> b
[1] 2
> a * b
[1] 10
```

We got the expected results. Note that to use this group of functions, the object needs to have the "quality" to be coerced. For example, I store my name in `m`. It is a `character`. In this case we fail the coercion to `numeric` because **R** does not know how to coerce a string of letters to a number.[6]

```
> m <- "massimiliano"
> class(m)
[1] "character"
> m <- as.numeric(m)
Warning message:
NAs introduced by coercion
> m
[1] NA
```

1.6.3 Case Sensitiveness

If we use the same name for an object, the second object overwrites the first object. Previously, we wrote

```
> b <- as.numeric(b)
```

In that case, we overwrote the previous `b` that was a `character`. However, observe the following example,

```
> b <- 3
> b
[1] 3
> b <- 2
> b
[1] 2
> B <- 4
> B
[1] 4
> b
[1] 2
```

[6] `NA` stands for `Not Available`. We will return to `NA` in Sect. 1.7.2 and `Warning message` in Sect. 1.6.8.

The object b initially stores 3. We overwrite it so that it stores 2. On the other hand, if we assign 4 to B this does not affect b. In fact, b and B are two different objects. In other words, **R** is a case sensitive language.

1.6.4 The c() Function

The c() function is used to concatenate items separated by a comma ,. For example,

```
> d <- c(1, 2, 3, 4, 5)
> d
[1] 1 2 3 4 5
> e <- c("a", "b", "c", "d", "e")
> e
[1] "a" "b" "c" "d" "e"
```

We can also concatenate the objects we generated. For example, we concatenate the objects d, a, and b. Note that the values of d, a and b are added to the new object, dab, in the order we concatenate them.

```
> dab <- c(d, a, b)
> dab
[1] 1 2 3 4 5 5 2
```

However, note the following

```
> de <- c(d,e)
> de
 [1] "1" "2" "3" "4" "5" "a" "b" "c" "d" "e"
```

Note the quotation marks around the numbers. What is the issue here? This happens because the c() function cannot store items with different classes. Consequently, **R** will coerce the different types of items to a common type. In this case, **R** coerced every item to be a character. Then, what about if we are not satisfied with this solution? We can use the list() function to store the objects in a single object keeping their characteristics.

```
> l <- list(d, e)
> l
[[1]]
[1] 1 2 3 4 5

[[2]]
[1] "a" "b" "c" "d" "e"

> class(l)
[1] "list"
> class(l[[1]])
[1] "numeric"
> class(l[[2]])
[1] "character"
```

1.6.5 The Square Bracket Operator `[ ]`

The square bracket operator `[ ]` has the function to subset, extract, or replace a part of an object such as a vector, a matrix or a data frame. For example, we select the first entry in the `e` object as follows

```
> e[1]
[1] "a"
```

Remember that the **R** language starts indexing from 1. Consequently, `"a"` is extracted because it is stored as the first entry in the `e` object.

If we run the `e` object again, we find that no modification has been made.

```
> e
[1] "a" "b" "c" "d" "e"
```

But as we said, `[ ]` can be used to replace an item from an object. In this case, we have just to assign a new value. For example,

```
> e[1] <- "m"
> e
[1] "m" "b" "c" "d" "e"
```

We replaced the first entry in `e`, i.e. `"a"` with `"m"`. That is, we overwrote the first element of `e`.

Let's rewrite the `e` object as before. Note that this time instead of typing each letter we are selecting them from the built-in object `letters`. Exactly, we are selecting the letters from 1 to (`:`) 5 that correspond to letters from *a* to *e*.

```
> e <- letters[1:5]
> e
[1] "a" "b" "c" "d" "e"
```

We can generate a new object, `e1`, and assign the first value from the `e` object as follows

```
> e1 <- e[1]
> e1
[1] "a"
```

If we want to subset for more that one value, we combine `[ ]` with the `c()` function. For example,

```
> e[c(1, 3)]
[1] "a" "c"
```

Subsets for the first element and third element of `e`, that are `"a"` and `"c"`, respectively.

If we want to subset for consecutive values we can use the `:` operator. For example, to select entries from 1 to 3

```
> e[1:3]
[1] "a" "b" "c"
```

This is what we did with the `letters` object.

Until now we worked with one dimension. Let's see a few examples with a data frame that is an object with two dimensions.[7] We use the `data.frame()` function

[7] You may think of a data frame as an Excel spreadsheet.

to create a data frame. We name this data frame as `df`. We create it by using `d` and `e` we created earlier. We set the column title for `d` and `e`, `numbers` and `letters`, respectively. Note that to create a data frame it is necessary that the objects we use—in this case `d` and `e`—have the same length, i.e. the same number of items. As `list()`, a data frame allows to store different types of object.

```
> df <- data.frame(numbers = d,
+                  letters = e)
> df
  numbers letters
1       1       a
2       2       b
3       3       c
4       4       d
5       5       e
```

The structure of `df` is rows per columns. Therefore, we need an index for the row and an index for the column. For example, if we want to select `d`, we observe that is located at row number 4 and column number 2. We use again the `[ , ]` but this time we add a comma `,` to separate the row dimension from the column dimension.

```
> df[4, 2]
[1] "d"
```

If we want to select more than one element, we use the `c()` function.

```
> df[4, c(1, 2)]
  numbers letters
4       4       d
> df[c(3, 5), 2]
[1] "c" "e"
> df[c(3, 5), c(1, 2)]
  numbers letters
3       3       c
5       5       e
```

In the first case, we selected one row, 4, and two column indexes, 1 for `numbers` and 2 for `letters`. In the second case, we selected two row indexes, 3 and 5, and one column index, 2. In the last case we selected two row indexes and two column indexes. What about selecting all the rows for the first column? We leave blank the spot for the row before the comma as follows

```
> df[, 1]
[1] 1 2 3 4 5
```

Consequently, if we leave blank the spot for the columns after the comma, we select all the columns for row indexes. For example,

```
> df[c(2, 4), ]
  numbers letters
2       2       b
4       4       d
```

Note that we can use the name of columns as well to extract the entries for the corresponding column. For example,

```
> df[, "numbers"]
[1] 1 2 3 4 5
> df[2, "letters"]
[1] "b"
```

We can replace an element from a data frame with the same pattern we saw before. Let's replace the entry in the first row and first column with 10.

```
> df[1, 1] <- 10
> df
  numbers letters
1      10       a
2       3       b
3       5       c
4       7       d
5       9       e
```

Additionally, note that `data.frame()` before **R** version 4.0.0 by default converted character vectors to factors. We can replicate it by setting `stringsAsFactors = TRUE` in the `data.frame()` function. Let's do it

```
> df <- data.frame(numbers = d,
+                  letters = e,
+                  stringsAsFactors = TRUE)
> df
  numbers letters
1       1       a
2       2       b
3       3       c
4       4       d
5       5       e
```

Note that now `letters` in `df` are stored as `factor`, i.e., categorical variables that take a limited number of different values. `levels` is an attribute that provides the identity of each category.

```
> class(df$letters)
[1] "factor"
> df[4, 2]
[1] d
Levels: a b c d e
```

Sometimes factors can be replaced by character data. We use the `as.character()` function to force it to be `character`. For example,

```
> df$letters <- as.character(df$letters)
> class(df$letters)
[1] "character"
```

Finally, note that we have other two operators acting on vectors, matrices, arrays, lists, and data frames to extract or replace parts: double square brackets `[[ ]]` and `$` operators.[8] The most important difference is that `[ ]` can select more than one element whereas the other two select a single element.

```
> l[[1]]
[1] 1 3 5 7 9
```

We extracted the content stored at index 1 of the list `l` we generated earlier.

[8] `$` works for lists and data frames.

Let's assign names to the objects stored in the list `l` with the `names()` function. Note that in **R** the order is extremely important. In our case, we assign two names, `numbers` and `letters`. The first name will be assigned to the first object stored at index 1 and the second name will be assigned to the second object stored at index 2. Then, we can select the object by name with `$`

```
> names(l) <- c("numbers", "letters")
> l
$numbers
[1] 1 2 3 4 5

$letters
[1] "a" "b" "c" "d" "e"

> l$numbers
[1] 1 2 3 4 5
```

With `$` operator, we can select the column of a data frame by its name

```
> df$numbers
[1] 1 3 5 7 9
```

In addition, we can use it to create a new column in the data frame by typing `$` after the name of the data frame and before the name of the column we choose, and with the values to be assigned to the new column

```
> df$new <- c(0, 1, 0, 1, 0)
> df
  numbers letters new
1       1       a   0
2       3       b   1
3       5       c   0
4       7       d   1
5       9       e   0
```

1.6.6 Loop, Vectorization, and the `apply()` Family Functions

Let's suppose we want to compute the multiplication table for 2, i.e, $2 \times 1, 2 \times 2, 2 \times 3, \ldots, 2 \times 10$. That is, we want to multiply 2 times 1 and print the result. Then, multiply 2 times 2 and print the result, and so on until 2 times 10. Basically, this is a loop. We can generate this kind of loops in **R** with the `for()` function. In the `for()` function we have three keys elements:

- `i` is a syntactical name for a value (as we will see later we can choose any name for it)
- `in` is an operator
- a sequence. In this example, we generate a sequence with the `seq()` function where we indicate the minimum and the maximum value and the increment amount between each value. We store the sequence in the `s` object.
- finally, note that the loop steps are enclosed in curly brackets.

```
> s <- seq(1, 10, 1)
> s
```

```
 [1]  1  2  3  4  5  6  7  8  9 10
> for(i in s){
+   res <- 2 * i
+   print(res)
+ }
[1] 2
[1] 4
[1] 6
[1] 8
[1] 10
[1] 12
[1] 14
[1] 16
[1] 18
[1] 20
```

What is happening? Basically, when the loop starts, `i` is 1. Therefore, `2 * 1` is multiplied, stored in `res` and printed with the `print()` function. Then, the loop moves to the second index in the sequence that in this case is 2. This means that now `i` is 2 and `2 * 2` is multiplied and so on. The loop stops at the end of the sequence, i.e. the last operation is when `i` is 10.

`for()` loop

Loops are generated by the `for()` function.

The structure of a `for()` loop is the following:

```
for(value in sequence){
        steps of commands
}
```

where:

- `value`: is an syntactical name for a value. It can be any name as we will see in a following example;
- `in`: is an operator that points where to look for the `value`;
- `sequence`: a vector or a data frame with values to loop over;
- `steps of commands`: the steps of commands you want the loop go through. They are enclosed by { }

However, in **R** we can avoid writing loops like the previous one because we can benefit from the *vectorization* of **R**. We can obtain the same results just multiplying 2 by a vector from 1 to 10 as follows. Note that in this case we use the colon operator : to generate the same sequence as before.

```
> n <- 1:10
> n
 [1]  1  2  3  4  5  6  7  8  9 10
> 2 * n
 [1]  2  4  6  8 10 12 14 16 18 20
```

However, extra care is needed when using vectorization. For example, in the previous case 2 is seen by **R** as a vector of length 1 that is multiplied by a vector of length 10. Therefore, **R** recycles its value to match the vector of length 10. In this case it is fine for us. But observe the following example

```
> v1 <- c(2, 3)
> v2 <- c(7, 9, 11)
> 100 + v1
[1] 102 103
> 100 + v2
[1] 107 109 111
> v1 + v2
[1]  9 12 13
Warning message:
In v1 + v2 :
  longer object length is not a multiple of shorter object length
> v1 * v2
[1] 14 27 22
Warning message:
In v1 * v2 :
  longer object length is not a multiple of shorter object length
```

The vectors `v1` and `v2` have different lengths. If we add each of these vector by 100, the value of 100 is recycled to match the length of the vectors and produce the expected results. However, if we add or multiply the two vectors with each other, a warning message is produce telling that the two objects have different lengths. The operations in both cases has been computed but note that in both cases the value 2 in `v1` is recycled to match the length of `v2`. In these cases we have an incomplete cycle. We need to be very careful to incomplete cycles in our computation when implementing vectorization.

Additionally, note that some functions in **R** are vectorized. For example, let's load the built-in data set `cars`. This is a data frame with 50 observations on 2 variables, speed and stopping distance. If we want to compute the mean of these two variables, we just use the `colMeans()` function

```
> data("cars")
> head(cars)
  speed dist
1     4    2
2     4   10
3     7    4
4     7   22
5     8   16
6     9   10
> colMeans(cars)
speed  dist
15.40 42.98
```

that is, the average speed is 15.40 mph and the average stopping distance is 42.98 ft.

Another kind of loop that is often used is the `while()` loop. The `while()` loop is trickier than the `for()` loop. The main difference is that the `for()` loop iterates over a sequence while the `while()` loop iterates over a conditional statement. The issue is that a sequence can be very long but it is finished, i.e. at the end of the sequence the loop will stop. On the other hand, if we wrongly define the conditional statement or we forget to write the step to modify the conditional statement in the `while()` function, the loop will iterate infinitely times. If this happens, just break the loop by clicking on the `stop` button that will appear in the console pane.

Let's consider a simple example. Let's say we want to print the numbers from 10 to 0 included with a `while()` loop. First, we assign the starting point, 10, to `x`. Then, we write the `while()` loop. The conditional statement in our case is that $x \geq 0$. That is, the loop has to iterate as long as x is greater or equal to 0. Now, keep in mind that we assigned 10 to `x`. That is, `x` is greater than 0. If we do not modify `x` in the `while()` loop so that at a given moment `x` will turn less than 0—and the fulfillment of this condition stops the loop—the loop will run infinitely times because `x` remains greater than 0. Note that also for the `while()` loop the steps of commands are enclosed by { } . In code,

```
> x <- 10
> while(x >= 0){
+   print(x)
+   x <- x - 1
+ }
[1] 10
[1] 9
[1] 8
[1] 7
[1] 6
[1] 5
[1] 4
[1] 3
[1] 2
[1] 1
[1] 0
```

As you can see, in the body of the `while()` function, `print(x)` prints out `x`. Then, we assign a new value to `x` every time the loop iterates. Again, let's go through each step. At the beginning, `x` is 10. Is 10 greater than 0? That's true. The conditional statement is satisfied. Then, `x` is printed, i.e. its value 10 is printed. Before the end of the loop we reassign a value for `x`. In this case we subtract 1 from `x` meaning that `x` becomes 9. Let's ask: is 9 greater than 0? Again, that's true. And again the conditional statement is satisfied and the same steps are implemented. But now, `x` becomes 8. That is still greater than 0. Now let's say that `x` has become 1. Its value is printed and the value 0 is assigned to `x`. The conditional statement that we wrote is true for $x \geq 0$. Meaning that the conditional statement is still satisfied. Therefore, 0 is printed out. But now `x` becomes -1. This violates the conditional statement. The conditional statement has turned false and this stops the loop.

If we implement the same task with the `for()` loop

```
> s <- 10:0
> for(i in s){
+   print(i)
+ }
[1] 10
[1] 9
[1] 8
[1] 7
[1] 6
[1] 5
[1] 4
[1] 3
[1] 2
[1] 1
[1] 0
```

As you can see, in this case we already know when the loop will eventually stop. A "side effect" of using a `for()` loop is that at the end of the loop the "unwanted" `i` object is created storing the last value—in this case 0.

`while() loop`

The `while()` loop is another common way to implement loop in **R**. The structure of a `while()` loop is the following:

```
while(conditional statement){
        steps of commands
        expression that will turn the conditional statement to false
}
```

where:

- `conditional statement`: the condition that activates the loop;
- `steps of commands`: the steps of commands you want the loop go through. They are enclosed by { }

Again, for this simple task we can avoid using any loop. In fact, by running the sequence `s` we generated, we obtain the countdown as well

```
> s
 [1] 10  9  8  7  6  5  4  3  2  1  0
```

Finally, the `apply()` family functions that include `apply()`, `lapply()`, `tapply()`, `vapply()`, and `mapply()` substitute the loop by applying another function to all elements in an object. For example, the object can be a matrix, an array or a data frame in the case of the `apply()` function; a vector, a data frame and a list in the case of `sapply()` and `lapply()`. The difference between `sapply()` and `lapply()` is that the former returns as result a vector, a matrix or a list, while the latter returns a list.

Let's write a function[9] `mean_dev()` to compute the deviation from the mean, i.e. how far the values of interest are from the average of those values

```
> mean_dev <- function(x){
+   x - mean(x)
+ }
```

Let's test it with the vector `v3 <- c(1, 4, 10)`

```
> v3 <- c(1, 4, 10)
> mean(v3)
[1] 5
> mean_dev(v3)
[1] -4 -1  5
```

We see that the average of the values of `v3` is 5. Consequently, the mean deviation is −4, −1, and 5.

[9] More on functions in Sect. 1.6.7.

Now our task is to apply the mean_dev() function to the columns of the cars data frame. We use the apply() function for this task. To make sense of the apply() family functions, I suggest that we read it from the last argument to the first argument, that is "apply the mean_dev() function to the columns (2) of the data frame cars"

```
head(apply(cars, 2, mean_dev))
      speed    dist
[1,] -11.4 -40.98
[2,] -11.4 -32.98
[3,]  -8.4 -38.98
[4,]  -8.4 -20.98
[5,]  -7.4 -26.98
[6,]  -6.4 -32.98
```

Note that we do not need to write the parentheses of the function in the apply() function and that 2 refers to the columns of the data frame while 1 refers to the rows of the data frame. We will see another example with sapply() in Sect. 1.6.7.

1.6.7 Functions

Now, let's continue with the example of the multiplication table and let's say we want to compute the multiplication table for 3 as well. And then for 4, 5, and so on.

```
> 3 * n
 [1]  3  6  9 12 15 18 21 24 27 30
> 4 * n
 [1]  4  8 12 16 20 24 28 32 36 40
> 5 * n
 [1]  5 10 15 20 25 30 35 40 45 50
```

In this code, we can observe that n is in common and the output changes based on the the inputs 3, 4, and 5. In this case, we may think to build a function to compute these calculations. We build a function with the function() function. We store it in an object, that in this case we call mtable.

```
> mtable <- function(x) x * n
```

Our function is now ready. If we want to compute the multiplication table for 2, we just need to write 2 in mtable(). This value will be used to replace x in x * n in the function.

```
> mtable(2)
 [1]  2  4  6  8 10 12 14 16 18 20
```

And, of course, if we want the multiplication table for 5 we write

```
> mtable(5)
 [1]  5 10 15 20 25 30 35 40 45 50
```

We can store the results of a function in an object as well. For example,

```
> mtab10 <- mtable(10)
> mtab10
 [1]  10  20  30  40  50  60  70  80  90 100
```

We can note two critical points of our function. First, `n` is defined outside the environment of the function. Second, `n` is not flexible. What about computing the multiplication table up to 15? and up to 20? We should rewrite `n` each time. Clearly, this would not be efficient. Let's try to fix `mtable()`.

```
> mtable <- function(x, w = 10){
+   n <- 1:w
+   res <- x*n
+   return(res)
+ }
```

We did what we wanted: (1) define `n` inside the environment of the function; and (2) make it flexible. But what did we do? We added a new argument to our function, `w`. Note that inside the function `w` is the end value of a sequence stored in `n` that starts with 1. In addition, we set w as a default argument. That is, it is set to 10. This choice depends on the fact that in most cases we want the multiplication table up to 10. So we do not want to bother ourselves typing every time 10. But this time, if we want a multiplication table up to 15, we just need to type 15 in the second entry of the function. Finally, note that we enclosed the code in curly brackets { }. We need them when we write the code of a function on multi-levels. However, it would have been more appropriate if we had used the curly brackets also for the first example of `mtable()`.

Functions

You can build your own functions using `function()`. For example, a structure of a function can be the following:

```
name_function <- function(x1, x2){
        step1 <- x1 and some operations
        step2 <- x2 and some operations
        output <- step1 + step2
        return(output)
}
```

where:

- `name_function`: you assign the function to an object;
- `function()`: in the parenthesis you type the arguments of the function, `x1` and `x2` in this example;
- `steps of commands`: the steps of commands you want the function go through. They are enclosed by { } ;
- `return()`: is a function that returns the object from inside the function to the workspace.

Basically, you type step by step what the function needs to do. It will take the arguments from inside the parentheses in `function`.

Now, let's see an example with the fixed `mtable()`. First, let's compute the multiplication table of 2 up to 10.

```
> mtable(2)
 [1]  2  4  6  8 10 12 14 16 18 20
```

And now up to 15.

```
> mtable(2, 15)
 [1]  2  4  6  8 10 12 14 16 18 20 22 24 26 28 30
```

Furthermore, note that the order of the arguments in the function matters unless we explicitly write the argument names. For example,

```
> mtable(15, 2)
[1] 15 30
> mtable(w = 15, x = 2)
 [1]  2  4  6  8 10 12 14 16 18 20 22 24 26 28 30
```

In the first case, 15 takes the place of `x` in `mtable()` while 2 takes the place of `w` in `mtable()`. On the other hand, we do not need to respect the positioning of the arguments if we explicitly write the names of the arguments in the function as in the second case. In other words, "**R** uses either named matching or positional matching to figure out the correct assignment" (Georgakopoulos, 2015, p. 28).

Additionally, note that `mtable()` computes the multiplication table for one input at a time. However, we know now that we can use the `apply()` functions to compute the multiplication tables for multiple values. Let's compute the multiplication table for 1 to 5 up to 8. Let's use the `sapply()` function. To use an argument of the function (in our case `w = 8`), we write it after the name of the function we want to use it. We nest the `sapply()` it in `t()` to transpose the results

```
> s <- 1:5
> t(sapply(s, mtable, w = 8))
     [,1] [,2] [,3] [,4] [,5] [,6] [,7] [,8]
[1,]    1    2    3    4    5    6    7    8
[2,]    2    4    6    8   10   12   14   16
[3,]    3    6    9   12   15   18   21   24
[4,]    4    8   12   16   20   24   28   32
[5,]    5   10   15   20   25   30   35   40
```

Finally, what I like about functions in **R** is that they can be seen as a neat correspondence of how we state mathematical functions. Let's consider a simple example. Let's suppose that the cost, C, of renting a car in dollars only depends on the number of days, d, we rent it and how many km, k, we drive. We are just expressing in English a function of two variables, $C = f(d, k)$. Let's say that renting a car costs 30$ per day and 0.15$ per km. We can write the functional form to compute the rental cost as $C = f(d, k) = 30d + 0.15k$. Therefore, what is the cost of renting a car for 2 days and driving it 100 km? Or, in other words, $C = f(d = 2, k = 100)$ (we can omit d and k as well, i.e., $C = f(2, 100)$).

In **R**, we set the function and find the solution as follows

```
> renting_car <- function(days, km){
+   res <- 30*days + 0.15*km
+   return(res)
+ }
> renting_car(2, 100)
[1] 75
```

This means that the cost of renting a car for 2 days and driving it 100 km is $75.

The final remark is that we could safely write `C <- function(d, k)`, and, consequently, `res <- 30*d + 0.15*k` and `C(2, 100)`. Naturally, `renting_car()` and `C()` produce the same results and they are both fine. However, clearly, the former is more readable and should be preferred.

1.6.8 Errors

I want to conclude this section talking about errors. When we make an error, we get an error message in red that can be intimidating and frustrating. When I started to learn **R** I have to admit it was quite discouraging. In addition, I learned **R** after learning a property statistical software that is objectively more user-friendly. Consequently, as a beginner in **R** I was making a lot of errors. As you can imagine, the errors indeed did not discourage me. I got even more passionate about **R** after solving the errors I was doing. I think, indeed, that when we solve errors we really learn how to use **R** (but this can be extended to any software). This short introduction about my experience is just to stress that everyone makes errors, above all at the beginning, and even the most expert users. Here I would like to talk about the most frequent errors I made when I started to learn **R**.

Syntax Errors

R is a language and as any language has its own grammar rules. For example, if in English I write "I, want to learn **R**" an English teacher would tell me I made an error because I put a comma between the subject and the verb. And something similar happens in **R**.

We can make "syntax errors" in **R**, i.e. errors due to write a part of code in the wrong place or to forget an essential element of the code. This kind of errors is the most recurrent case and, generally, it is extremely easy to fix. For example,

```
> a <- c(6, 7, 8, 9 10)
Error: unexpected numeric constant in "a <- c(6, 7, 8, 9 10"
```

Basically, we just forgot the comma `,` between 9 and 10.

Let's see another example. In **R**, we use many functions developed by the **R** Community members. All these functions come with documentation regarding their use. We access this documentation by typing a question mark before the name of the function or by using the `help()` function. For example,

```
> ?print
> ?"if"
> help("as.numeric")
```

For example, let's use the `lm()` function to fit a linear model. We generate some random data for the independent variable, `x`, by using the `rnorm()` function and then we generate the dependent variable `y`. We build then a data frame, `df`, with `x` and `y` and we print the first six entries with the `head()` function. Finally, we fit a linear model with the `lm()` function.

```
> x <- rnorm(100)
> y <- 10 + 5*x
> df <- data.frame(x, y)
> head(df)
           x         y
1 -1.1161285  4.419357
2  1.3803809 16.901904
3 -1.7812245  1.093877
4  0.9383783 14.691891
5 -0.4576268  7.711866
6 -1.7358237  1.320882
> model1 <- lm(y, x, data = df)
Error in formula.default(object, env = baseenv()) : invalid formula
```

However, we got an error. If we investigate the documentation for the `lm()` function, we find out that we incorrectly wrote the formula, i.e. the description of the model. In fact, we should have used the regression operator ∼ to separate the dependent variable from the independent variables. We will correctly use the `lm()` function from the next chapter.

class() Type Errors

This is the kind of error that we encountered when we tried to multiply a numeric value by a character value. If we compare this "class errors" with the "syntax errors", in this case we are correctly writing the code but the objects we use are not appropriate. Let's consider another example.

Let's build a data frame with the `data.frame()` function.

```
> df <- data.frame(a = c(1, 2),
+                  b = c(3, 4))
> df
  a b
1 1 3
2 2 4
```

Now this `df` object looks very similar to a matrix. Let's try to make a matrix multiplication with the operator `%*%`. To investigate the usage of this operator type `?"%*%"`.

Matrix Multiplication
Description

Multiplies two matrices, if they are conformable. If one argument is a vector, it will be promoted to either a row or column matrix to make the two arguments conformable. If both are vectors of the same length, it will return the inner product (as a matrix).

Usage

x %*% y

Arguments

x, y numeric or complex matrices or vectors.

After reading the documentation for `%*%`, do you think we can make a matrix multiplication between `df` and `df`? Let's try

```
> df %*% df
Error in df %*% df : requires numeric/complex matrix/vector arguments
```

As you correctly imagined, we got an error. As the documentation and the error message tell us, the operator `%*%` requires numeric or complex matrices or vectors. But we have a `data.frame` type object.

```
> class(df)
[1] "data.frame"
```

Since this object is very similar to a matrix, let's try to coerce it to a `matrix` type object by using this time the `as.matrix.data.frame()` function.

```
> df <- as.matrix.data.frame(df)
> class(df)
[1] "matrix" "array"
```

Now, let's compute the matrix multiplication again.

```
> df %*% df
      a  b
[1,]  7 15
[2,] 10 22
```

And as expected now it works.

We should keep in mind that in some cases we can apply operations only with some type of objects. Therefore, it is very important to be aware about the type of objects we are working with.

Warning Message

Let's write a conditional statement with the `if()` function. We create an object, `x`, and set it equal to 10. We tell **R** to print `"yes"` *if* `x == 10`.[10] Because `x` is 10, the conditional statement is true and, consequently, the function prints `"yes"`. Then, let's set `x <- 9`. In this case the function does nothing because now `x` is equal to 9 and therefore the conditional statement is false.

```
> x <- 10
> if(x == 10) print("yes")
[1] "yes"
> x <- 9
> if(x == 10) print("yes")
```

But note the following.[11]

```
> x <- 5:15
> x
 [1]  5  6  7  8  9 10 11 12 13 14 15
> if(x == 10) print("yes")
```

[10] Refer to Table 1.3 for logical operators.

[11] Note that if you have the latest version of **R** you will not able to replicate the warning message since the `if()` function returns an error in the latest version with the same example.

```
Warning message:
In if (x == 10) print("yes") :
  the condition has length > 1 and
  only the first element will be used
> if(x > 10) print("yes")
Warning message:
In if (x > 10) print("yes") :
  the condition has length > 1 and
  only the first element will be used
```

In these last cases, **R** prints a `Warning message.` We have to make a distinction between error and warning messages in **R**. When we get an error the function does not run. Instead, in the case of the warning message, it runs but **R** tells us something is unexpected.

In the example, the warning message says that `the condition has length > 1`, because we are working with an object that stores multiple values, and that `only the first element will be used`. In this case, the first value is 5 and therefore the function does nothing. But if the first value is 10 we have the following

```
> x <- 10:15
> if(x == 10) print("yes")
[1] "yes"
Warning message:
In if (x == 10) print("yes") :
  the condition has length > 1 and
  only the first element will be used
```

The function prints `"yes"` because the first value now is 10. To convince ourselves that the function is really working let's add an `else` expression. Let's rebuild the `x` object from 5 to 15.

```
> x <- 5:15
> if(x == 10){
+   print("yes")
+ } else{
+   print("no")
+ }
[1] "no"
Warning message:
In if (x == 10) { :
  the condition has length > 1 and
  only the first element will be used
```

And as you can see now the function prints `"no"` because the first element, 5, is not equal to 10. However, we still get the warning message.

We could work out this warning message by nesting the `any()` function in the `if()` function as follows

```
> x <- 5:15
> if(any(x == 10)) print("yes")
[1] "yes"
```

However, let's say we want something different, i.e. that the function is evaluated at each value of `x`. A better solution would consist in picking another function. In this case, the `ifelse()` function

```
> ifelse(x == 10, "yes", "no")
 [1] "no"  "no"  "no"  "no"  "no"  "yes" "no"  "no"  "no"  "no"  "no"
> ifelse(x > 10, "yes", "no")
 [1] "no"  "no"  "no"  "no"  "no"  "no"  "yes" "yes" "yes" "yes" "yes"
```

Finally, two pieces of advice. First, if we cannot solve the error after reading the documentation we simply can copy and paste the error or the warning message in a web search engine to look for more explanations and examples. You will find that in most of the cases your question has been already answered by the **R** Community. Second, since most of the **R** Community members communicate in English, it is convenient to set **R** in English. In this way **R** will print the error and warning messages in English. Consequently, we can find more examples for the case we are interested in.

No-Error Message Error

In this book, we will not code functions from scratch. However, we should be aware about the most difficult errors to deal with that mainly occur when we build our own functions: that is, the function we write runs but it does not do what we programmed it for. The main issue is that because it runs we do not get any error or warning message so we may wrongly think that it properly works. An important check when we build our own function is to test it to replicate well-known results and examples. For several examples on writing functions from scratch you may refer to *Introduction to Mathematics for Economics with R* (Porto, 2022).

1.7 Two Examples with R

In this section, we will go through some of the main features of **R** with two examples. In the first example in Sect. 1.7.1, we will see **R** as calculator, as programming language (interactive mode, loop and functions), as statistical software and as graphical software. In the second example in Sect. 1.7.2, we will focus on data management operations with two dummy data frames.

1.7.1 An Overview of R with a Step by Step Example

Suppose a student took a test made up of 50 questions. She gets 3 points for each correct answer. In total she gave 43 correct answers. She wants to know her total score. We can make this multiplication in **R**

```
> 43*3
[1] 129
```

Table 1.1 Math operators

Operator	Description	Example	Output
+	Addition	`2 + 5`	`7`
-	Subtraction	`5 - 2`	`3`
*	Multiplication	`5 * 2`	`10`
/	Division	`5 / 2`	`2.5`
^	Exponentiation	`5^2`	`25`
%%	Remainder	`5 %% 2`	`1`
%/%	Integer division	`5 %/% 2`	`2`

Table 1.2 Math functions

Operator	Description	Example	Output
`sum()`	Sum of vector elements	`sum(5, 2, 3)`	`10`
`cumsum()`	Cumulative sums	`cumsum(c(5, 2, 3))`	`5 7 10`
`min()`	Minima	`min(5, 2, 3)`	`2`
`max()`	Maxima	`max(5, 2, 3)`	`5`
`mean()`	Average	`mean(c(5, 2, 3))`	`3.333333`
`sqrt()`	Square root	`sqrt(25)`	`5`
`abs()`	Absolute value	`abs(-5)`	`5`

In this way, we are using **R** as calculator. Table 1.1 reports the most common operators. In addition, there are some built-in functions that extends the math capability. Refer to Table 1.2.[12]

Continuing with the example, we know that the total score of the student is 129.

However, if you skipped the first lines of the introduction to this section, this number would say nothing to you. Let's see how to reorganize the information. We generate an object, `n_correct_answer`, that stores the number of correct answers. We accomplish this task using the assignment operator `<-`. Then, we generate another object, `point`, that stores the points per correct answer. Finally, we multiply these two objects.

```
> n_correct_answer <- 43
> point <- 3
> n_correct_answer * point
[1] 129
```

Now the information is clearer. Let's add a new step. Let's store the result of the multiplication in a new object, `total_score`.

```
> total_score <- n_correct_answer * point
```

Note that now we do not see the output of the operation because it is stored in `total_score`. To see the output, we have to run the object

```
> total_score
[1] 129
```

[12] Note that `sum()`, `min()`, `max()` treat the collection of arguments as the vector. This is not the typical behaviour in **R**. In `cumsum()` and `mean()`, the `c()` function combines values into a vector (Burns, 2012, p. 8).

The number in the brackets points out the position of the printed element. In this case, 129 is the first element. Since we have only one element it may seem not a useful information. Let's see the output of `cumsum(1:25)`, where `:`, the colon operator, generates regular sequences, in this case, from 1 to 25. The output says that 120 is located at the 15th index.

```
> cumsum(1:25)
 [1]   1   3   6  10  15  21  28  36  45  55  66  78  91 105
[15] 120 136 153 171 190 210 231 253 276 300 325
```

Let's continue with the example. Suppose now we want to write a program that allows the students to enter their number of correct answers and calculates the total score. For this task, we use the `readline()` function. `readline()` reads a line from the terminal in interactive use.

We will assign to the object `n_correct_answer` the following input: `readline("Enter your number of correct answers: ")`. Note that the former score of the student will be overwritten.

When we run this object, **R** will ask to enter the input as follows

```
> n_correct_answer <- readline("Enter your number of correct answers: ")
Enter your number of correct answers:
```

If a student scored 39 she can enter it as follows.

```
> n_correct_answer <- readline("Enter your number of correct answers: ")
Enter your number of correct answers: 39
```

Now we multiply again the number of correct answers by the points, `point`.

```
> total_score <- n_correct_answer * point
Error in n_correct_answer * point :
  non-numeric argument to binary operator
```

But we got an error. The message says that we have a non-numeric argument even though we multiply 39 by 3. Why's that? Let's investigate our objects.

```
> class(point)
[1] "numeric"
```

By using the `class()` function we find out that `point` is a `numeric` class object. Let's check `n_correct_answer`.

```
> class(n_correct_answer)
[1] "character"
```

We found where the problem is. Even though we entered a number, 39, it is returned by the function as a `character`. Basically, we cannot multiply a number by a string. Therefore, we got an error. Let's solve the problem by coercing `n_correct_answer` from `character` to `numeric`. We do this by nesting the previous function in the `as.numeric()` function

```
> n_correct_answer <- as.numeric(
+   readline("Enter your number of correct answers: "))
Enter your number of correct answers: 39
```

Now, let's check again the score of the student.

```
> total_score <- n_correct_answer * point
> total_score
[1] 117
```

This student scored 117. We solved the problem. This example shows that it is important to know the `class` of an object we are dealing with because it can happen that some operations or functions work only with objects with a specific `class`.

Suppose now that we evaluate the tests of 7 students and collect the numbers of correct answers in the tests: 43, 39, 41, 36, 38, 48, 33. We want to calculate their scores.

We can do this by using a loop. First, we generate an object to collect the total score, `total_score`. Second, we collect all the numbers of correct answers in a vector using the `c()` function, `n_correct_answer`. Third, we define the object that stores the points, `point`.[13] Then we use a loop by using the `for()` function, where `i` is a syntactical name and `in` is an operator followed by a sequence. Note that the operations are enclosed in braces. The `print()` function prints out the output. How does the loop work? At the beginning, the `i` element is 43. This is multiplied by `point` and the result is stored in `total_score` and it is printed. Then, the loop starts again. Now the `i` element is 39. This is multiplied by `point` and the result is stored in `total_score` and then it is printed. This is repeated for the length of the sequence. In this case, 7 times.

```
> total_score <- 0
> n_correct_answer <- c(43, 39, 41, 36, 38, 48, 33)
> point <- 3
> for(i in n_correct_answer){
+   total_score <- i * point
+   print(total_score)
+ }
[1] 129
[1] 117
[1] 123
[1] 108
[1] 114
[1] 144
[1] 99
```

We obtained the scores for the 7 students. However, in this case the loop is not the best choice for this computation. We can just use the **R**'s vectorization feature. Basically, we just multiply the vector, `n_correct_answer`, by the scalar, `point`.

```
> names_stud <- c("Anne", "John", "Bob", "Emma",
+                 "Tony", "Sarah", "James")
> names(n_correct_answer) <- names_stud
> n_correct_answer
```

[13] Note that if you did not remove `point` or clear the objects from the workspace, you do not need to generate again `point` to make the loop work. However, we generate it again to make our work easy to understand. On the other hand, we do not really need to generate `total_score` out of the loop. We could remove it from the workspace with `rm()` and this would not affect the loop. However, when we want to store multiple results it is necessary to initialize it. We will talk again about the initialization of `total_score` in a few pages.

```
 Anne   John    Bob   Emma   Tony Sarah James
   43     39     41     36     38    48    33
> total_score <- n_correct_answer * point
> total_score
 Anne   John    Bob   Emma   Tony Sarah James
  129    117    123    108    114   144    99
```

Note also that we generated an object, `names_stud`, that contains the names of the students. By using the `names()` function, we set the names of `n_correct_answer`. Keep in mind that the order is key in **R**. For example, `Anne` is stored at index 1 in `names_stud`. Consequently, it is set as name of the item stored at index 1 in `n_correct_answer`.

Let's make another example with `for()` loop. Suppose that the students enter the number of correct answers in turn. We use the `readline()` function inside the loop.

```
> for(students in 1:length(names_stud)){
+   n_correct_answer <- as.numeric(
+     readline("Enter your number of correct answers: "))
+   total_score <- n_correct_answer * point
+   print(total_score)
+ }
Enter your number of correct answers: 43
[1] 129
Enter your number of correct answers: 39
[1] 117
Enter your number of correct answers: 41
[1] 123
Enter your number of correct answers: 36
[1] 108
Enter your number of correct answers: 38
[1] 114
Enter your number of correct answers: 48
[1] 144
Enter your number of correct answers: 33
[1] 99
```

In this example, first note that we use the name `students` as a syntactical name for a variable (basically, you can choose any name even though `i` for the first loop and `j` for the second loop are quite standard). Second, note how the sequence is written. We know that after `in` the sequence begins. We already know the meaning of the `:` operator. Basically, we generated a sequence that starts at 1 and ends at 7. Why seven? Because 7 is the length of the vector `names_stud`. In fact, it contains 7 elements, i.e. 7 students. Run `length(names_stud)` to verify it. `length()` gets or sets the length of vectors (including lists) and factors, and of any other **R** object for which a method has been defined.

```
> length(names_stud)
[1] 7
```

Additionally, instead of inputing the score after `Enter your number of correct answers:` , I write the score after the loop function in the **R Script** file like this

```
43
39
41
36
38
48
33
```

and run each of them them every time `Enter your number of correct answers:` is printed.

In the previous loop, we printed the results. However, in this way they cannot be used. Therefore, this time we run again the same loop but we remove the `print()` function. The results will be stored in `total_score`. Since we have more than one result to store, this time it is necessary to initialize the `total_score` object. In the previous example, we did not really need it because we just printed out each result every time the loop ran. Note that you can initialize the loop in different ways. In this example, we write `total_score <- numeric(length(names_stud))` that returns an object with seven 0, the length of `names_stud`. These zeros will be replaced by the result of each student every time the loop iterates.

In this regard, note how we write `total_score` inside the loop. We use the square brackets `[ ]` to replace the zeros with the results of the students when the loop iterates (more on this in a few lines). However, note that if we do not subset using the square brackets `[ ]` only the last score will be stored because each time the loop runs it will overwrite the previous value.

```
> point <- 3
> names_stud <- c("Anne", "John", "Bob", "Emma",
+                 "Tony", "Sarah", "James")
> total_score <- numeric(length(names_stud))
> total_score
[1] 0 0 0 0 0 0 0
> for(students in seq_along(names_stud)){
+   n_correct_answer <- as.numeric(
+     readline("Enter your number of correct answers: "))
+   total_score[students] <- n_correct_answer * point
+ }
Enter your number of correct answers: 43
Enter your number of correct answers: 39
Enter your number of correct answers: 41
Enter your number of correct answers: 36
Enter your number of correct answers: 38
Enter your number of correct answers: 48
Enter your number of correct answers: 33
> total_score
[1] 129 117 123 108 114 144  99
```

Finally, note the in `for()` we replaced `for(students in 1:length(x))` with `for(students in seq_along(names_stud))`. `seq_along()` also generates a sequence

```
> seq_along(names_stud)
[1] 1 2 3 4 5 6 7
```

Now let's break the loop down into pieces to analyse what it does.

First, let's again initialize the object to store the results of the loop

```
> total_score <- numeric(length(names_stud))
> total_score
[1] 0 0 0 0 0 0 0
```

When the loop starts, `students` is 1, that is the beginning of the sequence. Therefore, let's replace `students` with 1. The number of correct answers for the first student was 43. Consequently, the total score is replaced at the first entry.

```
> n_correct_answer <- as.numeric(
+   readline("Enter your number of correct answers: "))
Enter your number of correct answers: 43
> total_score[1] <- n_correct_answer * point
> total_score
[1] 129   0   0   0   0   0   0
```

What about if we run this last chunk of code to simulate the second iteration of the loop? Substitute `students` with 2 and give 39 as number of correct answers for the second student and check the output.

Until now the students know their score but they do not know yet if they passed the test. Let's find it out.

First, let's write the information we have, i.e. names of the students who took the test and their number of correct answers, in a data frame. Use the `data.frame()` function to build the data frame named `results_test`.

```
> names_stud <- c("Anne", "John", "Bob", "Emma",
+                 "Tony", "Sarah", "James")
> n_correct_answer <- c(43, 39, 41, 36, 38, 48, 33)
> results_test <- data.frame(names_stud,
+                            n_correct_answer)
> results_test
  names_stud n_correct_answer
1       Anne               43
2       John               39
3        Bob               41
4       Emma               36
5       Tony               38
6      Sarah               48
7      James               33
```

Now we build a function, `final_test`, that will return the score and the information about if the students passed the test.

```
> final_test <- function(n, data, tot_q,
+                        test_per, point = 3){
+   total_score <- data[, n] * point
+   full_score <- tot_q * point
+   threshold <- full_score * test_per
+   outcome <- ifelse(total_score > threshold,
+                     "PASS",
+                     "FAIL")
+   results_test_1 <- cbind(data, total_score, outcome)
+   return(results_test_1)
+ }
```

The function takes five arguments: `n`, `data`, `tot_q`, `test_per` and `point`. `n` refers to the column in the data set that contains the number of correct answer. It can be the name of the column as a string or the corresponding column index. In our case, the name of the column in the data frame is `n_correct_answer`. `data` is the name of the data set with the information about the test. In our case, the name of the data set is `results_test`. `tot_q` is the total number of questions in the test. `test_per` is the percentage that defines the passing threshold. Note that we set a default value, 3, for `point`. Between the braces, we define the steps of the function. First, we calculate the total score of the students, `total_score` as `n_correct_answer` multiplied by `point`. Note how we select the column with the number of correct answer in the data frame. We will talk about this shortly. Second, we calculate the maximum score, `full_score`, as tot_q multiply by point. Third, we calculate the threshold, threshold, as full_score multiplied by the passing percentage, test_per. Fourth, we generate a variable outcome that takes value "PASS" if the total_score is greater than the threshold, and "FAIL" otherwise. We use the ifelse() function to accomplish this task. Then, we combine by columns the data set, data, that represents our data set, with total_score and outcome by using the cbind() function. We assign this operation to a new object, results_test_1. Finally, we will use the return() function to return the data frame from inside the function to the workspace.

Now, we are ready to test it. Suppose that only the students who scored more than 80% of the maximum score pass the test. In this case

```
> final_test(n = "n_correct_answer",
+            data = results_test,
+            tot_q = 50,
+            test_per = 0.8)
  names_stud n_correct_answer total_score outcome
1       Anne               43         129    PASS
2       John               39         117    FAIL
3        Bob               41         123    PASS
4       Emma               36         108    FAIL
5       Tony               38         114    FAIL
6      Sarah               48         144    PASS
7      James               33          99    FAIL
```

Let's try the function by replacing the column name for n with the column index, in our case 2

```
> final_test(n = 2,
+            data = results_test,
+            tot_q = 50,
+            test_per = 0.8)
  names_stud n_correct_answer total_score outcome
1       Anne               43         129    PASS
2       John               39         117    FAIL
3        Bob               41         123    PASS
4       Emma               36         108    FAIL
5       Tony               38         114    FAIL
6      Sarah               48         144    PASS
7      James               33          99    FAIL
```

As expected, we obtain the same results. We have only three students who passed the test. Let's lower the percentage to 70%.

```
> final_test(n = "n_correct_answer",
+            data = results_test,
+            tot_q = 50,
+            test_per = 0.7)
  names_stud n_correct_answer total_score outcome
1       Anne               43         129    PASS
2       John               39         117    PASS
3        Bob               41         123    PASS
4       Emma               36         108    PASS
5       Tony               38         114    PASS
6      Sarah               48         144    PASS
7      James               33          99    FAIL
```

In this case, only one student did not pass the test.

Note that we can modify the default value for point as follows:

```
> final_test(n = "n_correct_answer",
```

```
+               data = results_test,
+               tot_q = 50,
+               test_per = 0.7,
+               point = 4)
  names_stud n_correct_answer total_score outcome
1       Anne               43         172    PASS
2       John               39         156    PASS
3        Bob               41         164    PASS
4       Emma               36         144    PASS
5       Tony               38         152    PASS
6      Sarah               48         192    PASS
7      James               33         132    FAIL
```

Let's go back to the first case, i.e. an 80% passing percentage. This time let's assign this operation to a new object, `results_test_def` to calculate some statistics about our data set. Remember that in this case, you have to run the object to see its content.

```
> results_test_def <- final_test(n = "n_correct_answer",
+                                data = results_test,
+                                tot_q = 50,
+                                test_per = 0.8)
> results_test_def
  names_stud n_correct_answer total_score outcome
1       Anne               43         129    PASS
2       John               39         117    FAIL
3        Bob               41         123    PASS
4       Emma               36         108    FAIL
5       Tony               38         114    FAIL
6      Sarah               48         144    PASS
7      James               33          99    FAIL
```

Let's investigate the structure of our data set with the `str()` function.

```
> str(results_test_def)
'data.frame':   7 obs. of  4 variables:
 $ names_stud      : chr  "Anne" "John" "Bob" "Emma" ...
 $ n_correct_answer: num  43 39 41 36 38 48 33
 $ total_score     : num  129 117 123 108 114 144 99
 $ outcome         : chr  "PASS" "FAIL" "PASS" "FAIL" ...
```

Note that `n_correct_answer` and `total_score` have numerical values. `names_stud` and `outcome` are characters.

Let's find, for example, the average score of the students. We use `$` to select the column of interest from the data set.

```
> mean(results_test_def$total_score)
[1] 119.1429
```

Let's find now the lowest and highest score:

```
> min(results_test_def$total_score)
[1] 99
> max(results_test_def$total_score)
[1] 144
```

A short-cut to obtain this information is through the `summary()` function.

```
> summary(results_test_def$total_score)
   Min. 1st Qu.  Median    Mean 3rd Qu.    Max.
   99.0   111.0   117.0   119.1   126.0   144.0
```

If we apply it to the whole data set:

```
> summary(results_test_def)
  names_stud        n_correct_answer  total_score        outcome
 Length:7           Min.   :33.00     Min.   : 99.0   Length:7
 Class :character   1st Qu.:37.00     1st Qu.:111.0   Class :character
 Mode  :character   Median :39.00     Median :117.0   Mode  :character
                    Mean   :39.71     Mean   :119.1
                    3rd Qu.:42.00     3rd Qu.:126.0
                    Max.   :48.00     Max.   :144.0
```

Let's coerce `outcome` to factors and let's apply again the `summary()` function to the data set (refer to Sect. 1.6.5 for the meaning of factors)

```
> results_test_def$outcome <- as.factor(results_test_def$outcome)
> results_test_def$outcome
[1] PASS FAIL PASS FAIL FAIL PASS FAIL
Levels: FAIL PASS
> summary(results_test_def)
  names_stud        n_correct_answer  total_score      outcome
 Length:7           Min.   :33.00     Min.   : 99.0   FAIL:4
 Class :character   1st Qu.:37.00     1st Qu.:111.0   PASS:3
 Mode  :character   Median :39.00     Median :117.0
                    Mean   :39.71     Mean   :119.1
                    3rd Qu.:42.00     3rd Qu.:126.0
                    Max.   :48.00     Max.   :144.0
```

As you can observe, now the `summary()` function prints how many passed and failed the test in the `outcome` column.

Now let's suppose we want to show only the personal result scored by the student. There are different ways we can extract information from a data frame. Basically, a data frame has two dimensions like a matrix. We can use the `[i, j]` indexes for rows and columns, respectively, where the square brackets `[ ]` subset the data frame.

Let's print again the data set.

```
> results_test_def
  names_stud n_correct_answer total_score outcome
1       Anne               43         129    PASS
2       John               39         117    FAIL
3        Bob               41         123    PASS
4       Emma               36         108    FAIL
5       Tony               38         114    FAIL
6      Sarah               48         144    PASS
7      James               33          99    FAIL
```

We see that student Anne is at row number 1 and column number 1. Therefore, to extract the name of student Anne

```
> results_test_def[1, 1]
[1] "Anne"
```

But if we want to extract all the info for student Anne, i.e. row 1 and all the columns associated

```
> results_test_def[1, ]
  names_stud n_correct_answer total_score outcome
1       Anne               43         129    PASS
```

Basically, we leave blank the space for the column entry after the comma `,`. Therefore, if we want to select only the column with the `total_score` we leave blank the space for the row entry before the comma, `,`

```
> results_test_def[, 3]
[1] 129 117 123 108 114 144  99
```

We can select the data also by column name in a data frame. For example, we could achieve the same previous task as follows:

```
> results_test_def[, "total_score"]
[1] 129 117 123 108 114 144  99
```

The selection of columns with the square bracket operator is alternative to `$`. However, with the square bracket operator we can select more columns with the `c()` function. For example, to select the first column and third column:

```
> results_test_def[, c(1, 3)]
  names_stud total_score
1       Anne         129
2       John         117
3        Bob         123
4       Emma         108
5       Tony         114
6      Sarah         144
7      James          99

> results_test_def[, c("names_stud", "total_score")]
  names_stud total_score
1       Anne         129
2       John         117
3        Bob         123
4       Emma         108
5       Tony         114
6      Sarah         144
7      James          99
```

Consequently, if we want to select more rows:

```
> results_test_def[c(2, 5), ]
  names_stud n_correct_answer total_score outcome
2       John               39         117    FAIL
5       Tony               38         114    FAIL
```

Now suppose we want to find the student who got the highest score:

```
> results_test_def[which.max(results_test_def$total_score), ]
  names_stud n_correct_answer total_score outcome
6      Sarah               48         144    PASS
```

Now the notation should be clear. We subset the data set by the row with the highest total score, i.e. 144, that it is located at row 6, and for all the columns. In fact,

```
> which.max(results_test_def$total_score)
[1] 6
```

Now suppose we want to rename the column names. We use the `colnames()` function.[14]

```
> colnames(results_test_def) <- c("Students", "Correct_Answer",
+                                  "Total_Score", "Outcome")
> results_test_def
  Students Correct_Answer Total_Score Outcome
```

[14] Note that it is better to avoid space in the names of the variables.

Table 1.3 Logical operators

Operator	Description
>	Greater than
<	Less than
>=	Greater or equal
<=	Less or equal
==	Exact equality
!=	Inequality

```
1      Anne          43           129     PASS
2      John          39           117     FAIL
3       Bob          41           123     PASS
4      Emma          36           108     FAIL
5      Tony          38           114     FAIL
6     Sarah          48           144     PASS
7     James          33            99     FAIL
```

But now we decide we want to change the name of `Outcome` in `PASSFAIL`:

```
> colnames(results_test_def) [
+   colnames(results_test_def) == "Outcome"] <- "PASSFAIL"
> results_test_def
  Students Correct_Answer Total_Score PASSFAIL
1     Anne             43         129     PASS
2     John             39         117     FAIL
3      Bob             41         123     PASS
4     Emma             36         108     FAIL
5     Tony             38         114     FAIL
6    Sarah             48         144     PASS
7    James             33          99     FAIL
```

Let's translate into plain English this line of code. We are telling **R** that "among all column names in the data set, the one whose name is equal to `Outcome` has to be renamed as `PASSFAIL`".

Note that == is a logical operator that means exact equality. Refer to Table 1.3 for more logical operators.

Let's see how we can replace column names in a different way. Let's change `PASSFAIL` to `PASS/FAIL`. Let's run only `colnames(results_test_def)`. This extracts the column names of the data frame or matrix. We observe that `PASSFAIL` is the 4th entry.

```
> colnames(results_test_def)
[1] "Students"         "Correct_Answer" "Total_Score"      "PASSFAIL"
```

Let's rename it by replacing its 4th entry

```
> colnames(results_test_def)[4] <- "PASS/FAIL"
> results_test_def
  Students Correct_Answer Total_Score PASS/FAIL
1     Anne             43         129      PASS
2     John             39         117      FAIL
3      Bob             41         123      PASS
4     Emma             36         108      FAIL
5     Tony             38         114      FAIL
6    Sarah             48         144      PASS
7    James             33          99      FAIL
```

Let's generate a new variable, `PASS`, that takes value 1 if the student passed, 0 otherwise. We use again the `ifelse()` function.

```
> results_test_def$PASS <- ifelse(
+   results_test_def$`PASS/FAIL` == "PASS",
+                                   1, 0)
> results_test_def
  Students Correct_Answer Total_Score PASS/FAIL PASS
1     Anne             43         129      PASS    1
2     John             39         117      FAIL    0
3      Bob             41         123      PASS    1
4     Emma             36         108      FAIL    0
5     Tony             38         114      FAIL    0
6    Sarah             48         144      PASS    1
7    James             33          99      FAIL    0
```

Let's conclude this section by plotting some information in the data set. We will plot using the `ggplot()` function from the `ggplot2` package.

We need to load the package before using it at the beginning of an **R** session. We use the `library()` function to load the package.

```
> library("ggplot2")
```

When we load a package some information about the package may be printed. For the sake of illustration we do not print them.

Now we are ready to use the `ggplot()` function. We will plot a bar plot and a box plot.

First, we will plot the total score of each student. Note again the code printed in the console pane for `ggplot()`. We have two +. One +, directly below the prompt symbol, >, means the the code is continuing on the next line in the console pane. This + is not part of the code we write. The other + is part of the `ggplot()` code and connect the different layers in `ggplot()`.

```
> ggplot(results_test_def, aes(x= Students, y = Total_Score,
+                              fill = `PASS/FAIL`)) +
+      geom_bar(position = "dodge", stat="identity") +
+      ylab("Total Score") + theme_classic() +
+      ggtitle("Total Score for a 50 question test") +
+      theme(legend.position = "bottom")
```

The first entry in `ggplot()` is the data set. In `aes()` we map the data for the x and y axes. We distinguish the values by whether the students passed the test by using `fill =`. We will return to the meaning of the backticks in `` `PASS/FAIL` `` in a moment. We choose to plot the data as a bar plot using `geom_bar()`. `position = "dodge"` puts the bars side-by-side. With `stat = "identity"` the heights of the bars represent values in the data. `ylab()` sets the label for the y-axis. In `ggtitle()` we type the title of the plot. `theme_classic()` is one of the possible options to define the layout of the plot. Finally, in `theme()` we set the position of the legend below the plot. The output is Fig. 1.12.

We can export it as image from **RStudio** as shown in Figs. 1.13 and 1.14

A feature of `ggplot()` is that its output can be stored. For example, if you plot using the built-in function in **R**, i.e. `plot()`, you cannot store its output.

In the next example, we will store the output of a box plot in the following object, `passed_boxplot`. Note the in `aes()`, we have to map `x` and `fill` to `` `PASS/FAIL` ``. Note that we have to enclose the variable name in ` ` because we included / in the column name. ` ` is also necessary when we write a column name with a space. For this reason, it is better to avoid spaces in the column names.

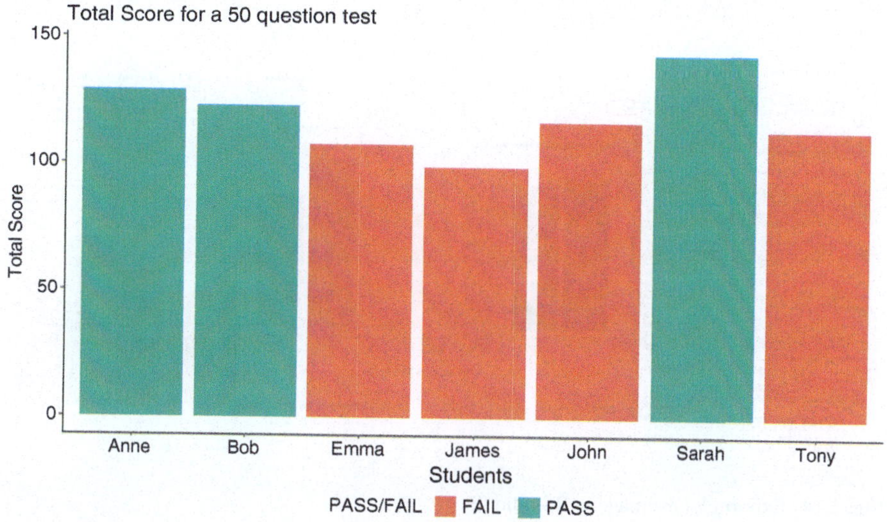

Fig. 1.12 Example of a bar plot

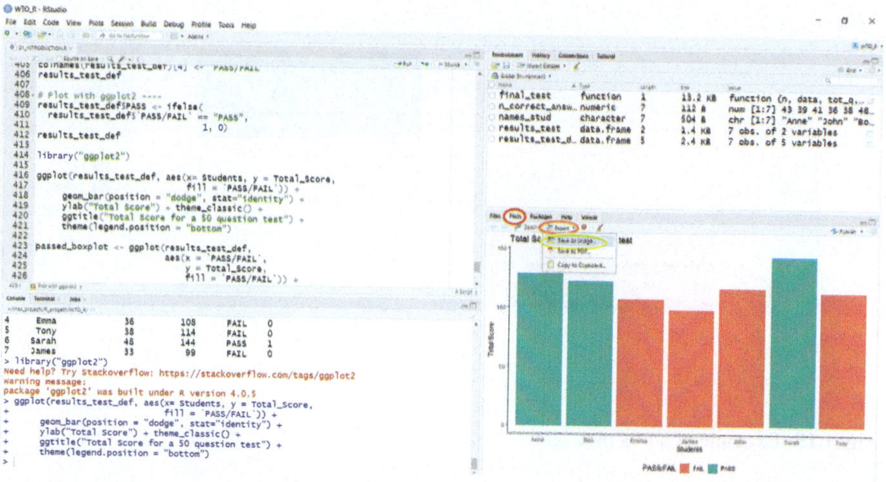

Fig. 1.13 Export plot as image in RStudio (1)

In addition, `xlab("")` removes the title of the *x*-axis while `legend.title = element_blank()` removes the title of the legend. Now, we have to run the object to see the plot (Fig. 1.15).

```
> passed_boxplot <- ggplot(results_test_def,
+                          aes(x = 'PASS/FAIL',
+                              y = Total_Score,
+                              fill = 'PASS/FAIL')) +
+   geom_boxplot() +
+   ylab("Total Score") + xlab("") +
+   ggtitle("Boxplot of Results (Fail, Pass)") +
```

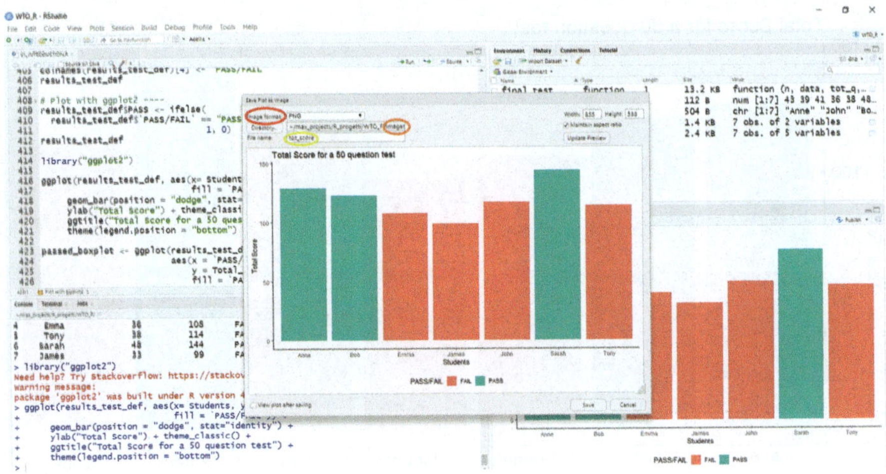

Fig. 1.14 Export plot as image in RStudio (2)

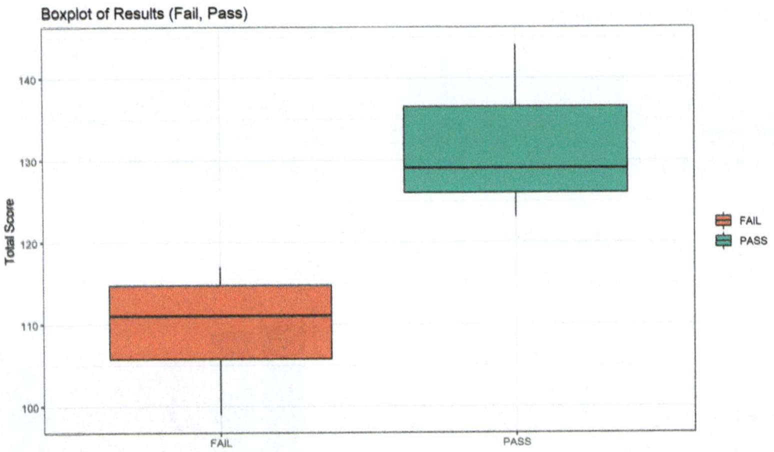

Fig. 1.15 Example of a box plot

```
+     theme_bw() +
+     theme(legend.title = element_blank())
> passed_boxplot
```

For this example, we use the `ggsave()` function from `ggplot2` to save the `ggplot2` plot. The first entry is the file name to create on the disk. Note that I specify the path to the `images` folder we created at the beginning. The second entry is the name of the plot we want to save. By default, it saves the last plot.[15]

---

[15] In the rest of the book I will not print the code to save the images. However, for `ggplot2` plots I use the `ggsave()` function. For other plots, I save them as shown in Figs. 1.13 and 1.14. To save 3D plots, you may use the `rgl.snapshot()` function from the `rgl` package. However, we will not make any 3D plot in this book.

```
> ggsave(filename = "images/passes_boxplot.png",
+         plot = passed_boxplot)
Saving 9.28 x 5.6 in image
```

Suppose we want to check the values of the boxplot. First, we can subset the data set using the `subset()` function. Since the `subset()` function is a built-in function, we do not need to load any package to use it. We create two objects. The first one contains the data only for the students who passed while the second one only for students who did not pass. The first entry in the `subset()` function is the data set. Then, we type the conditional statement. In this case, we subset the data set if the value in `'PASS/FAIL'` is equal to `"PASS"`. Note again the inclusion of `' '` around the column name. Note that for the object `FAIL` we use the inequality operator `!=`. We could also use `'PASS/FAIL' == "FAIL"` to accomplish the same task. Finally, we apply the `summary()` function to the value in `Total_Score`.

```
> PASS <- subset(results_test_def, 'PASS/FAIL' == "PASS")
> FAIL <- subset(results_test_def, 'PASS/FAIL' != "PASS")
> PASS
  Students Correct_Answer Total_Score PASS/FAIL PASS
1     Anne             43         129      PASS    1
3      Bob             41         123      PASS    1
6    Sarah             48         144      PASS    1
> FAIL
  Students Correct_Answer Total_Score PASS/FAIL PASS
2     John             39         117      FAIL    0
4     Emma             36         108      FAIL    0
5     Tony             38         114      FAIL    0
7    James             33          99      FAIL    0
> summary(PASS$Total_Score)
   Min. 1st Qu.  Median    Mean 3rd Qu.    Max.
  123.0   126.0   129.0   132.0   136.5   144.0
> summary(FAIL$Total_Score)
   Min. 1st Qu.  Median    Mean 3rd Qu.    Max.
   99.0   105.8   111.0   109.5   114.8   117.0
```

We read that the minimum value for `PASS` is 123, the beginning of the vertical line in Fig. 1.15. The first quartile corresponds to the beginning of the box, 126, while the third quartile corresponds to the end of the box, 136.5. The tick middle line corresponds to the median or middle quartile, 129. The end of the line corresponds to the maximum value, 144.

1.7.2 Main Data Management Operations

From the next chapter, we will repeatedly use functions to put information from several data frames of different sizes into a single data frame that will finally be analyzed. Since we will work with real data frames with thousands of rows and dozens of columns, it will be impossible to print the outcome of the individual functions.

Since I think it is very useful to clearly grasp how the functions modify the data frames we work with, in this section we implement the main data management operations to two small dummy data frames. We name the first data frame `trade`. It contains four columns: `year` containing information for years 2020, 2021, and 2022, `reporter` and `partner` containing information about 3 fictitious countries that we name as letters, and `export` containing the value of export from reporter to partner in million dollar. The second data frame is named `gdp` and contains the GDP values in billion dollar of four fictitious countries. Our goal is to put the info of these two different data frames in an single data frame and generate new variables to provide additional information.

We need to load the following packages before starting to write the code

```
library("data.table") # data management (melt, dcast)
library("tidyr") # data management (pivot_)
library("dplyr") # data management (case_when)
library("stringr") # string manipulation
library("zoo") # time series
```

Now let's build the two dummy data frames for the example

```
> set.seed(123)
> trade <- data.frame(year = rep(2020:2022, 6),
+                     reporter = rep(LETTERS[1:3], each = 6),
+                     partner = rep(c("B","C", "A", "C", "A", "B"),
+                                   each = 3),
+                     export = sample(50:150, 18, replace = TRUE))
> trade
   year reporter partner export
1  2020        A       B     80
2  2021        A       B    128
3  2022        A       B    100
4  2020        A       C     63
5  2021        A       C    116
6  2022        A       C     91
7  2020        B       A     99
8  2021        B       A     92
9  2022        B       A    150
10 2020        B       C     63
11 2021        B       C     74
12 2022        B       C    139
13 2020        C       A    140
14 2021        C       A    118
15 2022        C       A    140
16 2020        C       B    106
17 2021        C       B    141
18 2022        C       B     58

> set.seed(321)
> gdp <- data.frame(country = c(LETTERS[1:4]),
+                   isocode = paste0(LETTERS[1:4], 1:4),
+                   year2020 = sample(500:1000, 4),
+                   year2021 = sample(500:1000, 4),
+                   year2022 = sample(500:1000, 4))
> gdp
  country isocode year2020 year2021 year2022
1       A      A1      681      843      625
2       B      B2      997      963      772
3       C      C3      752      557      727
4       D      D4      832      851      546
```

Let's replace the entry for the *A* country for year 2021 with a missing value, NA

```
> gdp[1, 4] <- NA
> gdp
  country isocode year2020 year2021 year2022
1       A      A1      681       NA      625
2       B      B2      997      963      772
3       C      C3      752      557      727
4       D      D4      832      851      546
```

First, note that the `set.seed()` function is used to make the example reproducible with random number generation functions. Second, note that the `trade` data frame is in a long format while the `gdp` data frame is in a wide format. In the long format, values for years and id repeat in the columns. On the other hand, in the wide format, id values do not repeat in the columns, and each year is a column title.

Our goal is to merge `trade` and `gdp`. However, we cannot perform this operation with `gdp` in a wide format. Therefore the first step is to reshape it.

Reshaping Data Set Wide-Long

We can perform this task with different packages. We will see how to do it with the the `tidyr` package and with the `data.table` package.

Let's start with a simple case. Let's drop the `isocode` from `gdp`

```
> gdp2 <- gdp[, -2]
> gdp2
  country year2020 year2021 year2022
1       A      681       NA      625
2       B      997      963      772
3       C      752      557      727
4       D      832      851      546
```

The `country` column is our id column.

First, let's reshape it with the `pivot_longer()` function from the `tidyr` package. The esclamation mark `!` means that we are reshaping all the columns by using `country` as the id variable. In `names_to` we write the name of the column to be created the will store the names of the variables to be reshaped. In `vaues_to` we write the name of the column to be created the will store the reshaped values in the columns `year2020`, `year2021`, and `year2022`.

```
> gdp2_1 <- gdp2 %>%
+   pivot_longer(!country, # all columns but not country
+                names_to = "year",
+                values_to = "GDP")
> gdp2_1
# A tibble: 12 x 3
   country year       GDP
   <chr>   <chr>    <int>
 1 A       year2020   681
 2 A       year2021    NA
 3 A       year2022   625
 4 B       year2020   997
 5 B       year2021   963
 6 B       year2022   772
 7 C       year2020   752
 8 C       year2021   557
 9 C       year2022   727
```

```
10 D        year2020    832
11 D        year2021    851
12 D        year2022    546
```

The original data set `gdp2` has 4 rows and 4 columns. The reshaped data set `gdp2_l` has 12 rows and 3 columns. Now the values in `country` repeat, as the values in `year`. Note that in the `year` column we want numeric values. We will see how to adjust that in a moment. Finally, `GDP` is the column that we created and stores the GDP values corresponding to each country and year.

Additionally, note the role of `%>%`. This is the pipe operator. It is used to pipe an object forward into a function or call expression. We are using it to pass `gdp2` as the first argument in `pivot_longer()`. Note that we could just write as usual

```
> pivot_longer(gdp2,
+              !country, # all columns but not country
+              names_to = "year",
+              values_to = "GDP")
# A tibble: 12 x 3
   country year       GDP
   <chr>   <chr>    <int>
 1 A       year2020   681
 2 A       year2021    NA
 3 A       year2022   625
 4 B       year2020   997
 5 B       year2021   963
 6 B       year2022   772
 7 C       year2020   752
 8 C       year2021   557
 9 C       year2022   727
10 D       year2020   832
11 D       year2021   851
12 D       year2022   546
```

However, the pipe operator turns to be very useful to chain operations.

Ok, now `gdp2_l` is in the long format. What about if we want to reshape it in a wide format? We can use the `pivot_wider()` function from the `tidyr` package.

```
> gdp2_w <- gdp2_l %>%
+   pivot_wider(names_from = "year",
+               values_from = "GDP")
> gdp2_w
# A tibble: 4 x 4
  country year2020 year2021 year2022
  <chr>      <int>    <int>    <int>
1 A            681       NA      625
2 B            997      963      772
3 C            752      557      727
4 D            832      851      546
```

We are back to the wide format. However, note that the class of `gdp2` and `gdp2_w` is different

```
> class(gdp2)
[1] "data.frame"
> class(gdp2_w)
[1] "tbl_df"     "tbl"        "data.frame"
```

`gdp2_w` is a now a tibble object. Here, we define the `tbl_df` class as a special class of data frame. You may refer to Wickham (2019a, p. 58) for more details.

Now we implement the same operations with the `data.table` package. We use the `melt()` function to reshape the data set from wide to long, and the `dcast()` function to reshape from long to wide.

```
> gdp2_ldt <- melt(setDT(gdp2), id.vars = "country",
+                  measure.vars = 2:length(colnames(gdp2)),
+                  variable.name = "year",
+                  value.name = "GDP")
> gdp2_ldt
    country     year GDP
 1:       A year2020 681
 2:       B year2020 997
 3:       C year2020 752
 4:       D year2020 832
 5:       A year2021  NA
 6:       B year2021 963
 7:       C year2021 557
 8:       D year2021 851
 9:       A year2022 625
10:       B year2022 772
11:       C year2022 727
12:       D year2022 546
```

The `setDT()` function coerces lists and data.frames to data.table by reference.

In `id.vars` we indicate the id variables. It can be integer (corresponding id column numbers) or character (id column names) vector. In `measure.vars` we indicate the variables for melting. `variable.name` assigns the name for the measured variable names column. The default name is 'variable', while `value.name` assigns name for the molten data values column(s). The default name is 'value'.

By using `dcast()` we reshape the data set from wide back to long.

```
> gdp2_wdt <- dcast(gdp2_ldt, country ~ year,
+                   value.var = "GDP")
> gdp2_wdt
   country year2020 year2021 year2022
1:       A      681       NA      625
2:       B      997      963      772
3:       C      752      557      727
4:       D      832      851      546
```

In `dcast()` we need to use a formula of the form $LHS \sim RHS$. In our example, `country` is our id variable and `year` is casted away with the values of `GDP` fillig the corresponding entry in the data set.

Next, we repeat the same operations with the `pivot_longer()` function and with the `melt()` function to reshape the data set from wide to long. However, this time we specify the pattern in the data set.

```
> gdp2_l2 <- gdp2 %>%
+   pivot_longer(!country,
+                names_prefix = "year",
+                names_to = "year",
+                values_to = "GDP")
> gdp2_l2
# A tibble: 12 x 3
  country year    GDP
  <chr>   <chr> <int>
1 A       2020    681
2 A       2021     NA
3 A       2022    625
4 B       2020    997
5 B       2021    963
```

```
 6 B        2022    772
 7 C        2020    752
 8 C        2021    557
 9 C        2022    727
10 D        2020    832
11 D        2021    851
12 D        2022    546
```

By using `name_prefix` we removed the word `year` from the numeric year. However, note that the `year` column is character.

By using `measure = patterns()` in `melt()` we identify the column to melt by the pattern. Note that in this case we did not remove the word `year`. We will manipulate strings in Sect. 1.7.2.

```
> gdp2_ldt2 <- melt(setDT(gdp2), id = 1,
+                   measure = patterns("year"))
> gdp2_ldt2
    country variable value
 1:       A year2020   681
 2:       B year2020   997
 3:       C year2020   752
 4:       D year2020   832
 5:       A year2021    NA
 6:       B year2021   963
 7:       C year2021   557
 8:       D year2021   851
 9:       A year2022   625
10:       B year2022   772
11:       C year2022   727
12:       D year2022   546
```

Finally, we see how to reshape the data set with multiple id vars. We use the `gdp` data frame

```
> gdp
  country isocode year2020 year2021 year2022
1       A      A1      681       NA      625
2       B      B2      997      963      772
3       C      C3      752      557      727
4       D      D4      832      851      546
```

With `pivot_longer()`

```
> gdp_l <- gdp %>%
+   pivot_longer(cols = 3:length(colnames(gdp)),
+                names_prefix = "year",
+                names_to = "year",
+                values_to = "GDP",
+                values_drop_na = TRUE)
> gdp_l
# A tibble: 11 x 4
   country isocode year    GDP
   <chr>   <chr>   <chr> <int>
 1 A       A1      2020    681
 2 A       A1      2022    625
 3 B       B2      2020    997
 4 B       B2      2021    963
 5 B       B2      2022    772
 6 C       C3      2020    752
 7 C       C3      2021    557
 8 C       C3      2022    727
 9 D       D4      2020    832
10 D       D4      2021    851
11 D       D4      2022    546
```

Note that by setting `values_drop_na = TRUE` we removed the observation with the missing value. If we do not include it

```
> gdp %>%
+   pivot_longer(cols = 3:length(colnames(gdp)),
+                names_prefix = "year",
+                names_to = "year",
+                values_to = "GDP")
# A tibble: 12 x 4
   country isocode year    GDP
   <chr>   <chr>   <chr> <int>
 1 A       A1      2020    681
 2 A       A1      2021     NA
 3 A       A1      2022    625
 4 B       B2      2020    997
 5 B       B2      2021    963
 6 B       B2      2022    772
 7 C       C3      2020    752
 8 C       C3      2021    557
 9 C       C3      2022    727
10 D       D4      2020    832
11 D       D4      2021    851
12 D       D4      2022    546
```

Note that we just printed, but we did not store, the result of the previous operation.

To reshape from wide to long

```
> gdp_w <- gdp_l %>%
+   pivot_wider(names_prefix = "year",
+               names_from = "year",
+               values_from = "GDP",
+               names_sort = TRUE,
+               values_fill = NA)
> gdp_w
# A tibble: 4 x 5
  country isocode year2020 year2021 year2022
  <chr>   <chr>      <int>    <int>    <int>
1 A       A1           681       NA      625
2 B       B2           997      963      772
3 C       C3           752      557      727
4 D       D4           832      851      546
```

We are back to the wide format. Note that by setting `vales_fill = NA` we introduce the entry with the missing value in the data set.

Now we repeat the same operations with the `data.table` package

```
> gdp_l2 <- melt(setDT(gdp), id.vars = 1:2,
+               measure = 3:length(colnames(gdp)),
+               variable.name = "year",
+               value.name = "GDP",
+               na.rm = TRUE)
> gdp_l2
    country isocode     year GDP
 1:       A      A1 year2020 681
 2:       B      B2 year2020 997
 3:       C      C3 year2020 752
 4:       D      D4 year2020 832
 5:       B      B2 year2021 963
 6:       C      C3 year2021 557
 7:       D      D4 year2021 851
 8:       A      A1 year2022 625
 9:       B      B2 year2022 772
10:       C      C3 year2022 727
11:       D      D4 year2022 546
```

```
> gdp_w2 <- dcast(gdp_12, country + isocode ~ year,
+                 value.var = "GDP", fill = NA)
> gdp_w2
   country isocode year2020 year2021 year2022
1:       A      A1      681       NA      625
2:       B      B2      997      963      772
3:       C      C3      752      557      727
4:       D      D4      832      851      546
```

Working with Strings

We can use the `stringr` package to manipulate strings.[16] For example, let's remove the word year from the `year` column in `gdp2_l` by using the `str_remove_all()` function

```
> gdp2_l$year <- str_remove_all(gdp2_l$year, "year")
> gdp2_l
# A tibble: 12 x 3
   country year    GDP
   <chr>   <chr> <int>
 1 A       2020    681
 2 A       2021     NA
 3 A       2022    625
 4 B       2020    997
 5 B       2021    963
 6 B       2022    772
 7 C       2020    752
 8 C       2021    557
 9 C       2022    727
10 D       2020    832
11 D       2021    851
12 D       2022    546
```

We removed year but it is still a character. Let's convert into numeric

```
> gdp2_l$year <- as.numeric(gdp2_l$year)
> str(gdp2_l)
tibble [12 x 3] (S3: tbl_df/tbl/data.frame)
 $ country: chr [1:12] "A" "A" "A" "B" ...
 $ year   : num [1:12] 2020 2021 2022 2020 2021 ...
 $ GDP    : int [1:12] 681 NA 625 997 963 772 752 557 727 832 ...
```

There are several functions to work with strings in `stringr`. They start with `str_`. Read their documentation to learn more about them.

`case_when()` (if else)

Country `A` and country `B` belong to region `W`, while country `C` and country `D` belong to region `Z`. We want to add this information in the `gdp2_l` data set. We have already seen how to accomplish this task with the `ifelse()` function. In this case, however, it is more convenient to use the `case_when()` function from the `dplyr` package. This function allows you to vectorize multiple `if_else()` statements.

[16] In Sect. 2.4 we will work with the `stringi` package.

```
> gdp2_l <- gdp2_l %>%
+   mutate(region = case_when(
+     country == "A" | country == "B" ~ "W",
+     country == "C" | country == "D" ~ "Z",
+   ))
> gdp2_l
# A tibble: 12 x 4
   country  year   GDP region
   <chr>   <dbl> <int> <chr>
 1 A        2020   681 W
 2 A        2021    NA W
 3 A        2022   625 W
 4 B        2020   997 W
 5 B        2021   963 W
 6 B        2022   772 W
 7 C        2020   752 Z
 8 C        2021   557 Z
 9 C        2022   727 Z
10 D        2020   832 Z
11 D        2021   851 Z
12 D        2022   546 Z
```

Note that we nested `case_when()` in `mutate()`, another function from the `dplyr` package that allows to add new variables to the data set.

In `case_when()` we use a formula where the left hand side (LHS) determines which values match this case while the right hand side (RHS) provides the replacement value.

Grouping by One or More Variables

Often it happens that we have to perform operations per group of variables in a data set. For this task we can use the `group_by()` function from the `dplyr` package.

Let's say that we want to sum the GDP per country in `gdp2_l`. We can do as follow

```
> gdp2_l <- gdp2_l %>%
+   group_by(country) %>%
+   mutate(totalGDP = sum(GDP, na.rm = TRUE))
> gdp2_l
# A tibble: 12 x 5
# Groups:   country [4]
   country  year   GDP region totalGDP
   <chr>   <dbl> <int> <chr>     <int>
 1 A        2020   681 W          1306
 2 A        2021    NA W          1306
 3 A        2022   625 W          1306
 4 B        2020   997 W          2732
 5 B        2021   963 W          2732
 6 B        2022   772 W          2732
 7 C        2020   752 Z          2036
 8 C        2021   557 Z          2036
 9 C        2022   727 Z          2036
10 D        2020   832 Z          2229
11 D        2021   851 Z          2229
12 D        2022   546 Z          2229
```

Note that we need to set `na.rm = TRUE` in `sum()` because the series contains a missing value.

An alternative is to use the base function `ave()` as follows

```
> gdp2_ave <- gdp2_1
> gdp2_ave$totalGDPave <- ave(gdp2_ave$GDP,
+                            interaction(gdp2_ave$country),
+                            FUN = function(x) sum(x, na.rm = TRUE))
> gdp2_ave
# A tibble: 12 x 6
# Groups:   country [4]
   country  year   GDP region totalGDP totalGDPave
   <chr>   <dbl> <int> <chr>     <int>       <int>
 1 A        2020   681 W          1306        1306
 2 A        2021    NA W          1306        1306
 3 A        2022   625 W          1306        1306
 4 B        2020   997 W          2732        2732
 5 B        2021   963 W          2732        2732
 6 B        2022   772 W          2732        2732
 7 C        2020   752 Z          2036        2036
 8 C        2021   557 Z          2036        2036
 9 C        2022   727 Z          2036        2036
10 D        2020   832 Z          2229        2229
11 D        2021   851 Z          2229        2229
12 D        2022   546 Z          2229        2229
```

Merging Data Sets

Now we are ready to merge the `gdp2_1` data frame with the `trade` data frame. Let's print them again

```
> gdp2_1
# A tibble: 12 x 5
# Groups:   country [4]
   country  year   GDP region totalGDP
   <chr>   <dbl> <int> <chr>     <int>
 1 A        2020   681 W          1306
 2 A        2021    NA W          1306
 3 A        2022   625 W          1306
 4 B        2020   997 W          2732
 5 B        2021   963 W          2732
 6 B        2022   772 W          2732
 7 C        2020   752 Z          2036
 8 C        2021   557 Z          2036
 9 C        2022   727 Z          2036
10 D        2020   832 Z          2229
11 D        2021   851 Z          2229
12 D        2022   546 Z          2229
> trade
   year reporter partner export
1  2020        A       B     80
2  2021        A       B    128
3  2022        A       B    100
4  2020        A       C     63
5  2021        A       C    116
6  2022        A       C     91
7  2020        B       A     99
8  2021        B       A     92
9  2022        B       A    150
10 2020        B       C     63
11 2021        B       C     74
12 2022        B       C    139
13 2020        C       A    140
14 2021        C       A    118
15 2022        C       A    140
16 2020        C       B    106
17 2021        C       B    141
18 2022        C       B     58
```

Our goal is to put the data from the two data frames in a single data frame. We need an id column in both data frames to accomplish this task. In our case, we will use the `country` column in `gdp2_1` and the `reporter` column in `trade`. Note that two data frames to merge may not have exactly the same entries. This is the case for this example, where in `trade` we do not have any country `D`. This implies that we have to make a choice about keeping or dropping the values for `D`.

We will see several options to merge with the base `merge()` function, with the `dplyr` package and with the `data.table` package.

Let's start with the base `merge()` function. We refer to `gdp2_1` as the `x` data set and `trade` as the `y` data set. We merge them by using the info in `country` and `year` in the `x` data set and `reporter` and `year` in the `y` data set

```
> df <- merge(gdp2_1, trade,
+             by.x = c("country", "year"),
+             by.y = c("reporter", "year"))
> df
   country year GDP region totalGDP partner export
1        A 2020 681      W     1306       B     80
2        A 2020 681      W     1306       C     63
3        A 2021  NA      W     1306       B    128
4        A 2021  NA      W     1306       C    116
5        A 2022 625      W     1306       B    100
6        A 2022 625      W     1306       C     91
7        B 2020 997      W     2732       A     99
8        B 2020 997      W     2732       C     63
9        B 2021 963      W     2732       A     92
10       B 2021 963      W     2732       C     74
11       B 2022 772      W     2732       A    150
12       B 2022 772      W     2732       C    139
13       C 2020 752      Z     2036       A    140
14       C 2020 752      Z     2036       B    106
15       C 2021 557      Z     2036       A    118
16       C 2021 557      Z     2036       B    141
17       C 2022 727      Z     2036       A    140
18       C 2022 727      Z     2036       B     58
> class(df)
[1] "data.frame"
```

Note that the info for `D` has been dropped. To keep it we can set `all = TRUE`

```
> df2 <- merge(gdp2_1, trade,
+              by.x = c("country", "year"),
+              by.y = c("reporter", "year"),
+              all = TRUE)
> df2
   country year GDP region totalGDP partner export
1        A 2020 681      W     1306       B     80
2        A 2020 681      W     1306       C     63
3        A 2021  NA      W     1306       B    128
4        A 2021  NA      W     1306       C    116
5        A 2022 625      W     1306       B    100
6        A 2022 625      W     1306       C     91
7        B 2020 997      W     2732       A     99
8        B 2020 997      W     2732       C     63
9        B 2021 963      W     2732       A     92
10       B 2021 963      W     2732       C     74
11       B 2022 772      W     2732       A    150
12       B 2022 772      W     2732       C    139
13       C 2020 752      Z     2036       A    140
14       C 2020 752      Z     2036       B    106
15       C 2021 557      Z     2036       A    118
16       C 2021 557      Z     2036       B    141
17       C 2022 727      Z     2036       A    140
```

```
18          C 2022 727      Z      2036        B      58
19          D 2020 832      Z      2229     <NA>      NA
20          D 2021 851      Z      2229     <NA>      NA
21          D 2022 546      Z      2229     <NA>      NA
```

Now we kept `D` but obviously we have missing values for `partner` and `export` because we do not have `D` in `trade`.

Alternatively, to keep `D` we can set `all.x = TRUE` because `D` is in the `x` data set, i.e. in `gdp2_1`

```
> df3 <- merge(gdp2_1, trade,
+              by.x = c("country", "year"),
+              by.y = c("reporter", "year"),
+              all.x = TRUE)
> df3
   country year GDP region totalGDP partner export
1          A 2020 681      W     1306       B     80
2          A 2020 681      W     1306       C     63
3          A 2021  NA      W     1306       B    128
4          A 2021  NA      W     1306       C    116
5          A 2022 625      W     1306       B    100
6          A 2022 625      W     1306       C     91
7          B 2020 997      W     2732       A     99
8          B 2020 997      W     2732       C     63
9          B 2021 963      W     2732       A     92
10         B 2021 963      W     2732       C     74
11         B 2022 772      W     2732       A    150
12         B 2022 772      W     2732       C    139
13         C 2020 752      Z     2036       A    140
14         C 2020 752      Z     2036       B    106
15         C 2021 557      Z     2036       A    118
16         C 2021 557      Z     2036       B    141
17         C 2022 727      Z     2036       A    140
18         C 2022 727      Z     2036       B     58
19         D 2020 832      Z     2229    <NA>     NA
20         D 2021 851      Z     2229    <NA>     NA
21         D 2022 546      Z     2229    <NA>     NA
```

On the other hand, if we set `all.y = TRUE` we drop `D` because it is not in the `y` data set, i.e. in `trade`

```
> df4 <- merge(gdp2_1, trade,
+              by.x = c("country", "year"),
+              by.y = c("reporter", "year"),
+              all.y = TRUE)
> df4
   country year GDP region totalGDP partner export
1          A 2020 681      W     1306       B     80
2          A 2020 681      W     1306       C     63
3          A 2021  NA      W     1306       B    128
4          A 2021  NA      W     1306       C    116
5          A 2022 625      W     1306       B    100
6          A 2022 625      W     1306       C     91
7          B 2020 997      W     2732       A     99
8          B 2020 997      W     2732       C     63
9          B 2021 963      W     2732       A     92
10         B 2021 963      W     2732       C     74
11         B 2022 772      W     2732       A    150
12         B 2022 772      W     2732       C    139
13         C 2020 752      Z     2036       A    140
14         C 2020 752      Z     2036       B    106
15         C 2021 557      Z     2036       A    118
16         C 2021 557      Z     2036       B    141
17         C 2022 727      Z     2036       A    140
18         C 2022 727      Z     2036       B     58
```

Next we repeat the same operations with the functions from the `dplyr` package. We use again `x` and `y` to refer to the data set we input in the left argument and in the right argument in the function.

By using the `inner_join()` function, we include all the rows in `x` and `y`. We match the variables in the two data sets to join by with `by`

```
> df5 <- inner_join(gdp2_1, trade,
+                   by = c("country" = "reporter",
+                          "year" = "year"))
> df5
# A tibble: 18 x 7
# Groups:   country [3]
   country  year   GDP region totalGDP partner export
   <chr>   <dbl> <int> <chr>     <int> <chr>    <int>
 1 A        2020   681 W          1306 B           80
 2 A        2020   681 W          1306 C           63
 3 A        2021    NA W          1306 B          128
 4 A        2021    NA W          1306 C          116
 5 A        2022   625 W          1306 B          100
 6 A        2022   625 W          1306 C           91
 7 B        2020   997 W          2732 A           99
 8 B        2020   997 W          2732 C           63
 9 B        2021   963 W          2732 A           92
10 B        2021   963 W          2732 C           74
11 B        2022   772 W          2732 A          150
12 B        2022   772 W          2732 C          139
13 C        2020   752 Z          2036 A          140
14 C        2020   752 Z          2036 B          106
15 C        2021   557 Z          2036 A          118
16 C        2021   557 Z          2036 B          141
17 C        2022   727 Z          2036 A          140
18 C        2022   727 Z          2036 B           58
```

By using the `full_join()` function, we include all the rows in `x` or `y`

```
> df6 <- full_join(gdp2_1, trade,
+                  by = c("country" = "reporter",
+                         "year" = "year"))
> df6 # include D
# A tibble: 21 x 7
# Groups:   country [4]
   country  year   GDP region totalGDP partner export
   <chr>   <dbl> <int> <chr>     <int> <chr>    <int>
 1 A        2020   681 W          1306 B           80
 2 A        2020   681 W          1306 C           63
 3 A        2021    NA W          1306 B          128
 4 A        2021    NA W          1306 C          116
 5 A        2022   625 W          1306 B          100
 6 A        2022   625 W          1306 C           91
 7 B        2020   997 W          2732 A           99
 8 B        2020   997 W          2732 C           63
 9 B        2021   963 W          2732 A           92
10 B        2021   963 W          2732 C           74
# ... with 11 more rows
```

By using the `left_join()` function, we include all the rows in `x`

```
> df7 <- left_join(gdp2_1, trade,
+                  by = c("country" = "reporter",
+                         "year" = "year"))
> df7 # include D
# A tibble: 21 x 7
# Groups:   country [4]
   country  year   GDP region totalGDP partner export
   <chr>   <dbl> <int> <chr>     <int> <chr>    <int>
 1 A        2020   681 W          1306 B           80
```

```
 2 A          2020   681 W             1306 C              63
 3 A          2021    NA W             1306 B             128
 4 A          2021    NA W             1306 C             116
 5 A          2022   625 W             1306 B             100
 6 A          2022   625 W             1306 C              91
 7 B          2020   997 W             2732 A              99
 8 B          2020   997 W             2732 C              63
 9 B          2021   963 W             2732 A              92
10 B          2021   963 W             2732 C              74
# ... with 11 more rows
```

By using the `right_join()` function, we include all the rows in `y`

```
> df8 <- right_join(gdp2_1, trade,
+                       by = c("country" = "reporter",
+                              "year" = "year"))
> df8 # does not include D
# A tibble: 18 x 7
# Groups:   country [3]
   country  year   GDP region totalGDP partner export
   <chr>   <dbl> <int> <chr>     <int> <chr>    <int>
 1 A        2020   681 W          1306 B           80
 2 A        2020   681 W          1306 C           63
 3 A        2021    NA W          1306 B          128
 4 A        2021    NA W          1306 C          116
 5 A        2022   625 W          1306 B          100
 6 A        2022   625 W          1306 C           91
 7 B        2020   997 W          2732 A           99
 8 B        2020   997 W          2732 C           63
 9 B        2021   963 W          2732 A           92
10 B        2021   963 W          2732 C           74
11 B        2022   772 W          2732 A          150
12 B        2022   772 W          2732 C          139
13 C        2020   752 Z          2036 A          140
14 C        2020   752 Z          2036 B          106
15 C        2021   557 Z          2036 A          118
16 C        2021   557 Z          2036 B          141
17 C        2022   727 Z          2036 A          140
18 C        2022   727 Z          2036 B           58
```

Other two useful functions are `semi_join()` which returns all rows from `x` with a match in `y` and `anti_join()` which returns all rows from `x` without a match in `y`.

Finally, we implement the same operations with the `merge()` function from the `data.table` package. The arguments of this function are the same as the base `merge()` function. Before merging the data frames, we set them as `data.table` objects

```
> gdp2_ldt <- setDT(gdp2_l)
> trade_dt <- setDT(trade)
> dfdt <- merge(gdp2_ldt, trade_dt,
+               by.x = c("country", "year"),
+               by.y = c("reporter", "year"))
> dfdt
    country year GDP region totalGDP partner export
 1:       A 2020 681      W     1306       B     80
 2:       A 2020 681      W     1306       C     63
 3:       A 2021  NA      W     1306       B    128
 4:       A 2021  NA      W     1306       C    116
 5:       A 2022 625      W     1306       B    100
 6:       A 2022 625      W     1306       C     91
 7:       B 2020 997      W     2732       A     99
 8:       B 2020 997      W     2732       C     63
 9:       B 2021 963      W     2732       A     92
```

```
10:        B 2021 963      W      2732       C      74
11:        B 2022 772      W      2732       A     150
12:        B 2022 772      W      2732       C     139
13:        C 2020 752      Z      2036       A     140
14:        C 2020 752      Z      2036       B     106
15:        C 2021 557      Z      2036       A     118
16:        C 2021 557      Z      2036       B     141
17:        C 2022 727      Z      2036       A     140
18:        C 2022 727      Z      2036       B      58
> class(dfdt)
[1] "data.table" "data.frame"
> df2dt <- merge(gdp2_ldt, trade_dt,
+                by.x = c("country", "year"),
+                by.y = c("reporter", "year"),
+                all = TRUE)
> df2dt
    country year GDP region totalGDP partner export
 1:       A 2020 681      W     1306       B     80
 2:       A 2020 681      W     1306       C     63
 3:       A 2021  NA      W     1306       B    128
 4:       A 2021  NA      W     1306       C    116
 5:       A 2022 625      W     1306       B    100
 6:       A 2022 625      W     1306       C     91
 7:       B 2020 997      W     2732       A     99
 8:       B 2020 997      W     2732       C     63
 9:       B 2021 963      W     2732       A     92
10:       B 2021 963      W     2732       C     74
11:       B 2022 772      W     2732       A    150
12:       B 2022 772      W     2732       C    139
13:       C 2020 752      Z     2036       A    140
14:       C 2020 752      Z     2036       B    106
15:       C 2021 557      Z     2036       A    118
16:       C 2021 557      Z     2036       B    141
17:       C 2022 727      Z     2036       A    140
18:       C 2022 727      Z     2036       B     58
19:       D 2020 832      Z     2229    <NA>     NA
20:       D 2021 851      Z     2229    <NA>     NA
21:       D 2022 546      Z     2229    <NA>     NA
    country year GDP region totalGDP partner export

> df3dt <- merge(gdp2_ldt, trade_dt,
+                by.x = c("country", "year"),
+                by.y = c("reporter", "year"),
+                all.x = TRUE)
> df3dt
    country year GDP region totalGDP partner export
 1:       A 2020 681      W     1306       B     80
 2:       A 2020 681      W     1306       C     63
 3:       A 2021  NA      W     1306       B    128
 4:       A 2021  NA      W     1306       C    116
 5:       A 2022 625      W     1306       B    100
 6:       A 2022 625      W     1306       C     91
 7:       B 2020 997      W     2732       A     99
 8:       B 2020 997      W     2732       C     63
 9:       B 2021 963      W     2732       A     92
10:       B 2021 963      W     2732       C     74
11:       B 2022 772      W     2732       A    150
12:       B 2022 772      W     2732       C    139
13:       C 2020 752      Z     2036       A    140
14:       C 2020 752      Z     2036       B    106
15:       C 2021 557      Z     2036       A    118
16:       C 2021 557      Z     2036       B    141
17:       C 2022 727      Z     2036       A    140
18:       C 2022 727      Z     2036       B     58
19:       D 2020 832      Z     2229    <NA>     NA
20:       D 2021 851      Z     2229    <NA>     NA
21:       D 2022 546      Z     2229    <NA>     NA
```

```
   country year GDP region totalGDP partner export
```

```
> df4dt <- merge(gdp2_ldt, trade_dt,
+               by.x = c("country", "year"),
+               by.y = c("reporter", "year"),
+               all.y = TRUE)
> df4dt
    country year GDP region totalGDP partner export
 1:       A 2020 681      W     1306       B     80
 2:       A 2020 681      W     1306       C     63
 3:       A 2021  NA      W     1306       B    128
 4:       A 2021  NA      W     1306       C    116
 5:       A 2022 625      W     1306       B    100
 6:       A 2022 625      W     1306       C     91
 7:       B 2020 997      W     2732       A     99
 8:       B 2020 997      W     2732       C     63
 9:       B 2021 963      W     2732       A     92
10:       B 2021 963      W     2732       C     74
11:       B 2022 772      W     2732       A    150
12:       B 2022 772      W     2732       C    139
13:       C 2020 752      Z     2036       A    140
14:       C 2020 752      Z     2036       B    106
15:       C 2021 557      Z     2036       A    118
16:       C 2021 557      Z     2036       B    141
17:       C 2022 727      Z     2036       A    140
18:       C 2022 727      Z     2036       B     58
```

Aggregating Data

Another operation that we often implement consists in aggregating some variables in the data frame. In this example, we compute the mean of `GDP` and `export` by `country` and `partner` in `df4`. Again, we show how we can accomplish this task with the base `aggregate()` function, with `dplyr`, and with `data.table`

In `aggregate()`, in a `list()` we indicate the variables to aggregate, in `by` a list of grouping elements, and in `FUN` the function to use to aggregate.

```
> df4agg <- aggregate.data.frame(list(GDP_mean = df4$GDP,
+                                     export_mean = df4$export),
+                              by = list(country = df4$country,
+                                        partner = df4$partner),
+                              FUN = function(x) mean(x, na.rm = T))
> df4agg
  country partner GDP_mean export_mean
1       B       A 910.6667    113.6667
2       C       A 678.6667    132.6667
3       A       B 653.0000    102.6667
4       C       B 678.6667    101.6667
5       A       C 653.0000     90.0000
6       B       C 910.6667     92.0000
```

With the `dplyr` package, we combine `group_by()` with `summarize()`. Here, I show you two ways. You can refer to https://dplyr.tidyverse.org/reference/summarise_all.html for additional examples.

```
> df4agg2 <- df4 %>%
+   group_by(country, partner) %>%
+   summarize(GDP_mean = mean(GDP, na.rm = TRUE),
+             export_mean = mean(export, na.rm = TRUE))
`summarise()` regrouping output by 'country' (override with `.groups` argument)
> df4agg2
```

```
# A tibble: 6 x 4
# Groups:   country [3]
  country partner GDP_mean export_mean
  <chr>   <chr>      <dbl>       <dbl>
1 A       B            653        103.
2 A       C            653         90
3 B       A            911.       114.
4 B       C            911.        92
5 C       A            679.       133.
6 C       B            679.       102.
> df4agg2 <- df4 %>%
+   group_by(country, partner) %>%
+   summarize(across(c("GDP", "export"),
+                    ~ mean(.x, na.rm = TRUE)))
`summarise()` regrouping output by 'country' (override with `.groups` argument)
> df4agg2
# A tibble: 6 x 4
# Groups:   country [3]
  country partner   GDP export
  <chr>   <chr>   <dbl>  <dbl>
1 A       B         653   103.
2 A       C         653    90
3 B       A         911.  114.
4 B       C         911.   92
5 C       A         679.  133.
6 C       B         679.  102.
```

Finally, with `data.table`

```
> df4dtagg <- df4dt[, list(GDP_mean = mean(GDP, na.rm = TRUE),
+                          export_mean = mean(export, na.rm = TRUE)),
+                   by = list(country, partner)]
> df4dtagg
   country partner GDP_mean export_mean
1:       A       B 653.0000    102.6667
2:       A       C 653.0000     90.0000
3:       B       A 910.6667    113.6667
4:       B       C 910.6667     92.0000
5:       C       A 678.6667    132.6667
6:       C       B 678.6667    101.6667
```

Detecting Missing Values

In `gdp2_1` we have a missing value. We can clearly see it in this small data frame. But how can we detect it in a larger data frame?

First, we can run the `summary()` function

```
> summary(gdp2_1)
   country              year           GDP             region
 Length:12          Min.   :2020   Min.   :546.0   Length:12
 Class :character   1st Qu.:2020   1st Qu.:653.0   Class :character
 Mode  :character   Median :2021   Median :752.0   Mode  :character
                    Mean   :2021   Mean   :754.8
                    3rd Qu.:2022   3rd Qu.:841.5
                    Max.   :2022   Max.   :997.0
                                   NA's   :1
    totalGDP
 Min.   :1306
 1st Qu.:1854
 Median :2132
 Mean   :2076
 3rd Qu.:2355
 Max.   :2732
```

We see that GDP has one missing value.

Alternatively, we can use the `is.na()` function. The TRUE value indicates the presence of the missing value

```
> is.na(gdp2_1)
      country  year   GDP region totalGDP
 [1,]   FALSE FALSE FALSE  FALSE    FALSE
 [2,]   FALSE FALSE  TRUE  FALSE    FALSE
 [3,]   FALSE FALSE FALSE  FALSE    FALSE
 [4,]   FALSE FALSE FALSE  FALSE    FALSE
 [5,]   FALSE FALSE FALSE  FALSE    FALSE
 [6,]   FALSE FALSE FALSE  FALSE    FALSE
 [7,]   FALSE FALSE FALSE  FALSE    FALSE
 [8,]   FALSE FALSE FALSE  FALSE    FALSE
 [9,]   FALSE FALSE FALSE  FALSE    FALSE
[10,]   FALSE FALSE FALSE  FALSE    FALSE
[11,]   FALSE FALSE FALSE  FALSE    FALSE
[12,]   FALSE FALSE FALSE  FALSE    FALSE
```

Let's locate it by nesting `is.na()` in the `which()` function

```
> which(is.na(gdp2_1))
[1] 26
```

The output indicates that the missing value is the 26th value by counting from top to down from the first column. Still is quite hard to spot it in a large data set. To get a better location for the missing value, we add `arr.ind = TRUE` to the previous function to return the indices for the matrix

```
> which(is.na(gdp2_1), arr.ind = TRUE)
     row col
[1,]   2   3
```

Now we know that the missing value is located at row 2 and column 3.

In the next part of this section, we simply learn a few functions to work with missing values.

First, we can omit the observation with the missing value by using `na.omit()`

```
> gdp_NAomit <- na.omit(gdp2_1)
> gdp_NAomit
    country year GDP region totalGDP
 1:       A 2020 681      W     1306
 2:       A 2022 625      W     1306
 3:       B 2020 997      W     2732
 4:       B 2021 963      W     2732
 5:       B 2022 772      W     2732
 6:       C 2020 752      Z     2036
 7:       C 2021 557      Z     2036
 8:       C 2022 727      Z     2036
 9:       D 2020 832      Z     2229
10:       D 2021 851      Z     2229
11:       D 2022 546      Z     2229
```

We dropped the observation for country A and year `2021`.

Alternatively, we can use `complete.cases()` which returns a logical vector indicating which cases are complete, i.e. have no missing values

```
> gdp2_1[complete.cases(gdp2_1), ]
    country year GDP region totalGDP
 1:       A 2020 681      W     1306
 2:       A 2022 625      W     1306
 3:       B 2020 997      W     2732
 4:       B 2021 963      W     2732
```

```
 5:        B 2022 772       W      2732
 6:        C 2020 752       Z      2036
 7:        C 2021 557       Z      2036
 8:        C 2022 727       Z      2036
 9:        D 2020 832       Z      2229
10:        D 2021 851       Z      2229
11:        D 2022 546       Z      2229
```

Without going into detail of missing data analysis, let's see how we can simply replace the missing value. For example, we can forward the previous value. For this task we use the `na.locf()` function from the `zoo` package. Since we have to make sure that the previous value belong to the same country, we use `group_by()`

```
> gdp2_1 %>%
+   group_by(country) %>%
+   mutate(gdp_NAomit = na.locf(GDP))
# A tibble: 12 x 6
# Groups:   country [4]
   country  year   GDP region totalGDP gdp_NAomit
   <chr>   <dbl> <int> <chr>     <int>      <int>
 1 A        2020   681 W          1306        681
 2 A        2021    NA W          1306        681
 3 A        2022   625 W          1306        625
 4 B        2020   997 W          2732        997
 5 B        2021   963 W          2732        963
 6 B        2022   772 W          2732        772
 7 C        2020   752 Z          2036        752
 8 C        2021   557 Z          2036        557
 9 C        2022   727 Z          2036        727
10 D        2020   832 Z          2229        832
11 D        2021   851 Z          2229        851
12 D        2022   546 Z          2229        546
```

In this example, we generated a new column `gdp_NAomit` where we replaced the missing value. Instead of forwarding, we can backward a value. We use the same function as before but we add `fromLast = TRUE`

```
> gdp2_1 %>%
+   group_by(country) %>%
+   mutate(gdp_NAomit = na.locf(GDP,
+                               fromLast = TRUE))
# A tibble: 12 x 6
# Groups:   country [4]
   country  year   GDP region totalGDP gdp_NAomit
   <chr>   <dbl> <int> <chr>     <int>      <int>
 1 A        2020   681 W          1306        681
 2 A        2021    NA W          1306        625
 3 A        2022   625 W          1306        625
 4 B        2020   997 W          2732        997
 5 B        2021   963 W          2732        963
 6 B        2022   772 W          2732        772
 7 C        2020   752 Z          2036        752
 8 C        2021   557 Z          2036        557
 9 C        2022   727 Z          2036        727
10 D        2020   832 Z          2229        832
11 D        2021   851 Z          2229        851
12 D        2022   546 Z          2229        546
```

Alternatively, we can replace it with the average of the previous and following value. We can use `na.approx()` for this task. Note that this is a generic function for replacing each NA with interpolated values.

```
> gdp3 <- gdp2_1 %>%
+   group_by(country) %>%
```

```
+   mutate(GDP = na.approx(GDP))
> gdp3
# A tibble: 12 x 5
# Groups:   country [4]
   country  year   GDP region totalGDP
   <chr>   <dbl> <dbl> <chr>     <int>
 1 A        2020   681 W          1306
 2 A        2021   653 W          1306
 3 A        2022   625 W          1306
 4 B        2020   997 W          2732
 5 B        2021   963 W          2732
 6 B        2022   772 W          2732
 7 C        2020   752 Z          2036
 8 C        2021   557 Z          2036
 9 C        2022   727 Z          2036
10 D        2020   832 Z          2229
11 D        2021   851 Z          2229
12 D        2022   546 Z          2229
```

Another alternative to replace missing values is to use `fill()`

```
> gdp2_1 %>%
+   group_by(country) %>%
+   fill(GDP, .direction = "up")
# A tibble: 12 x 5
# Groups:   country [4]
   country  year   GDP region totalGDP
   <chr>   <dbl> <int> <chr>     <int>
 1 A        2020   681 W          1306
 2 A        2021   625 W          1306
 3 A        2022   625 W          1306
 4 B        2020   997 W          2732
 5 B        2021   963 W          2732
 6 B        2022   772 W          2732
 7 C        2020   752 Z          2036
 8 C        2021   557 Z          2036
 9 C        2022   727 Z          2036
10 D        2020   832 Z          2229
11 D        2021   851 Z          2229
12 D        2022   546 Z          2229
```

Creating Lag Variables

There are different options to create lag variables but in this example we will see only a case with the `lag()` function from `dplyr`. We will use another approach in Sect. 2.2 with the `plm` package.

Since we have different countries, we have to make sure that the lag variable belongs to the appropriate country. Consequently, we need to use `group_by()` to group the series by `country`. Note that we use `dplyr::lag` to tell **R** that we want to use the `lag()` function from the `dplyr` package. Since there are more than one functions named `lag()`, by specifying the package we avoid possible errors. In `lag()`, `n` gives the number of positions to lead or lag by.

```
> gdp3 <- gdp3 %>%
+   group_by(country) %>%
+   mutate(Lgdp = dplyr::lag(GDP, n = 1))
> gdp3
# A tibble: 12 x 6
# Groups:   country [4]
```

```
   country  year   GDP region totalGDP  Lgdp
   <chr>   <dbl> <dbl> <chr>     <int> <dbl>
 1 A        2020   681 W          1306    NA
 2 A        2021   653 W          1306   681
 3 A        2022   625 W          1306   653
 4 B        2020   997 W          2732    NA
 5 B        2021   963 W          2732   997
 6 B        2022   772 W          2732   963
 7 C        2020   752 Z          2036    NA
 8 C        2021   557 Z          2036   752
 9 C        2022   727 Z          2036   557
10 D        2020   832 Z          2229    NA
11 D        2021   851 Z          2229   832
12 D        2022   546 Z          2229   851
```

Subsetting a Data Frame

We have already seen how to subset by using `subset()`

```
> gdp3W <- subset(gdp3, region == "W")
> gdp3W
# A tibble: 6 x 6
# Groups:   country [2]
  country  year   GDP region totalGDP  Lgdp
  <chr>   <dbl> <dbl> <chr>     <int> <dbl>
1 A        2020   681 W          1306    NA
2 A        2021   653 W          1306   681
3 A        2022   625 W          1306   653
4 B        2020   997 W          2732    NA
5 B        2021   963 W          2732   997
6 B        2022   772 W          2732   963
> gdp3Z <- subset(gdp3, region != "W")
> gdp3Z
# A tibble: 6 x 6
# Groups:   country [2]
  country  year   GDP region totalGDP  Lgdp
  <chr>   <dbl> <dbl> <chr>     <int> <dbl>
1 C        2020   752 Z          2036    NA
2 C        2021   557 Z          2036   752
3 C        2022   727 Z          2036   557
4 D        2020   832 Z          2229    NA
5 D        2021   851 Z          2229   832
6 D        2022   546 Z          2229   851
```

An alternative is to use `filter()` from `dplyr`

```
> gdp3C <- gdp3 %>%
+   filter(country == "C")
> gdp3C
# A tibble: 3 x 6
# Groups:   country [1]
  country  year   GDP region totalGDP  Lgdp
  <chr>   <dbl> <dbl> <chr>     <int> <dbl>
1 C        2020   752 Z          2036    NA
2 C        2021   557 Z          2036   752
3 C        2022   727 Z          2036   557
```

1.8 Retrieve the Data Sets from the WTO

After reviewing the main features of **R** and the main data management operations, we are almost ready to start. We need to retrieve the data sets from the WTO for replication. We have two options. The first option is to visit the WTO website at https://www.wto.org/english/res_e/publications_e/practical_guide12_e.htm and download the files from the link "Download application and exercises files". The second option is to download the data sets directly from **R**. Let's use this second option. First, we download the files that are zipped. Please note that the download can last several minutes because we are downloading quite large data sets. Second, we unzip the files. Following, I show both the code from the **R Script** file

```
download.file("https://www.wto.org/english/res_e/reser_e/PracticalGuideFiles.
                    zip", destfile = "PracticalGuideFiles.zip")
unzip("PracticalGuideFiles.zip")
```

and from the console pane

```
> download.file("https://www.wto.org/english/res_e/reser_e/PracticalGuideFiles.
  zip", +                 destfile = "PracticalGuideFiles.zip")
trying URL 'https://www.wto.org/english/res_e/reser_e/PracticalGuideFiles.zip'
Content type 'application/x-zip-compressed' length 467548975 bytes (445.9 MB)
downloaded 445.9 MB

> unzip("PracticalGuideFiles.zip")
```

The files downloaded include all the data sets, the Stata do files where the code is written in Stata, and other files. Since we only use a few data sets, we create a new directory, `datWTO`, where we move the data sets of interest.

```
dir.create("datWTO")
```

We have to copy the data sets from the folder where they are stored into `datWTO`. We will use a `for()` loop for this task. First, we store the name of the data sets we use in `dat1`, `dat2`, and `dat3`. The corresponding data sets are stored in three different folders. Second, we generate a list that contains these three objects. Third, we use the `for()` loop where we define the path to the three folders where the data sets are stored and the path to `datWTO`

```
dat1 <- c("aBilateralTrade.dta", "BilateralTrade.dta",
          "comtrade_exports_all_countries_2000.dta",
          "germany_trade_2004_hs6.dta",
          "GravityData.dta",
          "openness.dta",
          "TPP.dta",
          "unctad_tot_data.dta")

dat2 <- "PMA_MEX.dta"

dat3 <- c("dist_cepii224.dta", "Religion.dta",
          "tradeflows.csv", "joinwto.txt",
          "GDP.csv")

datList <- list(dat1, dat2, dat3)

for(i in 1:3){
  p <- paste0("Practical guide to TPA/Chapter", i,
              "/Datasets/")
```

```
  file.copy(from = paste0(p, datList[[i]]),
            to = paste0("datWTO/", datList[[i]]))
}
```

Note the loop can take a few seconds to copy all the data sets.
Now we are ready to work.

Chapter 2
Analyzing Trade Flows

2.1 Openness Across Countries

Learning Objectives

- Import a Stata file
- Generate new variables
- Replace variables
- Subset a data set
- Run a regression
- Reproduce Stata robust standard errors
- Plot with `plot()` and `ggplot()`
- Generate new variables with `ifelse()`
- Handle missing values

In this section we replicate the UNCTAD & WTO's Stata code in **R** for assessing and estimating trade openness across countries.[1]

Country's trade openness is defined as

$$\text{Openness}_i = \frac{\text{Export}_i + \text{Import}_i}{\text{GDP}_i} \tag{2.1}$$

[1] The corresponding Stata code is available in openness.do.

© The Author(s), under exclusive license to Springer Nature Switzerland AG 2023

M. Porto, *Using R for Trade Policy Analysis*,
https://doi.org/10.1007/978-3-031-35044-3_2

Table 2.1 Openness for G20 countries, 2016

Country	GDP	Export	Import	EXP/GDP	IMP/GDP	Openness
ARG	554.8	57.7	55.6	10.4%	10.0%	20.4%
AUS	1208.0	189.6	189.4	15.7%	15.7%	31.4%
BRA	1793.9	185.2	137.5	10.3%	7.7%	18.0%
CAN	1535.7	389.0	402.9	25.3%	26.2%	51.6%
CHN	11190.9	2097.6	1587.9	18.7%	14.2%	32.9%
FRA	2465.1	488.8	560.5	19.8%	22.7%	42.6%
DEU	3477.7	1340.7	1060.6	38.6%	30.5%	69.1%
IND	2274.2	260.3	356.7	11.4%	15.7%	27.1%
IDN	932.2	144.4	135.6	15.5%	14.6%	30.0%
ITA	1859.3	461.5	404.5	24.8%	21.8%	46.6%
JPN	4949.2	644.9	606.9	13.0%	12.3%	25.3%
KOR	1414.8	495.4	406.1	35.0%	28.7%	63.7%
MEX	1077.7	373.9	387.0	34.7%	35.9%	70.6%
RUS	1284.7	285.4	182.2	22.2%	14.2%	36.4%
SAU	644.9	183.6	140.1	28.5%	21.7%	50.2%
ZAF	295.7	74.1	74.7	25.1%	25.3%	50.3%
TUR	863.7	142.5	198.6	16.5%	23.0%	39.5%
GBR	2650.8	411.4	636.3	15.5%	24.0%	39.5%
USA	18624.4	1450.4	2248.2	7.8%	12.1%	19.9%

Source: GDP data from the World Bank. Trade data from COMTRADE
Note: Values in billion US dollars

Trade openness measures the integration of an economy into the world trade circuit. Table 2.1 reports the openness indicator for the G20 countries for the 2016. We observe different degrees of openness. Mexico and Germany record the highest degree of openness, around 70%, while United States and Brazil the lowest, around 20%.

Open a new script file in **RStudio** and save it as `02_openness_2edn`.

Let's load the following packages by using the `library()` function.

```
library("haven") # import STATA .dta file
library("ggplot2") # plot with ggplot
library("ggpubr") # combine ggplot plots
library("sandwich") # replicate Stata robust standard errors
library("lmtest") # replicate Stata robust standard errors
library("estimatr") # estimation with Stata robust standard errors
```

We start by importing the WTO's `openness.dta` data set in **R** by using `read_dta()` from the `haven` package. Next, follow these steps:

1. Check the class of the imported data set with `class()`;
2. View the data set using `View()`;
3. Retrieve the dimension of the data set with `dim()`;
4. Obtain additional information about the structure of the data set using the `str()` function.

```
#' Note I assume that you set up the R project as described
#' in the introductory chapter and that you saved the data sets
#' in datWTO as shown in the last section in the introductory
#' chapter.
openness <- read_dta("datWTO/openness.dta")
class(openness)
View(openness)
dim(openness)
str(openness)
```

`openness` is a tibble data frame[2] with 3161 observations and 10 variables such as reporter, `ccode`, year, `year`, trade openness in current terms, `openc`, trade openness in real terms, `openk`, total population, `pop`, GDP in current terms, `gdp_current`, landlocked, i.e. if a country has no access to the sea, `ldlock`, island, i.e. if a country is an island country, `island`, remoteness, `remoteness`, and remoteness as defined by Head, `remoteness_head`. Data cover the years 1976–2004.

Let's start preparing the data set for the analysis. First, we create new variables. We do this simply by adding `$` to the data set before the name of the new variable. Then we use the assignment operator `<-` to assign values to the new variable. In the first line of the next code block, for example, we create `gdppc`, GDP per capita, dividing `gdp_current`, current GDP, by `pop`, population, in the data set `openness`.

Then, we create new variables as the logarithm of existing variables by using the `log()` function. Finally, we scale the variable for GDP capita, `gdppc`, dividing by 1000. We simply assign a new value to replace it.

```
# GDP per capita (gdppc)
openness$gdppc <- openness$gdp_current / openness$pop

# Log of variables
openness$ln_open <- log(openness$openc)
openness$ln_gdp <- log(openness$gdp_current)
openness$ln_gdppc <- log(openness$gdppc)
openness$ln_pop <- log(openness$pop)
openness$ln_remot <- log(openness$remoteness)
openness$ln_remot_head <- log(openness$remoteness_head)

# Replace gdppc and ln_gdppc
openness$gdppc <- openness$gdppc / 1000
openness$ln_gdppc <- log(openness$gdppc)
```

Our aim is to plot the data for year 2000 for countries whose trade openness in current terms, `openc`, is less or equal to 200. The first step is to subset the data set. We use the `subset()` function to subset the original data set if `year` is 2000 and if `openc` is less or equal to 200.

```
# subset openness data set with year = 2000 and openc <= 200
openness_2000 <- subset(openness, year == 2000 & openc <= 200)
dim(openness_2000)
```

Note that we create a new data set, `openness_2000`, to not overwrite the original data set. In the `subset()` function, first we enter the name of the data

[2] Here, we just refer to it as a special class of data frame. You may refer to Wickham (2019a, p. 58) for more details.

set to subset and then the conditional statement, i.e., in this case, `year` equal to 2000 (double equal sign) and `openc` less than or equal to 200.

Now we are ready to plot. For this first example, we will plot by using the basic `plot()` function and the `ggplot()` function to highlight some differences. Afterwards, we will use `ggplot()` in the rest of this section and in the rest of the book. We will use again `plot()` only in Sect. 2.6.

```
# Linear regression
openness_2000_lm <- lm(openc ~ gdppc, data = openness_2000)

# Basic plot
plot(openness_2000$gdppc, openness_2000$openc,
     xlab = "GDP per Capita",
     ylab = "Openness",
     main = "Trade Openness")
abline(openness_2000_lm, col ="red")

# ggplot
ggplot(openness_2000, aes(x=gdppc, y=openc)) +
  geom_point() +
  stat_smooth(method = "lm", col ="red") +
  labs(x = "GDP per Capita", y = "Openness",
       title = "Trade Openness")
```

The entries of the `plot()` function are the *x* and *y* coordinates of points in the plot. Then we add labels for the *x*-axis and *y*-axis, `xlab =` and `ylab =` respectively, and the main title, `main =` . We add a regression line with the `abline()` function. Note that we run a linear regression and store its results in an object called `openness_2000_lm`. This is the first entry of the `abline()` function. More on regression in Sects. 3.2 and 4.2. The argument `col =` specify the color of the line.

In `ggplot()` we first identify the data set that must be a data frame. Second we map the data to the *x*-axis and *y*-axis in `aes()`. Then we specify the kind of plot we want to create. In this case, `geom_point()` is used to create scatter-plots. Then we add the regression line using `stat_smooth()` and specifying `method = "lm"`. In the argument `labs()` we set axes labels and title. Figure 2.1 shows the outcome of these plots.

A feature of the `ggplot()` function is that the + operator is part of the code and it is used to combine the different layers of the plot. For example, observe the commands in the console pane for `plot()` and `ggplot()` after running the code in the script file.

```
> plot(openness_2000$gdppc, openness_2000$openc,
+      xlab = "GDP per Capita",
+      ylab = "Openness",
+      main = "Trade Openness")

> ggplot(openness_2000, aes(x=gdppc, y=openc)) +
+   geom_point() +
+   stat_smooth(method = "lm", col ="red") +
+   labs(x = "GDP per Capita", y = "Openness",
+        title = "Trade Openness")
`geom_smooth()` using formula 'y ~ x'
Warning messages:
1: Removed 1 rows containing non-finite values (stat_smooth).
2: Removed 1 rows containing missing values (geom_point).
```

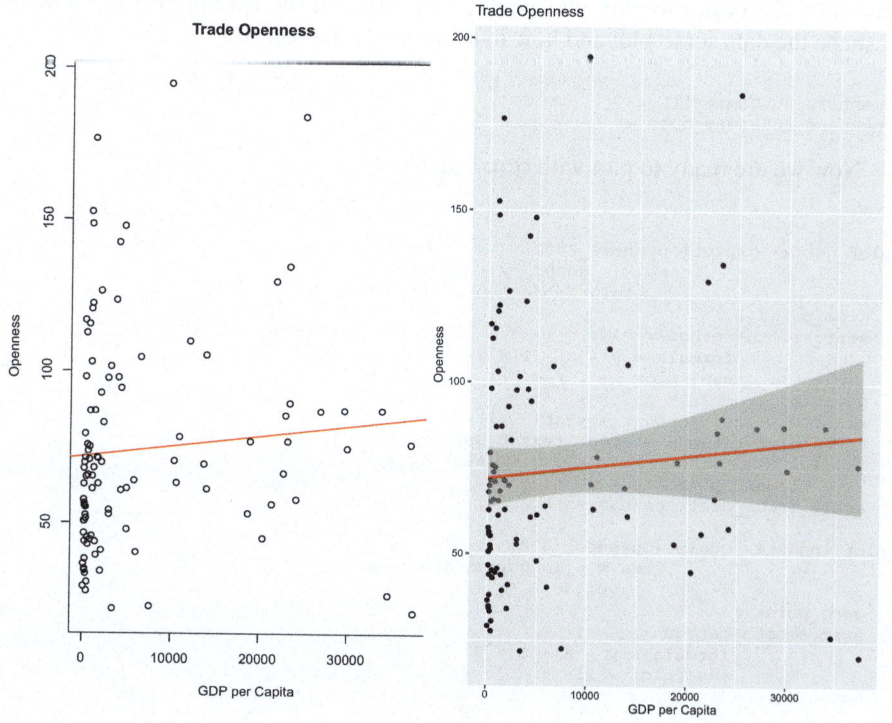

(a) (b)

Fig. 2.1 Comparing basic plot and ggplot layout. (**a**) Plot function. (**b**) ggplot function

The command line for `plot()` reports a + that is not in the code. This + just signals that the code continues on the second line. We do not need it when we edit in the **R Script** file. On the other hand, the command line for `ggplot()` reports a double +. This is due to the fact the one + is part of the code of the `ggplot()` while the second + just signals that the code continues on the second line. We do not need the second + when we edit in the **R Script** file.

Finally, note that `ggplot()` prints that `geom_smooth()` uses the formula `y ~ x` because we did not explicitly write the formula we want. However, we are fine with this choice (more on the formula shortly).

The following codes generate the plots with a quadratic fit using `ggplot()`, without and with log transformation, respectively `plot_qdt` and `plot_lnqdt`. Note that in `ggplot()` the `x` value is mapped to `gdppc` in `plot_qdt` while to `ln_gdppc` in `plot_lnqdt`. `ln_gdppc` is the log transformation of `gdppc` generated at the beginning.

Before plotting, we create new variables that store a character value. This will be use for mapping the color and legend in `aes()` in `ggplot()`. In this section, we introduce the basics to plot with `ggplot()`. We will see later in Sect. 2.3 how to reshape the data set to plot and how to set properly the legend.

```
# add variables to openness_2000 for mapping in aes() in ggplot()
openness_2000$map_fit <- "fitted"
openness_2000$map_open <- "openness"
```

Now we are ready to plot with `ggplot()`.

```
# Plot

plot_qdt <- ggplot(openness_2000,
                   aes(x = gdppc, y = openc,
                       color = "openness")) +
  geom_point() +
  stat_smooth(method = "lm",
              formula = y ~ x + I(x^2),
              aes(color = "fitted")) +
  ggtitle("Quadratic fit") +
  xlab("GDP per capita") + ylab(" ") +
  theme(plot.title = element_text(hjust = 0.5,
                                  size = 10),
        legend.position = "bottom") +
  scale_color_discrete(name="Legend")

plot_lnqdt <- ggplot(openness_2000,
                     aes(x = ln_gdppc, y = openc,
                         color = "openness")) +
  geom_point() +
  stat_smooth(method = "lm",
              formula = y ~ x + I(x^2),
              aes(color = "fitted")) +
  ggtitle("Quadratic fit after log transformation") +
  xlab("GDP per capita") + ylab(" ") +
  theme(plot.title = element_text(hjust = 0.5, size = 10),
        legend.position = "bottom") +
  scale_color_discrete(name="Legend")

plot_qdt
plot_lnqdt

## combine plots
ggarrange(plot_qdt, plot_lnqdt,
          ncol = 1, nrow = 2)
```

Note that this time in `stat_smooth()` we specify the `method = "lm"` and we define a quadratic formula for the quadratic fit line, `formula = y ~ x + I(x^2)`.[3] Furthermore, note that we add new lines of code. For example, the labels are written in *ad hoc* arguments, `xlab()`, `ylab()` and the title of the plot in `ggtitle()`. This method is alternative to the one we coded in Fig. 2.1. It is recommended if we change other scale options. In `theme(plot.title = element_text())` we set the horizontal adjustment, `hjust =` and the size, `size =` for the title. The last two arguments manage color and the legend. We say more about them in Sects. 2.2 and 2.3. Note that we store the plots in two objects. Therefore, to view the plots we have to run the objects. Finally, we combine the two plots with `ggarrange()` from the `ggpubr` package to reproduce the outcome

[3] The `I()` function is used to inhibit the interpretation of operators such as "+", "-", "*" and "^" as formula operators, so they are used as arithmetical operators.

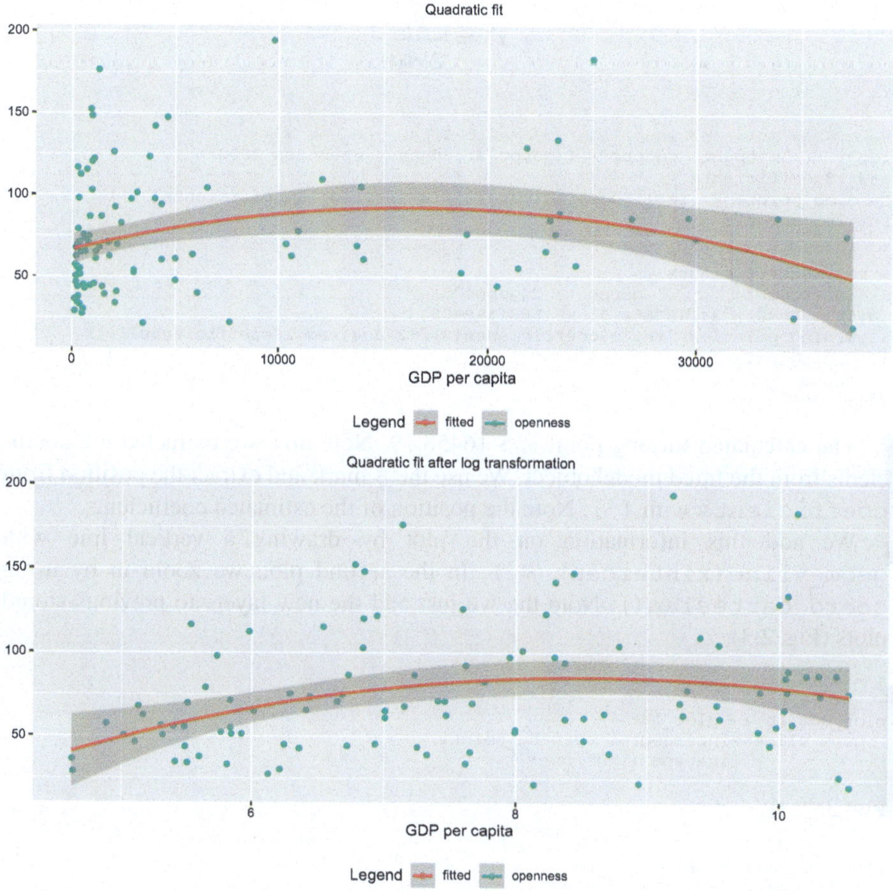

Fig. 2.2 Adding a quadratic fit to a ggplot

as in Fig. 2.2. We specify the number of rows, `nrow` and the number of columns, `ncol`, to arrange the plot grid in two rows and one column.[4] The plots are shown in Fig. 2.2.

Note that the different appearance of the two plots is due to the log transformation. In the second plot, the influence of the outliers is reduced.

Next, we compute the turning point for the quadratic estimation. In an estimated quadratic equation with $\hat{\beta}_1 > 0$ and $\hat{\beta}_2 < 0$, the turning point (or maximum of the function) is always achieved at the coefficient on x over twice the absolute value of the coefficient on x^2 (Wooldridge, 2012, p.195)

[4] Note that a plot generated by `plot()` cannot be stored in an object. I combined the plots in Fig. 2.1 directly when editing this book in LaTeX.

$$x^* = \frac{\hat{\beta}_1}{2|\hat{\beta}_2|} \tag{2.2}$$

```
# turning point of equation "quadratic fit"
reg_1 <- lm(openc ~ gdppc + I(gdppc^2), data = openness_2000)
reg_1$coefficients
turning_point1 <- reg_1$coefficients[2]/(2*abs(reg_1$coefficients[3]))
turning_point1
```

```
> reg_1$coefficients
  (Intercept)         gdppc    I(gdppc^2)
 6.683052e+01  3.146966e-03 -9.560138e-08
> turning_point1 <- reg_1$coefficients[2]/(2*abs(reg_1$coefficients[3]))
> turning_point1
   gdppc
16458.79
```

The calculated turning point is \$ 16458.79. Note how we extracted the coefficients from the fitted model object. We use the $ mark and extract the position from `coefficients` with `[ ]`. Note the position of the estimated coefficients.

We add this information on the plot by drawing a vertical line with `geom_vline(xintercept = )`. In the second plot, we zoom in by using `coord_cartesian()`. Note the we just add the new layers to previous stored plots (Fig. 2.3).

```
# Plot with vertical line at turning point

plot_qdt_tp <- plot_qdt +
  geom_vline(xintercept = turning_point1,
             linetype = "dotted" )

plot_qdt_tp

### zoom-in
plot_qdt_zoom <- plot_qdt_tp +
  coord_cartesian(xlim = c(10000, 25000),
                  ylim = c(75, 110)) +
  labs(caption = "zoom in")

ggarrange(plot_qdt_tp, plot_qdt_zoom,
          ncol = 1, nrow = 2,
          common.legend = TRUE,
          legend = "bottom")
```

Note that in `ggarange()` we set `common.legend` equal `TRUE` so that the two plots share the same legend.

Now, let's add another kind of information to our plots. Suppose we want to identify which countries have a trade openness greater than 150 and add this information to our plots. We can add this information as label, `geom_label()`, or text, `geom_text()` to the plot.

In the following code, we create a new object, `openness_2000sub`, which is a subset of `openness_2000` data set by countries with a trade openness greater than 150. This object stores the information we want to add to the plot (Fig. 2.4).

```
# add text to ggplot()
## subset if openc > 150
openness_2000sub <- openness_2000[openness_2000$openc > 150, ]
```

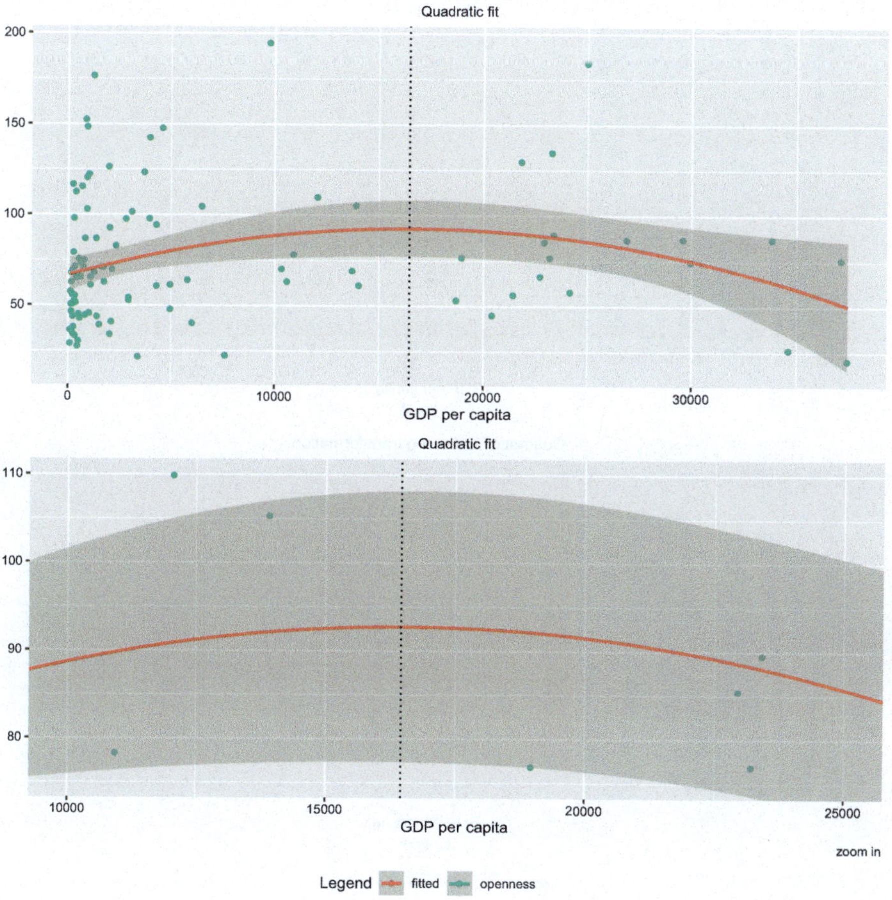

Fig. 2.3 Adding an x intercept line to a ggplot

```
head(openness_2000sub)

plot_qdt_lbl <- plot_qdt +
  geom_label(aes(gdppc, openc, label = ccode),
             size = 2.5, data = openness_2000sub) +
  labs(caption = "a) label") +
  theme(plot.title = element_text(hjust = 0.5, size = 11.5),
        plot.caption = element_text(hjust = 0.5, size = 12))


plot_lnqdt_txt <- plot_lnqdt +
  labs(caption = "b) text") +
  theme(plot.title = element_text(hjust = 0.5, size = 11.5),
        plot.caption = element_text(hjust = 0.5, size = 12),
        legend.position = "bottom") +
  geom_text(aes(ln_gdppc, openc, label = ccode),
            size = 2.5, data = openness_2000sub,
            alpha= 0.5, hjust = 1.2)
```

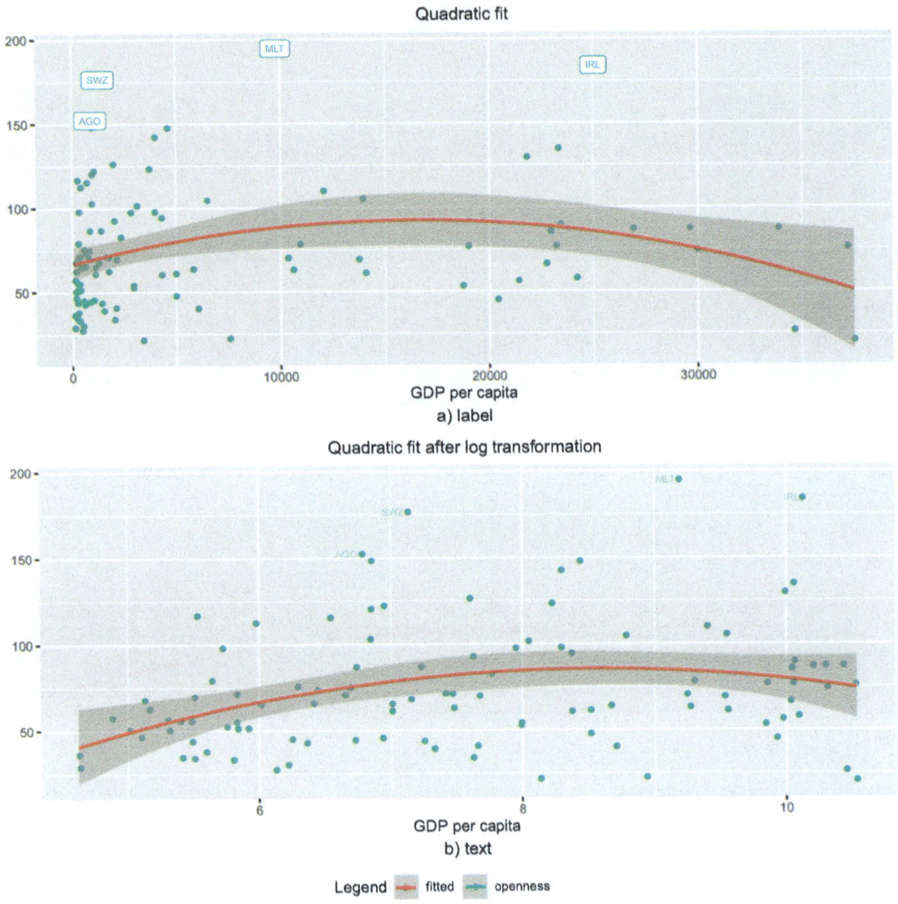

Fig. 2.4 Adding labels and text to a ggplot

```
plot_qdt_lbl
plot_lnqdt_txt

ggarrange(plot_qdt_lbl, plot_lnqdt_txt,
          ncol = 1, nrow = 2,
          common.legend = TRUE,
          legend.grob = get_legend(plot_lnqdt_txt),
          legend = "bottom")
```

In the second part of this example, we compare the observed values with fitted values to check how much a country trades relatively to how much it can be expected. First, we estimate the following equation

$$ln\_open = \beta_0 + \beta_1 ln\_gdppc + \beta_2 ln\_pop + \beta_3 ccode + u \tag{2.3}$$

First, we use the `lm()` function that is a base **R** function. The first entry is the model, i.e. is the dependent variable separated by the independent variables by a tilde, ~. Between independent variables we insert a + operator. Finally, we include `data =` with the name of the database where these variables are located.

Let's store the result in a new object, `open_reg`. To see the result we use the `summary()` function. Note that to reproduce robust standard errors as in Stata we have to call for another function, `coeftest()` in `lmtest` package and choose the option `vcov = vcovHC(x, "HC1")`, where `x` represents a fitted model object.

```
open_reg <- lm(ln_open ~ ln_gdppc + ln_pop + factor(ccode),
               data = openness)
summary(open_reg)
coeftest(open_reg, vcov = vcovHC(open_reg, "HC1"))
```

Now, we replicate the same results with the `lm_robust()` function from the `estimatr` package. With this function, we just need to write `se_type = "stata"` to reproduce Stata robust standard errors.

```
open_reg_rob <- lm_robust(ln_open ~ ln_gdppc + ln_pop + factor(ccode),
                          data = openness,
                          se_type = "stata")
summary(open_reg_rob)
```

Let's continue the example with `open_reg`. Let's extract the fitted values and store in a new variable in the `openness` data set. If we do it, we get the following error.

```
> openness$fitted <- open_reg$fitted.values # error
Error: Assigned data `open_reg$fitted.values` must be compatible with existing
    data.
x Existing data has 3161 rows.
x Assigned data has 3039 rows.
i Only vectors of size 1 are recycled.
Run `rlang::last_error()` to see where the error occurred.
```

We read the the data set has 3161 rows and the fitted values 3039. Let's check the dimension of the data set and the length of the fitted values.

```
> dim(openness)
[1] 3161   17
> length(open_reg$fitted.values)
[1] 3039
```

Note that when we run the regression with the `lm()` function, we can add the argument `na.action`, a function which indicates what should happen when the data contain `NA`s. The default is set by the `na.action` setting of options, and is `na.fail` if that is unset. The 'factory-fresh' default is `na.omit`. Another possible value is `NULL`, no action. Value `na.exclude` can be useful.

In the next step we omit the missing values from our data set with `na.omit()`. Note that before omitting the missing values we test the values with the function `is.na()`. It returns `TRUE` for values with missing values and `FALSE` otherwise. We nested the `is.na()` in `any()` and `which()` to obtain more info about the missing values.

```
# omit data with missing values
is.na(openness)
any(is.na(openness))
which(is.na(openness), arr.ind = TRUE)
```

Note that if we call for the `summary()` function, it provides the number of missing values, `NA`. For example,

```
> summary(openness$ln_gdppc)
   Min. 1st Qu.  Median    Mean 3rd Qu.    Max.    NA's
  4.203   6.027   7.173   7.413   8.644  10.910     122
```

Note that the number of `NA` is the difference between 3161 and 3039.

```
openness_omit <- na.omit(openness)
```

`openness_omit` has 3039 observations.

```
> nrow(openness_omit)
[1] 3039
```

Then, we add a new variable to the data set that contains the result of fitted values from our previous regression. To access these values, we extract them from `open_reg`, the object that stores our results from the regression analysis. We use `$` to extract fitted values from the regression object and assign them to the new variable `fitted` which we generate in the `openness_omit` data set.

Finally, we compare the observed values with the fitted values. We generate a new column in our data set, `trade_more` with the `ifelse()` function. The first entry of the function states the conditional statement. In this case, if the observed values are greater than the fitted values. If they are greater, it assigns 1 to `trade_more`, 0 otherwise. Finally, we table the results by using the `table()` function. Note that we nest `table()` in `with()` and `head()`. `with()` evaluates an **R** expression in an environment constructed from data. Therefore, it allows us to avoid writing the name of the data set for the two variables. `head()` allows us to view the first entries of the data set. By default `head()` shows the first 6 entries. Here, we set `head()` to show the first 15 entries.[5]

```
# Predict
openness_omit$fitted <- open_reg$fitted.values

# check if trade more
openness_omit$trade_more <- ifelse(openness_omit$ln_open >
                                   openness_omit$fitted,
                                   1, 0)

# crosstable
head(with(openness_omit, table(ccode, trade_more)), 15)
```

```
> head(with(openness_omit, table(ccode, trade_more)), 15)
     trade_more
ccode  0  1
  AGO  7 13
  ARE 14 13
  ARG 16 13
  AUS 17 12
  AUT 18 11
```

[5] Note that some results for `0` (trade less) differ from the output in Stata. The reason is that Stata is comparing the observed values with the fitted values even though the value is indeed missing. It assigns the result of this comparison to `0`. If you drop the missing values for fitted values in Stata you will get the same results as in **R**.

```
BDI 12 17
BEN 16 13
BFA 15 14
BGD 18 11
BOL 19 10
BRA 16 13
BWA 15 14
CAF 15 14
CAN 18 11
CHE 15 14
```

2.2 Geographical Orientation of Exports

Learning Objectives

- Import a Stata file
- Conversion of objects
- Generate new variables
- Group operations with `ave()`
- Group operations with `group_by()`
- Sort data set by variables
- Collapse a data set with `aggregate()`
- Rename column names
- Label variables
- Generate lag variables in a panel data set
- Merge two data sets with `merge()`
- Replace if
- Subset a data set
- Plot with `ggplot()`

In this section we replicate the UNCTAD & WTO's Stata code in **R** for plotting the geographical orientation of exports of Colombia and Pakistan.[6]

Open a new script file in **RStudio** and save it as `03_growth_orientation_of_exports_2edn`.

Let's load the following packages by using the `library()` function.

```
library("haven") # import Stata .dta file
library("Hmisc") # for label
library("ggplot2") # plot with ggplot
```

[6] The corresponding Stata code is available in growth_orientation_of_exports.do.

```
library("plm") # for making lag variables in panel data
library("dplyr") # data management
library("ggpubr") # combine ggplot plots
```

We start by importing the data set `aBilateralTrade.dta` as `aBT` in **R**. `aBT` is a data frame with 403,135 observations and 5 variables: reporter, `ccode`, partner, `pcode`, year, `year`, export value, `exp_tv`, and import value, `imp_tv`. Data cover the years 1976–2004.

```
aBT <- read_dta("datWTO/aBilateralTrade.dta")
class(aBilateralTrade)
View(aBT)
dim(aBT)
str(aBT)
```

We generate a new variable, `tot_exp`, that is the total value of exports of an exporter towards all partners by year. To calculate it, we need to sum the export value, `exp_tv`, by country, `ccode`, for a given year, `year`. We group these two operations using the `ave()` function.[7] The first entry of `ave()` is the variable we want to operate, i.e., `exp_tv` in this case. In the term `interaction()` we define the grouping variables. In this case, `ccode`, for the exporting country, and `year`, for the year. Finally, we define a function to apply for each level combination. In this case we define a `sum()` function. Note that `x` refers to `exp_tv`, the first entry of `ave()`, and `na.rm = T` removes missing values.

Then, we create a new variable, `export_share` as export value, `exp_tv`, divided by total value of exports, `tot_exp`. Finally, we sort the `aBT` data set by `ccode` and `year` with the `order()` function.

```
## Generate total export value
aBT$tot_exp <- ave(aBT$exp_tv, interaction(aBT$ccode, aBT$year),
                   FUN = function(x) sum(x, na.rm = T))
aBT$export_share <- aBT$exp_tv / aBT$tot_exp
aBT <- aBT[order(aBT$ccode, aBT$year), ]

summary(aBT$export_share)
```

The following is the output of the `summary()` function applied to `export_share`. **R** signals the presence of missing values, NA.

```
> summary(aBT$export_share)
   Min. 1st Qu.  Median    Mean 3rd Qu.    Max.    NA's
  0.000   0.000   0.000   0.008   0.002   1.000    3567
```

In the next step, let's label the variable `export_share` with the `upData()` function from the `Hmisc` package. In the first entry we input the data set. Then, in `label =` we set a label to the variable of interest. The `label()` function shows the labels of your variables in the data set. If you `View()` the data set, you will note that the label has been also added below the variable name.

```
aBT <- upData(aBT, labels = c(export_share =
                              "pcode's share in ccode's total exports"))
label(aBT)
View(aBT)
```

[7] We will implement another approach with the `dplyr` package to group by later in this section.

```
> label(aBT)
                                       ccode                                   pcode
                              "Country code"                          "Partner code"
                                        year                                  exp_tv
                                      "Year"                         "(sum) exp_tv"
                                      imp_tv                                 tot_exp
                              "(sum) imp_tv"                         "(sum) exp_tv"
                                export_share
"pcode's share in ccode's total exports"
```

Next, we use again the `ave()` function to generate the sum of total imports, `tot_imppcode`, by partner, `pcode`, and year, `year`. Then, we label it as reported in the following code.

```
aBT$tot_imppcode <- ave(aBT$exp_tv, interaction(aBT$year, aBT$pcode),
                        FUN = function(x) sum(x, na.rm = T))
aBT <- upData(aBT, labels = c(tot_imppcode =
                              "total import of importing country (pcode)"))
label(aBT)
View(aBT)
```

Next, we collapse the data set by aggregating `tot_imppcode` by `pcode` and `year`. We use the `aggregate()` function. The first argument of `aggregate()` is the variables to be summarized, the second argument is a list containing the variables to be used for grouping, and the third argument is the function to be used to summarize the data. We assign this operation to a new data set, `aBTc`, to not overwrite `aBT`.

```
aBTc <- aggregate(list(tot_imppcode = aBT$tot_imppcode),
                  by = list(pcode = aBT$pcode, year = aBT$year),
                  mean, na.rm = T)
View(aBTc)
```

In the next lines of code, we generate a new variable for the year over year change, `gamma_totimppcode`. For this task we need to create a lag variable for `tot_imppcode`. First, we sort the data set `aBTc` by `pcode` with the `order()` function. Second, we make the `aBTc` data set as a panel data frame object by using the function `pdata.frame()` from the `plm` package. The `index` attribute describes its individual and time dimensions. Third, we use the `lag()` function from the `plm` package to create the lag variable for `imppcode`, `lag_totimppcode`. Again, note that we specify that **R** has to use the `lag()` function from the `plm` package. Finally, we create the new variable, `gamma_totimppcode` and replace infinity value `Inf` with `NA`.

```
# making lag variable in panel data
aBTc <- aBTc[order(aBTc$pcode),]

aBTc <- pdata.frame(aBTc, index = c("pcode", "year"))
class(aBTc)
str(aBTc)
View(aBTc)

aBTc$lag_totimppcode <- plm::lag(aBTc$tot_imppcode)
aBTc$gamma_totimppcode <- (aBTc$tot_imppcode / aBTc$lag_totimppcode) - 1

# replace Inf with NA
any(is.infinite(aBTc$gamma_totimppcode))
aBTc$gamma_totimppcode[is.infinite(aBTc$gamma_totimppcode)] <- NA
```

If you noted, when we run `str(aBTc)` the variable `year` is reported as a factor. Here, we show how to convert factor into a numeric value. We nest the `level()` function in `as.numeric()`. This is the advice from FAQ on CRAN to convert factors to numeric.[8]

```
# change factor to numeric
aBTc$year <- as.numeric(levels(aBTc$year))[aBTc$year]
```

In the next lines of code, we create new variables that represent average for all the years of the data set, 1974–2004 (`avg_imp_g_1974_2004`), for the period 1990–2000 (`avg_imp_g_1990_2000`), and for the period 1994–2004 (`avg_imp_g_1994_2004`). We use the `dplyr` package. We use `group_by()` to group the data by `pcode`. Then, we compute just the mean for `avg_imp_g_1974_2004` by making sure to remove the missing values for the computation. The other two variables are generated by using the `case_when()` function from `dplyr`. When the year corresponds to our period of interest, we compute the mean for `gamma_totimppcode` for that period.[9]

```
# create average variables ----

aBTc <- aBTc %>%
  group_by(pcode) %>%
  mutate(avg_imp_g_1974_2004 = mean(gamma_totimppcode, na.rm = T),
         avg_imp_g_1990_2000 = case_when(
           year >= 1990 & year <= 2000 ~ mean(
             gamma_totimppcode[year >= 1990 & year <= 2000], na.rm = T)
         ),
         avg_imp_g_1994_2004 = case_when(
           year >= 1994 & year <= 2004 ~ mean(
             gamma_totimppcode[year >= 1994 & year <= 2004], na.rm = T)
         ))


View(aBTc)
```

Next, we use `merge()` to merge the data in `aBT` and `aBTc`. We define the keyword for the merge in `by =`. Note that in this case, we have the same column titles for the two data sets. That's why the code differs from the example from section "Merging Data Sets" where the column titles had different names.

```
# merge aBT and aBTc -> aBTm

aBTm <- merge(aBT, aBTc,
              by = c("pcode", "year", "tot_imppcode"),
              all = TRUE)
View(aBTm)
```

Next, we generate the logarithm of `export_share` and `avg_imp_g_1990_2000`. When we check the summary, we see that some `-Inf` values are returned for `ln_x`. This is caused by taking the log of 0. We replace these

---

[8] See https://cran.r-project.org/doc/FAQ/R-FAQ.html#How-do-I-convert-factors-to-numeric_003f.

[9] Note that this chunk of code differs from the code in the first edition. I found out that the function I wrote for the first edition did not return the correct results for `avg_imp_g_1990_2000` for about 15% of the countries. It seems that the issued I overlooked was related to the fact that for those countries the series of data starts after 1990.

values with NA. Note again that [ ] is a subset operator. Therefore, in aBTm$ln_x[is.infinite(aBTm$ln_x)] <- NA we are replacing the value of ln_x with NA if this value is equal to infinity. We label this new variable as Log of export share to destination j with upData().

Finally, we create two variables for mapping the legend in the plots, fitted and log, which store the text that will appear in the legend.

```
aBTm$ln_x <- log(aBTm$export_share)
aBTm$ln_y <- log(aBTm$avg_imp_g_1990_2000)

summary(aBTm$ln_x)
summary(aBTm$ln_y)

any(is.infinite(aBTm$ln_x))
aBTm$ln_x[is.infinite(aBTm$ln_x)] <- NA

summary(aBTm$ln_x)

# label
aBTm <- upData(aBTm,
        labels = c(ln_x = "Log of export share to destination j"))

aBTm$fitted <- "Fitted"
aBTm$log <- "log average import growth of destination j, 1990-2000"
```

To plot the geographical orientation of exports of Colombia and Pakistan we first subset the data set for Colombia and year 2000 and then for Pakistan and year 2000 with the subset() function.

```
# select only Colombia and year == 2000
aBTm_col <- subset(aBTm, ccode == "COL" & year == 2000)
View(aBTm_col)

# select only Pakistan and year == 2000
aBTm_pak <- subset(aBTm, ccode == "PAK" & year == "2000")
View(aBTm_pak)
```

Finally, we create two plots and then combine them. We add more options with respect to the plots we made in Sect. 2.1. In particular, we control for the legend with aes() and with the options in theme(), we add a new format for the the title and define a new background, theme_classic(). Add the options gradually to see what they do. Note that n in the title splits a title over two lines (Fig. 2.5).

```
# plot Geographical orientation of Colombia's exports, 2000

plot_col <- ggplot(aBTm_col, aes(x = ln_x, y = ln_y)) +
  geom_point(shape = 1, color = "blue",
             aes(fill = factor(log))) +
  geom_smooth(method=lm, aes(color = "Fitted")) +
  geom_text(aes(label = pcode), size = 2, hjust=0, vjust=1) +
  theme_classic() +
  xlab("log of export share to destination j") + ylab("") +
  ggtitle("Geographical orientation of \n Colombia's exports, 2000") +
  theme(plot.title = element_text(hjust = 0.5, size = 10, face="bold"),
        axis.title.x = element_text(size = 7.5)) +
  theme(legend.position = "bottom", legend.box = "vertical",
        legend.text = element_text(size = 7.5),
        legend.key.size = unit(0.2, "cm"),
        legend.title = element_blank())
```

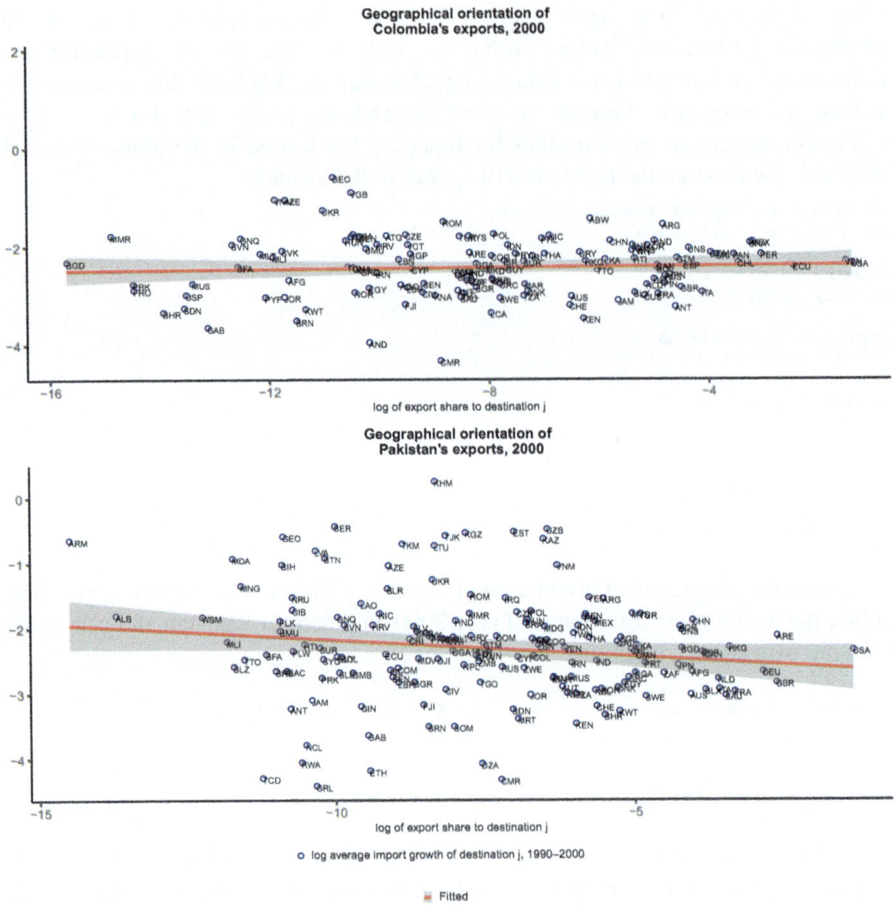

Fig. 2.5 More elaborated plots with `ggplot2`

```
# plot Geographical orientation of Pakistan's exports, 2000

plot_pak <- ggplot(aBTm_pak, aes(x = ln_x, y = ln_y)) +
  geom_point(shape = 1, color = "blue",
             aes(fill = factor(log))) +
  geom_smooth(method=lm, aes(color = "Fitted")) +
  geom_text(aes(label = pcode), size = 2, hjust=0, vjust=1) +
  theme_classic() +
  xlab("log of export share to destination j") + ylab("") +
  ggtitle("Geographical orientation of \n Pakistan's exports, 2000") +
  theme(plot.title = element_text(hjust = 0.5, size = 10, face="bold"),
        axis.title.x = element_text(size = 7.5)) +
  theme(legend.position = "bottom", legend.box = "vertical",
        legend.text = element_text(size = 7.5),
        legend.key.size = unit(0.2, "cm"),
        legend.title = element_blank())
```

```
ggarrange(plot_col, plot_pak,
          ncol = 1, nrow = 2,
          common.legend = TRUE,
          legend = "bottom")
```

2.3 Sectoral Orientation of Exports

Learning Objectives

- Import a Stata file
- Conversion of objects
- Generate new variables
- Group operations with `ave()`
- Sort data set by variables
- Generate ranking for variables
- Generate group id
- Reshape the data set
- Subset a data set
- Plot with `ggplot()`

In this section we replicate the UNCTAD & WTO's Stata code in **R** to plot the sectoral orientation of exports of Colombia.[10]

Open a new script file in **RStudio** and save it as `04_sectoral_geographical_orientation_of_trade_2edn`.

Let's load the following packages by using the `library()` function.

```
library("haven") # import Stata .dta file
library("dplyr") # group id
library("data.table") # reshape the dataset with dcast
library("ggplot2") # plot with ggplot
```

Let's import the data set `TPP.dta` in **R**. `TPP` is a data frame with 81,200 observations and 40 variables. Data cover the years 1976–2004.

```
TPP <- read_dta("datWTO/TPP.dta")
class(TPP)
View(TPP)
dim(TPP)
str(TPP)
```

[10] The corresponding Stata code is available in sectoral_geographical_orientation_of_trade.do.

We generate total export variable, `total_export`, with the `ave()` function. Refer to Sect. 2.2 for details on the `ave()` function. Then, we generate the export share, `export_share`, as export value, `exp_tv`, divided by total export, `total_export`. Finally, we sort the `TPP` dataset by `ccode`, `year` and `export_share` using the `order()` function. Note that the `-` operator before the variable sorts it in descending order. The `summary()` function applied to `export_share` shows that `export_share` has missing values, `NA`.

```
## Main export sectors, Colombia, 1990 and 2000

TPP$total_export <- ave(TPP$exp_tv, interaction(TPP$ccode, TPP$year),
                        FUN = function(x) sum(x, na.rm = T))
TPP$export_share <- TPP$exp_tv / TPP$total_export

# ordering:minus (-) before the variable for descending order
TPP <- TPP[order(TPP$ccode, TPP$year, -TPP$export_share),]

summary(TPP$export_share)
```

In the next line of code, we generate a ranking for export share, `ranking`, by `ccode` and `year`, nesting the `rank()` function in the `ave()` function. Note that the `-` operator before `x` in the `rank()` function sorts the ranking in descending order.

```
# ranking
TPP$ranking <- ave(TPP$export_share, interaction(TPP$ccode, TPP$year),
                   FUN = function(x) rank(-x))
```

We keep only `ranking`, `sector`, `ccode`, `year`, and `export_share` by applying `[ ]` to `TPP` data set. Let's assign this operation to a new object, `TPP2`.

We generate group id variable, `id`, by `ccode` and `sector` using the `cur_group_id()` function from the `dplyr` package.[11] Let's copy the `TPP2` in a new object, `TPP3`.

Finally, we have to reshape the data set wide. We want to generate new columns with the ranking per each year and the export share per each year for id, country (`ccode`) and sector. For this operation, I prefer to use the `dcast()` function from the `data.table` package. You can refer to Sect. 1.7.2 for an alternative method. Note that before reshaping the data set, we convert the data set in a `data.table` using `setDT()` from the `data.table` package. The first entry in `dcast` is a data set that must be a `data.table` or a `data.frame`. Note that when casting multiple variables it is better to have the data set as `data.table`. The variables on the left hand side of $\sim$ will be in rows while the variables on the right hand side of $\sim$ will become column names. The argument `value.var =` assigns the name of the column whose values will be filled to cast.

```
TPP2 <- TPP[, c("ranking", "sector", "ccode", "year", "export_share")]

# generate group id by ccode & sector
TPP2 <- TPP2 %>%
```

[11] The `cur_group_id()` function replaces `group_indices()` that was used in the first edition because it is now a deprecated function.

```
  group_by(ccode, sector) %>%
  mutate(id = cur_group_id())

View(TPP2)

# make the dataset wide
## convert the dataset in a data.table before using dcast
TPP3 <- setDT(TPP2)

TPP3s <- dcast(TPP3, id + ccode + sector ~ year,
               value.var = c("ranking", "export_share"))

View(TPP3s)
```

Now we can prepare the data set for plotting. We plot the data for Colombia only. Therefore, the first step consists in subsetting by Colombia using `subset()`. This operation is stored in a new object, `TPP_col`. We keep only the following variables: `ccode`, `sector`, `ranking_1990`, `ranking_2000`, `export_share_1990`, and `export_share_2000`. We use `[ ]` for this operation and we assign it to a new object, `TPP_col2`.

To plot the following bar plot we need to reshape the data long. We use `melt()` from `data.table` package. The first entry is the data set to be reshaped. The argument `id.vars =` is a vector of id variables, i.e., the variables that identify individual rows of data. It can be integer (variable position) or string (variable name). The argument `measure.vars =` is a vector of measured variables. It can be integer (variable position) or string (variable name). By default, `melt()` names the new variables `variable` and `value`. You can rename using `variable.name =` and `value.name =`. Finally, we sort the data set by `ranking` using `order()`.

```
# subset for Colombia
TPP_col <- subset(TPP3s, ccode == "COL")
View(TPP_col)

TPP_col2 <- TPP_col[, c("ccode", "sector", "ranking_1990", "ranking_2000",
                        "export_share_1990", "export_share_2000")]

dim(TPP_col2)
View(TPP_col2)

## make dataset long with melt()
TPP_col3 <- melt(TPP_col2, id.vars = c("sector", "ccode",
                                       "ranking_1990", "ranking_2000"),
                 measure.vars  = c("export_share_1990",
                                   "export_share_2000"))

TPP_col3 <- TPP_col3[order(TPP_col3$ranking_1990),]
head(TPP_col3)
```

By using `head()` we see the first six entries of the data set as reported in the following output.[12]

[12] Note that I shortened the name for sector to show the output in a more readable way. The name of the sector should be Petroleum refineries, Food products, and Iron and steel.

```
> head(TPP_col3)
      sector ccode ranking_1990 ranking_2000          variable      value
1: Petroleum   COL            1            1 export_share_1990 0.22075888
2: Petroleum   COL            1            1 export_share_2000 0.14273302
3:      Food   COL            2            2 export_share_1990 0.15854882
4:      Food   COL            2            2 export_share_2000 0.12791253
5:      Iron   COL            3            6 export_share_1990 0.09223055
6:      Iron   COL            3            6 export_share_2000 0.06149664
```

Now we are ready to plot a bar plot with `ggplot()`. Note that the general structure is the same as the previous plots with `ggplot()`. Here, we describe the different arguments.

`reorder()` in `aes()` order the `sector` by `ranking_1990`. If you want to reverse the order of the bars, from high to low, remove the - before `ranking_1990`.

`fill` = maps the color conditional on a variable. In this case, this variable is called `variable`. It is the column name in the `TPP_col3` dataset that contains the values `export_share_1990` and `export_share_2000`.

To generate a bar plot we use `geom_bar()`. `position = "dodge"` puts the bars side-by-side. Remove it to see the different output. With `stat = "identity"` the heights of the bars represent values in the data. `coord_flip()` flips the plot.

In `xlab()` and `ylab()` we only insert " " because we do not want any label for *x* and *y* axis. If we do not include `xlab()` and `ylab()` with " ", **R** will generate default labels for the axes.

With `scale_fill_manual()` we define manually the labels name and colors.

Figure 2.6 shows the outcome of this plot.

```
# plot

plot_TPP_col <- ggplot(TPP_col3,
                       aes(x = reorder(sector, -ranking_1990),
                           y = value, fill = variable)) +
  geom_bar(position = "dodge", stat="identity") +
  coord_flip() +
  xlab("") + ylab("") + theme_classic() +
  ggtitle("Sectoral share in total exports, 1990-2000") +
  scale_fill_manual(labels = c("Share 1990", "Share 2000"),
                    values = c("blue", "red")) +
  theme(plot.title = element_text(hjust = 0.5, size = 10,
                                  face="bold"),
        axis.title.x = element_text(size = 7.5),
        axis.text.y = element_text(size = 7.5)) +
  theme(legend.position = "bottom", legend.box = "vertical",
        legend.text = element_text(size = 7.5),
        legend.key.size = unit(0.2, "cm"),
        legend.title = element_blank())

plot_TPP_col
```

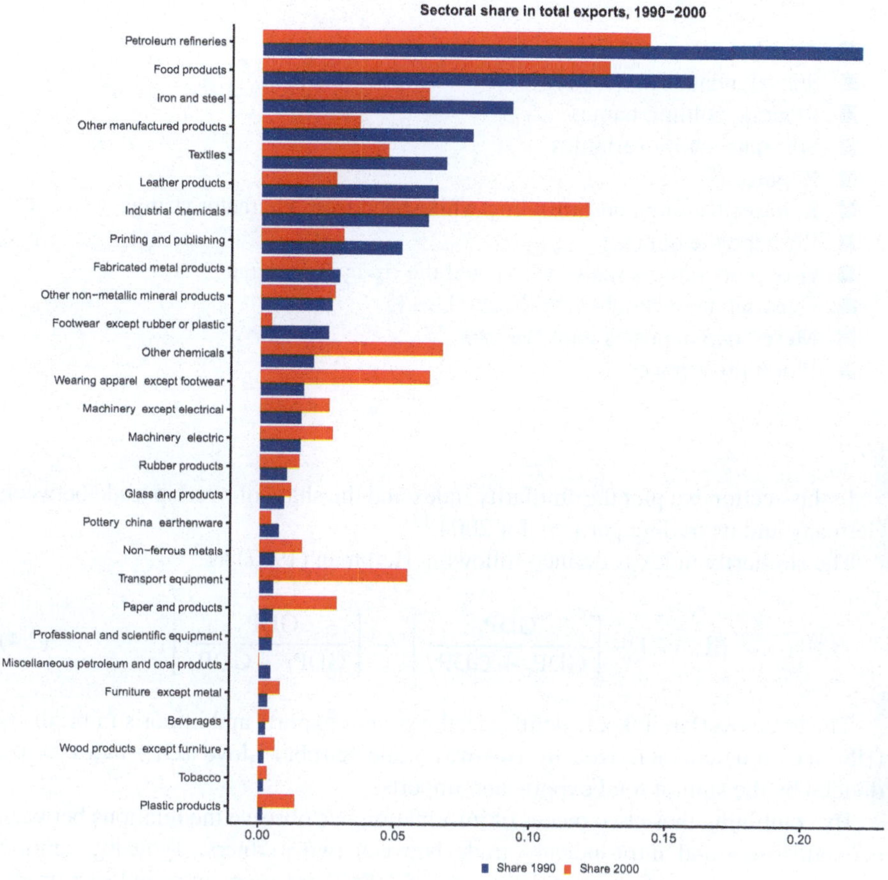

Fig. 2.6 Bar plot with `ggplot2`

2.4 Overlap Trade and Similarity Index

Learning Objectives

- Import a Stata file
- Conversion of objects
- Generate new variables
- Drop duplicates

(continued)

- Attach a data set
- Subset a data set
- Rename column names
- Sort data set by variables
- Replace if
- Remove leading and/or trailing whitespace from character strings
- Reshape the data set
- Group operations with `ave()` and the `dplyr` package
- Generate new variables with `ifelse()`
- Merge two data sets with `merge()`
- Plot with `ggplot()`

In this section we plot the similarity index and the share of overlap trade between Germany and its trading partners for 2004.[13]

The similarity index is defined following Helpman (1987) as

$$\mathrm{SI}_{ij} = 1 - \left[\frac{\mathrm{GDP}_i}{\mathrm{GDP}_i + \mathrm{GDP}_j}\right]^2 - \left[\frac{\mathrm{GDP}_j}{\mathrm{GDP}_i + \mathrm{GDP}_j}\right]^2 \tag{2.4}$$

The trade overlap index is defined as the sum of exports and imports in products (HS, six digit) characterized by two-way trade (Grubel-Lloyd (GL) index > 0), divided by the sum of total exports and imports.

By combining these two pieces of information, we observe the relations between economic size and intra-industry trade between two partners. Typically, similar countries (in terms of economic size, e.g. GDP) share more intra-industry trade. Refer to UNCTAD & WTO (2012, p. 20) for more insights.

Open a new script file in **RStudio** and save it as `05_overlap_trade_2edn`. Let's load the following packages by using the `library()` function.

```
library("haven") # import Stata .dta file
library("stringi") # count the number of code points
library("data.table") # reshape the data set
library("dplyr") # data management
library("ggplot2") # plot with ggplot
library("ggpubr") # combine ggplot plots
```

First, we build the similarity index. Let's import the UNCTAD & WTO's `GravityData.dta` as `GravityData` in **R** by using `read_dta()` from the `haven` package. `GravityData` has 3,950,635 observations and 27 variables. Data cover the years 1976–2004. Since it is quite big, we make a copy and work with `GD`. Therefore, in case we make an error, it is not necessary to import it again because we do not modify `GravityData`.

[13] The corresponding Stata code is available in overlap_trade.do.

```
GravityData <- read_dta("datWTO/GravityData.dta")
class(GravityData)
GD <- GravityData
dim(GD)
str(GD)
```

We keep only the following columns: ccode, pcode, year, cgdp_c2000, and pgdp_c2000. Then, we drop the duplicates using the unique function. This last operation may take a while.

```
GD <- GD[, c("ccode", "pcode", "year", "cgdp_c2000", "pgdp_c2000")]
GD <- unique(GD)
```

We attach the data set GD by using the attach() function. This means that the database is searched by **R** when evaluating a variable, so objects in the database can be accessed by simply giving their names. Then, we detach the data set by using the detach() function before moving on.

Next, we build the similarity index, simil_index, as in Eq. (2.4).

Then, we keep only the following variables: ccode, pcode, year, and simil_index. We assign this operation to a new object, GD2. Then, we subset it by year equal 2004 and country equal Germany (ccode == "DEU"). We store the results in GDger. Let's sort the data set by ccode, pcode, and year by using the order() function. Finally, we check basic statistics for simil_index.

```
attach(GD)
GD$temp1 <- cgdp_c2000 / (cgdp_c2000 + pgdp_c2000)
GD$temp2 <- pgdp_c2000 / (cgdp_c2000 + pgdp_c2000)
detach(GD)

GD$simil_index <- 1 - GD$temp1^(2) - GD$temp2^(2)
GD2 <- GD[, c("ccode", "pcode", "year", "simil_index")]
GDger <- subset(GD2, year == "2004" & ccode == "DEU")
GDger <- GDger[order(GDger$ccode, GDger$pcode, GDger$year),]
summary(GDger$simil_index)
```

In this part, we build the trade overlap index. Let's import the UNCTAD & WTO's germany_trade_2004_hs6.dta as GT_2004HS6 in **R** by using read_dta() from the haven package. GT_2004HS6 has 874,975 observations and 11 variables.

```
GT_2004HS6 <- read_dta("datWTO/germany_trade_2004_hs6.dta")
class(GT_2004HS6)
View(GT_2004HS6)
dim(GT_2004HS6)
str(GT_2004HS6)
```

We rename reporter as ccode and partner as pcode using the colnames() function. Then, we replace the value Gross Exp. in flow_name as Exports and the value Gross Imp. in flow_name as Imports. Finally, we drop the first column.

```
colnames(GT_2004HS6)[2] <- "ccode"
colnames(GT_2004HS6)[4] <- "pcode"
GT_2004HS6$flow_name[GT_2004HS6$flow_name == "Gross Exp."] <- "Exports"
GT_2004HS6$flow_name[GT_2004HS6$flow_name == "Gross Imp."] <- "Imports"
GT_2004HS6 <- GT_2004HS6[, -1]
```

Next, we remove leading and/or trailing whitespace from product using the trimws() function. By default, trimws() removes both leading and trailing whitespace. However, it is possible to remove only the leading or trailing whitespace, specifying in the function `"left"` or `"right"`, respectively.

```
GT_2004HS6$product <- trimws(GT_2004HS6$product)
```

Next, we drop observations from the data set if `product` is equal to `Total`. Then, we subset again if the length of the values in the `product` column is longer than 6. We use the `stri_length()` function from the `stringi` package to accomplish this step. Finally, we remove the `rowname` column.

```
GT_2004HS6_2 <- subset(GT_2004HS6, !product == "Total")
GT_2004HS6_3 <- subset(GT_2004HS6_2,
                       stri_length(product) >= "6")
GT_2004HS6_3 <- GT_2004HS6_3[, -10]
```

Next, we reshape the data set wide by using the `dcast()` function from the `data.table` package. Refer to Sect. 2.3 for the use of `dcast()`. We assign this operation to a new object, `overlap_temp`.

```
overlap_temp <- dcast(setDT(GT_2004HS6_3),
                      ccode + pcode + year + product ~
                      flow_name,
                      value.var = "trade_value")
```

After sorting the data set by `pcode` and `product`, we build the Grubel-Lloyd (GL) index. The GL index is defined as follows:

$$GL_{ij,k} = 1 - \frac{|X_{ij,k} - M_{ij,k}|}{X_{ij,k} + M_{ij,k}} \tag{2.5}$$

where

- $X_{ij,k}$ is i's exports to j in sector k
- $M_{ij,k}$ is i's imports from j in sector k

By definition, we have $0 \leq GL \leq 1$. $GL = 0$ means that a country does not engage in intra-industry trade, i.e. either $X_{ij,k} = 0$ or $M_{ij,k} = 0$. $GL = 1$ means that a country exports and imports the good in sector k in equal amounts, i.e. $X_{ij,k} = M_{ij,k}$. Consequently, a greater GL index indicates a larger intra-industry trade between two countries.

We replace the `NA` values of the GL index, `gl_i_j_k`, with 0 and sort the dataset by `pcode`.

```
overlap_temp <- overlap_temp[order(overlap_temp$pcode,
                                   overlap_temp$product), ]

## Grubel-Lloyd (GL) Index
overlap_temp$gl_i_j_k <- 1 - (abs(overlap_temp$Exports - overlap_temp$Imports) /
                              (overlap_temp$Exports + overlap_temp$Imports))
overlap_temp$gl_i_j_k[is.na(overlap_temp$gl_i_j_k)] <- 0
overlap_temp <- overlap_temp[order(overlap_temp$pcode), ]
```

In the next lines of code, we generate two new variables, `x1` and `x2`, which are given by the sum of `Exports` and `Imports`, respectively, by partner, `pcode`. We accomplish these operations with the `ave()` function that we encountered in Sects. 2.2 and 2.3. Then, we generate the denominator, `denom`, as the sum between x1 and x2. Finally, we generate a new variable, dd, which reports the max value of denom by pcode. We use again the ave() function. Note that now the function to apply for each factor level combination is max.

```
overlap_temp$x1 <- ave(overlap_temp$Exports, overlap_temp$pcode,
                       FUN = function(x) sum(x, na.rm = T))
overlap_temp$x2 <- ave(overlap_temp$Imports, overlap_temp$pcode,
                       FUN = function(x) sum(x, na.rm = T))

overlap_temp$denom <- overlap_temp$x1 + overlap_temp$x2

overlap_temp$dd <- ave(overlap_temp$denom, overlap_temp$pcode, FUN = max)
```

Next, we generate two new variables, x11 and x22 which are given by the sum of Exports and Imports, respectively, by partner, pcode, as x1 and x2, but subject to the condition that gl_i_j_k is greater than 0. Remember that this is the condition stated in the definition of the trade overlap index.

In this case, instead, we sum the values by using functions from the dplyr package as in Sect. 2.2.

```
overlap_temp <- overlap_temp %>%
  group_by(pcode) %>%
  mutate(x11 = ifelse(gl_i_j_k > 0,
                      sum(Exports[gl_i_j_k > 0], na.rm = T),
                      NA),
         x22 = ifelse(gl_i_j_k > 0,
                      sum(Imports[gl_i_j_k > 0], na.rm = T),
                      NA))
```

Note again that %>% is an operator which pipes a value forward into an expression or function call. The group_by() function performs the operation by groups of observations within a data set. The mutate() function adds new variables that are functions of existing variables and preserves existing variables. We use in mutate() the ifelse() function to state the conditional statement of the operation, i.e. GL index greater than 0.

Next, we generate the numerator, numer, as the sum between x11 and x22, and the variable nn. Conceptually, nn is similar to dd in terms of code. However, we need to take care of missing values and infinite values.

Then, we generate the trade overlap index, overlap, as the ratio between nn and dd. Finally, we create a new data set, overlap, which contains 4 variables from overlap_temp: ccode, pcode, year, and overlap.

```
overlap_temp$numer <- overlap_temp$x11 + overlap_temp$x22
overlap_temp <- overlap_temp %>%
  group_by(pcode) %>%
  mutate(nn = max(numer, na.rm = T))

overlap_temp$nn[is.infinite(overlap_temp$nn)] <- NA

overlap_temp$overlap <- overlap_temp$nn / overlap_temp$dd

overlap <- overlap_temp[, c("ccode", "pcode", "year", "overlap")]
```

Now, we are ready to merge overlap and GDger, the data set that stores the similarity index for Germany. We use the merge() function. We assign this operation to a new object, overlap_m. After merging, we drop the duplicates.

```
overlap_m <- merge(overlap, GDger,
```

```
                   by = c("ccode", "pcode", "year"),
                   all.x = T, all.y = F)

overlap_m <- unique(overlap_m)
```

Before plotting, we add two new columns to the dataset `overlap_m` for mapping the legend in the plots, `Fitted` and `leg_overlap`, that store the text that will appear in the legend.

```
overlap_m$Fitted <- "Fitted Values"
overlap_m$leg_overlap <- "Share of overlap trade"
```

The following code generates Fig. 2.7.

```
plot_lft <- ggplot(overlap_m,
                   aes(x = simil_index, y = overlap)) +
  geom_point(shape = 1, color = "blue",
             aes(fill = factor(leg_overlap))) +
  geom_smooth(method = lm, aes(color = "Fitted Values")) +
  geom_text(aes(label = pcode), size = 2, hjust = 0, vjust = 1) +
  theme_classic() +
  xlab("Share of overlap trade") + ylab(" ") +
  ggtitle("Similarity index") + labs(caption = "a) linear fit") +
  theme(plot.title = element_text(hjust = 0.5, size = 10, face="bold"),
        plot.caption = element_text(hjust = 1, size = 10),
        axis.title.x = element_text(size = 7.5)) +
  theme(legend.position = "bottom", legend.box = "vertical",
        legend.text = element_text(size = 7.5),
        legend.title = element_blank(),
        legend.key.height = unit(0.1, "cm"))


plot_lft


plot_qft <- ggplot(overlap_m,
                   aes(x = simil_index, y = overlap)) +
  geom_point(shape = 1, color = "blue",
             aes(fill = factor(leg_overlap))) +
  geom_smooth(method = lm, formula = y ~ x + I(x^2),
              aes(color = "Fitted Values")) +
  geom_text(aes(label = pcode), size = 2, hjust = 0, vjust = 1) +
  theme_classic() +
  xlab("Share of overlap trade") + ylab(" ") +
  ggtitle("Similarity index") +labs(caption = "b) quadratic fit") +
  theme(plot.title = element_text(hjust = 0.5, size = 10, face="bold"),
        plot.caption = element_text(hjust = 1, size = 10),
        axis.title.x = element_text(size = 7.5)) +
  theme(legend.position = "bottom", legend.box = "vertical",
        legend.text = element_text(size = 7.5),
        legend.title = element_blank(),
        legend.key.height = unit(0.1, "cm"))

plot_qft

ggarrange(plot_lft, plot_qft,
          ncol = 1, nrow = 2,
          common.legend = TRUE,
          legend = "bottom")
```

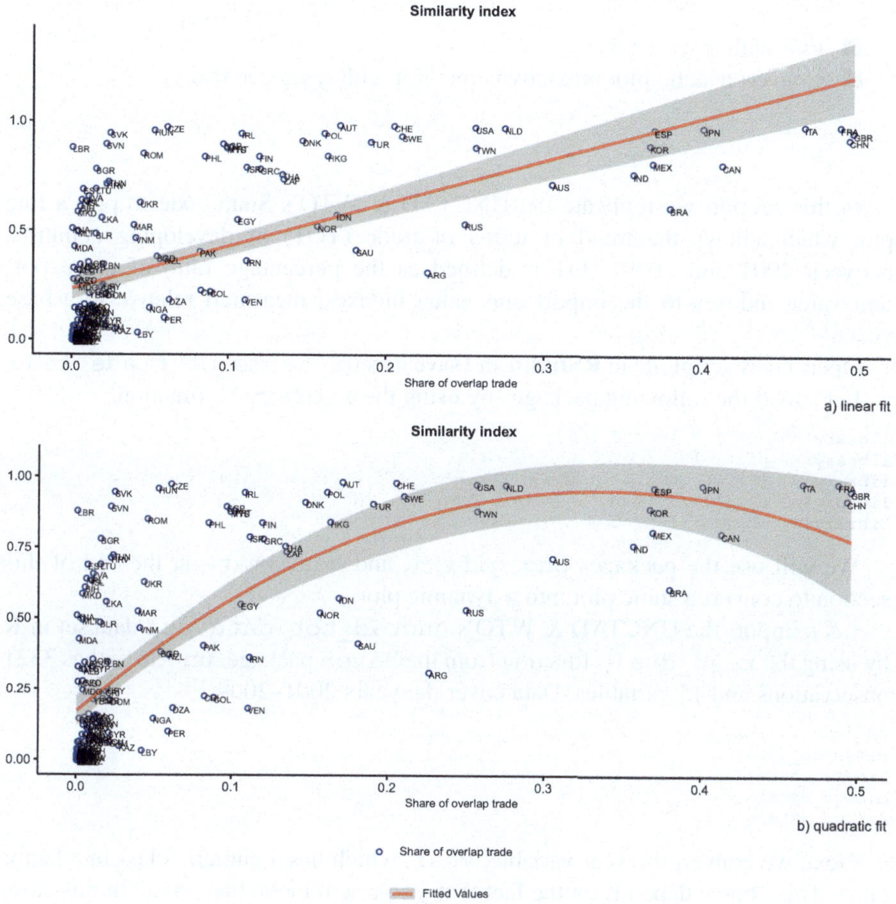

Fig. 2.7 Scatterplot with linear and quadratic fitted lines with `ggplot2`

2.5 Terms of Trade

> **Learning Objectives**
>
> - Import a Stata file
> - Conversion of objects
> - Subset a data set

(continued)

- Plot with `ggplot()`
- Convert a static plot into a dynamic plot with `gganimate()`

In this section we replicate the UNCTAD & WTO's Stata code to plot a line plot which shows the trend of terms of trade (TOT) of developing countries between 2001 and 2009. TOT is defined as the percentage ratio of the export unit value indexes to the import unit value indexes, measured relative to a base year.[14]

Open a new script file in **RStudio** and save it as `06_terms_of_trade_2edn`.

Let's load the following packages by using the `library()` function.

```
library("haven") # import Stata .dta file
library("ggplot2") # plot with ggplot
library("png") # graphics devices for BMP, JPEG, PNG and TIFF format bitmap
library("gifski") # converts image frames to high quality GIF animations
library("gganimate") # animated plot
```

We will use the packages `png`, `gifski`, and `gganimate` at the end of this section to convert a static plot into a dynamic plot.

Let's import the UNCTAD & WTO's `unctad_tot_data.dta` data set in **R** by using the `read_dta()` function from the `haven` package. `un_data` has 3321 observations and 15 variables. Data cover the years 2001–2009.

```
un_data <- read_dta("datWTO/unctad_tot_data.dta")
class(un_data)
View(un_data)
dim(un_data)
str(un_data)
```

Next, we convert the year variable, `year`, which has a numeric class in a factor class. This choice depends on the fact that `year` will be on the *x*-axis. In this case, it is useful to treat it as a categorical variable instead of a numeric one. Note that if the *x*-axis variable is continuous, it should be kept as numeric.

```
un_data$year <- as.factor(un_data$year)
```

Next we subset `un_data` by countries of interest by using the `subset()` function.

```
un_data_s <- subset(
  un_data,
  country=="Selected exporters of agricultural products (TDR)" |
    country=="Selected exporters of manufactured goods and primary commodities
    (TDR)" |
    country=="Selected exporters of minerals and mining products (TDR)" |
    country=="Selected manufactured goods exporters (TDR)" |
    country=="Selected petroleum exporters (TDR)")
```

Now we are ready to plot. We use `geom_line()` in `ggplot()` to generate a line plot. We have new layers compared to previous plots. `group` groups data

[14] The corresponding Stata code is available in terms_of_trade.do.

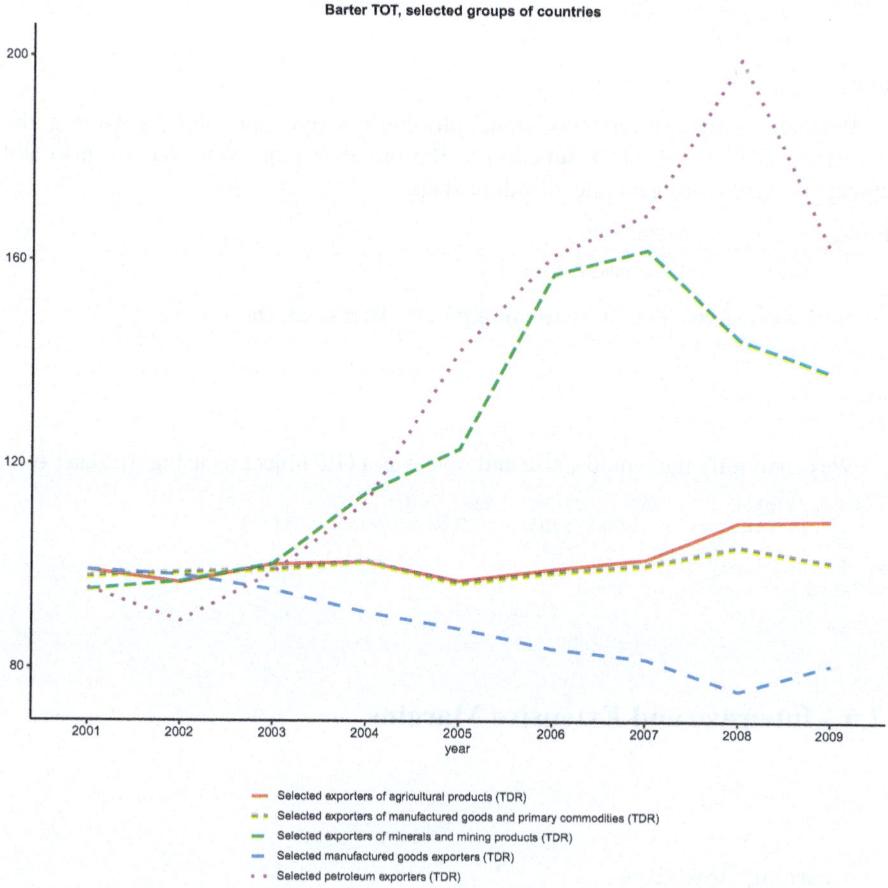

Fig. 2.8 Line plot with `ggplot2` (static version of the dynamic plot)

points so that `ggplot()` knows which points to connect. Note that we grouped them by `country`. We use `country` to set `colour`, `shape`, and `linetype` as well. `legend.direction` indicates the direction of the legend, "horizontal" or "vertical". Figure 2.8 illustrates the outcome.

```
plot_line <- ggplot(un_data_s, aes(x = year, y = tot,
                                    group = country,
                                    shape = country,
                                    colour = country)) +
  geom_line(aes(linetype = country), size = 1) +
  theme_classic() +
  ylab(" ")  +
  ggtitle("Barter TOT, selected groups of countries") +
  theme(plot.title = element_text(hjust = 0.5, size = 10, face="bold"),
        axis.title.x = element_text(size = 8.5)) +
  theme(legend.position = "bottom", legend.box = "vertical",
        legend.direction = "vertical",
        legend.text = element_text(size = 8),
```

```
        legend.key.size = unit(0.5, "cm"),
        legend.title = element_blank())

plot_line
```

We can easily convert this static plot into a dynamic plot by adding the `transition_reveal()` function to the previous plot. Note that we also add `geom_point()` to generate a leading shape

```
plot_line_anim <- plot_line +
  geom_point(size = 2) +
  transition_reveal(as.numeric(year))
```

Now we can visualize it by running `plot_line_anim`

```
> plot_line_anim

Frame 100 (100%)
Finalizing encoding... done!
```

We can modify the window size and save it as a GIF object by using `animate()`

```
> animate(plot_line_anim, height = 538, width = 866,
+         renderer = gifski_renderer("images/gganim.gif"))

Frame 100 (100%)
Finalizing encoding... done!
```

2.6 Intensive and Extensive Margins

Learning Objectives

- Import a Stata file
- Conversion of objects
- Generate new variables
- Group operations with `ave()`
- Subset a data set
- Collapse a data set with `aggregate()`
- Replace if
- Drop duplicates
- Rename column names
- Plot with `plot()`

In this section we replicate the UNCTAD & WTO's Stata code in **R** to calculate and plot extensive and intensive margins of diversification.

Open a new script file in **RStudio** and save it as `06_IM_EM_hummels_klenow_2edn`.[15] Let's load the following package by using the `library()` function.

```
library("haven") # import Stata .dta file
```

Let's import the data set `comtrade_exports_all_countries_2000.dta` as `exp2000` in **R**. `exp2000` has 358,871 observations and 9 variables. Variables identifies reporter, `reporter` and `reporter_name`, partner, `partner` and `partner_name`, year, `year`, product name, `product_name`, flow name, `flow_name`, trade value, `trade_value`, and product, `product`. Data cover the year 2000.

```
exp2000 <- read_dta("datWTO/comtrade_exports_all_countries_2000.dta")
class(exp2000)
dim(exp2000)
View(exp2000)
str(exp2000)
```

In the next lines of code we build the intensive and extensive margin of diversification based on the Hummels-Klenow decomposition for products and geographical markets.

The intensive margin for products is given by

$$IM^i = \frac{\sum_{K^i} X_k^W}{\sum_{K^i} X_k^W}$$

The extensive margin for products is given by

$$EM^i = \frac{\sum_{K^i} X_k^i}{\sum_{K^W} X_k^W}$$

where

- K^i is the set of products exported by country i
- X_k^i is the dollar value of i's exports of product k to the world
- X_k^W is the dollar value of world exports of product k

Note that we use the `ave()` function. Refer to Sects. 2.2 and 2.3 for description of the `ave()` function.

```
exp2000$x_i_k <- exp2000$trade_value

### Sum of i's export of all products exported by i
exp2000$sum_i_x_i_k <- ave(exp2000$x_i_k,
                           interaction(exp2000$reporter, exp2000$year),
                           FUN = function(x) sum(x, na.rm = T))
exp2000 <- exp2000[order(exp2000$reporter, exp2000$year), ]

exp2000$temp1 <- ifelse(exp2000$reporter == "All",
```

[15] The corresponding Stata code is available in IM_EM_hummels_klenow.do.

```
                   exp2000$x_i_k, NA)

### World exports of product k in year t
exp2000$temp2 <- ave(exp2000$temp1,
                     interaction(exp2000$year, exp2000$product),
                     FUN = function(x) max(x, na.rm = T))

### Total world exports of all products exported by i
exp2000$sum_i_x_w_k <- ave(exp2000$temp2,
                     interaction(exp2000$reporter, exp2000$year),
                     FUN = function(x) sum(x, na.rm = T))

### Total world exports of all products in the world
exp2000$sum_w_x_w_k <- ave(exp2000$x_i_k,
                     interaction(exp2000$year),
                     FUN = function(x) sum(x, na.rm = T))

exp2000$im_i <- exp2000$sum_i_x_i_k / exp2000$sum_i_x_w_k
exp2000$em_i <- exp2000$sum_i_x_w_k / exp2000$sum_w_x_w_k

summary(exp2000$im_i)
summary(exp2000$em_i)
```

We keep only `reporter`, `year`, `im_i`, and `em_i`. We store the results of this operation in a new object, `exp2000_2`. Then, we drop the duplicates by using the `unique()` function. Finally, multiply the intensive margin, `im_i`, and the extensive margin, em_i, by 100.

```
exp2000_2 <- exp2000[, c("reporter", "year", "im_i", "em_i")]

# drop duplicates
exp2000_3 <- unique(exp2000_2)
dim(exp2000_2)
dim(exp2000_3)

exp2000_3$im_i <- exp2000_3$im_i*100
exp2000_3$em_i <- exp2000_3$em_i*100

summary(exp2000_3$im_i)
summary(exp2000_3$em_i)
```

The intensive margin for geographical markets is given by

$$IM^i = \frac{\sum_{D^i} X_d^W}{\sum_{D^i} X_d^W}$$

The extensive margin for geographical markets is given by

$$EM^i = \frac{\sum_{D^i} X_d^i}{\sum_{D^W} X_d^W}$$

where

- D^i is the set of destination markets where i exports
- X_d^i is the dollar value of i's total exports to destination d
- X_d^W is the dollar value of world exports to destination d
- D^W is the set of all destination countries

To calculate it, we need to import the data set `BilateralTrade.dta` in **R**. We work on a new object, `BT` that has 5,563,268 observations and 11 variables. Data cover the years 1976–2004.

```
# Geographical decomposition ----

## Construction of IM and EM
BilateralTrade <- read_dta("datWTO/BilateralTrade.dta")
BT <- BilateralTrade
class(BT)
dim(BT)
View(BT)
str(BT)
```

In this last part, we focus on how to plot with `plot()`.

In the next lines of code, we use `aggregate()`, `ave()`, and `unique()` functions. Note that this time we indicate two variables, `exp_tv` and `imp_tv`, to aggregate in the data set. We include both variables in `list()` in the first entry of the `aggregate()` function.

```
BT$tt <- sum(BT$exp_tv, na.rm = T)
summary(BT$tt)

BTc <- aggregate(list(exp_tv = BT$exp_tv,
                      imp_tv = BT$imp_tv),
                 by = list(ccode = BT$ccode,
                           pcode = BT$pcode,
                           year = BT$year),
                 FUN = function(x) sum(x, na.rm = T))
dim(BTc)

BTc2 <- BTc
BTc2$x_i_d <- BTc2$exp_tv

# Sum of ccode's export to all its destinations
BTc2$sum_i_x_i_d <- ave(BTc2$exp_tv,
                        interaction(BTc2$ccode, BTc2$year),
                        FUN = function(x) sum(x, na.rm = T))

# Total world exports to each destination
BTc2$x_w_d <- ave(BTc2$exp_tv,
                  interaction(BTc2$pcode, BTc2$year),
                  FUN = function(x) sum(x, na.rm = T))

# Total world exports to all destinations served by ccode
BTc2$sum_i_x_w_d <- ave(BTc2$x_w_d,
                        interaction(BTc2$ccode, BTc2$year),
                        FUN = function(x) sum(x, na.rm = T))

# Total world exports to all destinations in the world
BTc2$sum_w_x_w_d <- ave(BTc2$exp_tv,
                        interaction(BTc2$year),
                        FUN = function(x) sum(x, na.rm = T))

BTc2$em_i <- BTc2$sum_i_x_w_d / BTc2$sum_w_x_w_d
BTc2$im_i <- BTc2$sum_i_x_i_d / BTc2$sum_w_x_w_d

summary(BTc2$em_i)
summary(BTc2$im_i)

BTc3 <- BTc2[, c("ccode", "year", "em_i", "im_i")]
BTc3 <- unique(BTc3)
dim(BTc3)

BTc3$em_i <- BTc3$em_i * 100
```

```
BTc3$im_i <- BTc3$im_i * 100

summary(BTc3$em_i)
summary(BTc3$im_i)
```

We build a double *y*-axis plot with the intensive margin on the left side *y*-axis and the extensive margin on the right side *y*-axis margin. It is possible to plot a double *y*-axis plot with `ggplot()`. However, to my knowledge, `ggplot()` does not allow the rescale of the second *y*-axis. With `ggplot()` we need to transform the data for representation. However, the transformation of the data in the two *y*-axes is a $1:1$ transformation. On the other hand, `plot()` automatically rescales the second *y*-axis. Therefore, to reproduce the same plot as in Stata, this time we use `plot()`.

We plot the intensive and extensive margins for four countries: Argentina, Colombia, Mexico, and Spain. We use `subset()` to subset `BTc3` by each of these countries and assign each of them to new objects.

```
# plot double y-axis with plot() for ARG, COL, MEX and ESP
### subset ccode == "ARG"
BT_arg <- subset(BTc3, ccode == "ARG")
summary(BT_arg$em_i)
summary(BT_arg$im_i)

### subset ccode == "COL"
BT_col <- subset(BTc3, ccode == "COL")
summary(BT_col$em_i)
summary(BT_col$im_i)

### subset ccode == "MEX"
BT_mex <- subset(BTc3, ccode == "MEX")
summary(BT_mex$em_i)
summary(BT_mex$im_i)

### subset ccode == "ESP
BT_esp <- subset(BTc3, ccode == "ESP")
summary(BT_mex$em_i)
summary(BT_mex$im_i)
```

The first lines of code draw the plot for Argentina. Note the use of `par()`. `par()` can be used to set or query graphical parameters. In the first line of code, we use the parameter `mfrow =` to define the arrangement of the plotting space by number of rows and number of columns. In this specific case, we are arranging a 2 x 2 space where to draw the four plots. Note that at the very last line we code `par(mfrow = c(1,1))` to set back the plotting space to the whole area.

In the second line, we modify the margins inside `par()`. `xpd = TRUE` sets all plotting clipped to the figure region. `mar = par()$mar + c(0, 0, 0, 2)` expands the margins on the right. Note that at the end of the code for each plot we restore the margins.

In `plot()`, the first entries represent the coordinates of points in the plot. In this case, we use ~. This allows to plot formula, such as `y ~ x`. `pch =` define a plotting character. `las =` sets the label style, where 1 means *always horizontal*. `cex =` indicates the amount by which plotting text and symbols should be scaled relative to the default that is 1. Therefore, `cex.main =` and `cex.axis =` define the magnification to be used for main title and axis notation.

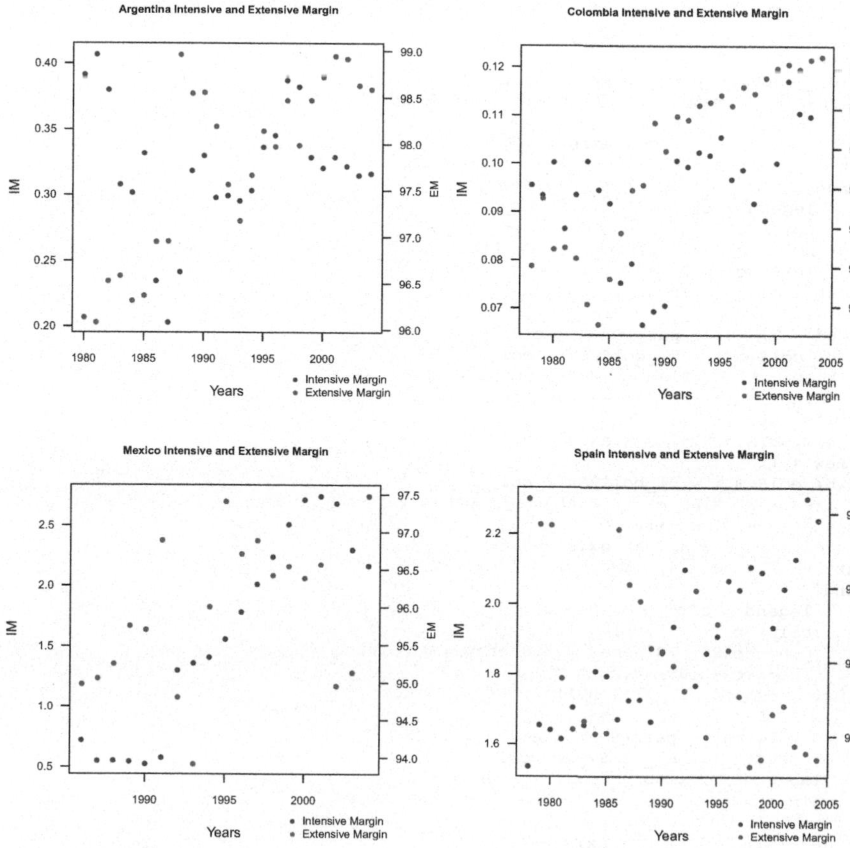

Fig. 2.9 A double *y*-axis plot

We set `par(new = T)` to not clean the first plot. Therefore, the new plot is added in the same frame. In fact, now we code the second plot. Note that for the *y*-axis we use the extensive margin, `em_i`, while in the first plot we used the intensive margin, `im_i`. We add two arguments, `axis()` and `mtext()`. Note the both have `side = 4`. This means that the options in these arguments apply to the second *y*-axis.

Finally, we define the legend. Note that with `inset =` we define the position of the legend outside the box. `bty` defines the box style. The value `n` suppress the box around the plot.

Repeat this codes for the other three countries to reproduce Fig. 2.9.

```
# plot

par(mfrow = c(2,2))
par(xpd = T, mar = par()$mar + c(0, 0, 0, 2))
plot(BT_arg$im_i ~ BT_arg$year, col = "blue",
     ylab = "IM", xlab = "Years", pch = 20,
     main = "Argentina Intensive and Extensive Margin",
```

```
     las = 1,
     cex.main = 0.8, cex.axis = 0.8)
par(new = T)
plot(BT_arg$em_i ~ BT_arg$year, col = "red",
     axes = F, xlab = "", ylab = "", pch = 20)
axis(side = 4, las = 1,
     cex.main = 0.8, cex.axis = 0.8)
mtext("EM", side = 4, line = 2.5, cex = 0.7)
legend("bottomright",
       legend = c("Intensive Margin", "Extensive Margin"),
       col = c("blue", "red"),
       pch = c(20, 20), cex = 0.8, bty = "n",
       inset=c(-0.05,-0.25))
par(mar = c(5, 4, 4, 2) + 0.1)

par(xpd = T, mar = par()$mar + c(0, 0, 0, 2))
plot(BT_col$im_i ~ BT_col$year, col = "blue",
     ylab = "IM", xlab = "Years", pch = 20,
     main = "Colombia Intensive and Extensive Margin",
     las = 1,
     cex.main = 0.8, cex.axis = 0.8)
par(new = T)
plot(BT_col$em_i ~ BT_col$year, col = "red",
     axes = F, xlab = "", ylab = "", pch = 20)
axis(side = 4, las = 1,
     cex.main = 0.8, cex.axis = 0.8)
mtext("EM", side = 4, line = 2.5, cex = 0.7)
legend("bottomright",
       legend = c("Intensive Margin", "Extensive Margin"),
       col = c("blue", "red"),
       pch = c(20, 20), cex = 0.8, bty = "n",
       inset=c(-0.05,-0.25))
par(mar = c(5, 4, 4, 2) + 0.1)

par(xpd = T, mar = par()$mar + c(0, 0, 0, 2))
plot(BT_mex$im_i ~ BT_mex$year, col = "blue",
     ylab = "IM", xlab = "Years", pch = 20,
     main = "Mexico Intensive and Extensive Margin",
     las = 1,
     cex.main = 0.8, cex.axis = 0.8)
par(new = T)
plot(BT_mex$em_i ~ BT_mex$year, col = "red",
     axes = F, xlab = "", ylab = "", pch = 20)
axis(side = 4, las = 1,
     cex.main = 0.8, cex.axis = 0.8)
mtext("EM", side = 4, line = 2.5, cex = 0.7)
legend("bottomright",
       legend = c("Intensive Margin", "Extensive Margin"),
       col = c("blue", "red"),
       pch = c(20, 20), cex = 0.8, bty = "n",
       inset=c(-0.05,-0.25))
par(mar = c(5, 4, 4, 2) + 0.1)

par(xpd = T, mar = par()$mar + c(0, 0, 0, 2))
plot(BT_esp$im_i ~ BT_esp$year, col = "blue",
     ylab = "IM", xlab = "Years", pch = 20,
     main = "Spain Intensive and Extensive Margin",
     las = 1,
     cex.main = 0.8, cex.axis = 0.8)
par(new = T)
plot(BT_esp$em_i ~ BT_esp$year, col = "red",
     axes = F, xlab = "", ylab = "", pch = 20)
axis(side = 4, las = 1,
     cex.main = 0.8, cex.axis = 0.8)
mtext("EM", side = 4, line = 2.5, cex = 0.7)
legend("bottomright",
       legend = c("Intensive Margin", "Extensive Margin"),
```

```
        col = c("blue", "red"),
        pch = c(20, 20), cex = 0.8, bty = "n",
        inset=c(-0.05,-0.25))
par(mar = c(5, 4, 4, 2) + 0.1)
par(mfrow = c(1,1))
```

Chapter 3
Analyzing Trade Tariffs

3.1 Summary of Tariff Statistics

Learning Objectives

- Import a Stata file
- Conversion of objects
- Generate new variables
- Describe variables
- Export data set
- Reshape the data set
- Subset a data set
- Plot with `ggplot()`
- Make an interactive plot with `ggplotly()`

In this section we summarize, reorganize and export basic statistics for tariffs. We conclude the section by plotting tariffs for Colombia and Japan using histogram, density plot and scatter plot.[1]

Open a new script file in **RStudio** and save it as `08_tariff_statistics_2edn`.

Let's load the following packages by using the `library()` function.

```
library("haven") # import Stata .dta file
```

[1] The code in this section is base on the Stata code available in AnalyzingTradePolicy.do.

© The Author(s), under exclusive license to Springer Nature Switzerland AG 2023
M. Porto, *Using R for Trade Policy Analysis*,
https://doi.org/10.1007/978-3-031-35044-3_3

```
library("Hmisc") # describe variable
library("data.table") # reshape the data set
library("dplyr") # combine operations
library("doBy") # summarise by
library("ggplot2") # plot with ggplot
library("plotly") # interactive plot
```

Let's import the UNCTAD & WTO's `TPP.dta` data set in **R**. `TPP` is a data frame with 81,200 observations and 40 variables. Data cover the years 1976–2004.

```
TPP <- read_dta("datWTO/TPP.dta")
class(TPP)
View(TPP)
dim(TPP)
str(TPP)
```

We access basic statistics by using the general function `summary()`. In the following lines of code, we obtain basic statistics for Colombia and Japan. We obtain information such as minimum, 1st quartile, median, mean, 3rd quartile, maximum, and, if present, number of missing values. Note that we can obtain information about a variable also with the `describe()` function from the `Hmisc` package.

```
# summary statistics for Colombia and Japan
summary(subset(TPP, ccode == "COL"))
summary(subset(TPP, ccode == "JPN"))

describe(TPP$isic3d_3dig)
```

In the next lines of code, we compute mean, media, standard deviation, minimum and maximum for tariffs for Colombia and Japan.

First, we subset the data set for Colombia and Japan, respectively. Then, we keep only the following variables: sector, `sector`, simple average of applied tariffs on imports, `tar_savg_ahs`, weighted average of applied tariffs on imports, `tar_iwahs`, simple average import tariff for most favored nation MFN `tar_savg_mfn`, and weighted average tariff rate for MFN `tar_iwmfn`.

```
TPP_col <- subset(TPP, ccode == "COL")
TPP_col <- TPP_col[, c("sector", "tar_savg_ahs", "tar_iwahs",
                       "tar_savg_mfn", "tar_iwmfn")]

TPP_jpn <- subset(TPP, ccode == "JPN")
TPP_jpn <- TPP_jpn[, c("sector", "tar_savg_ahs", "tar_iwahs",
                       "tar_savg_mfn", "tar_iwmfn")]
```

We use the `summaryBy()` function from the `doBy` package. This is a function to calculate group wise summary statistics The first entry is a formula object. In this case, we calculate statistics by each tariff per sector. We indicate the data set in the second entry. Then, we include the list of functions that we want to apply. The argument `na.rm=TRUE` will remove the missing values.[2] The calculations for each tariff will be stored in a new object.

```
tar_col <- summaryBy(tar_savg_ahs + tar_iwahs +
                       tar_savg_mfn + tar_iwmfn ~ sector,
                     TPP_col, na.rm = T,
                     FUN=c(mean, median, sd, min, max))
```

[2] `na.rm` = is passed as an extra argument to the function. We need to be sure the all the functions in `FUN` accept the extra argument to pass it.

```
View(tar_col)

tar_jpn <- summaryBy(tar_savg_ahs + tar_iwahs +
                     tar_savg_mfn + tar_iwmfn ~ sector,
          TPP_jpn, na.rm = T,
          FUN=c(mean, median, sd, min, max))

View(tar_jpn)
```

Finally, we export the data sets as a tab delimited text files using `write.table()`.

```
## export dataset as tab delimited txt file
write.table(tar_col, "AverageTariff_COL.txt",
            row.names = F, sep="\t")
write.table(tar_jpn, "AverageTariff_JPN.txt",
            row.names = F, sep="\t")
```

Following, we plot the data. We use a histogram for Colombia's tariffs distribution, a density plot for Japan's tariffs distribution, and a scatter plot for Japan split by tariffs.[3]

The first step to plot the histogram for Colombia's tariffs distribution is to reshape the data set long. We use the `melt()` function from the `data.table` package. Refer to Sect. 2.3 for details about the function.

```
TPP_col_l <- melt(setDT(TPP_col), id.vars = "sector",
                  measure.vars = c("tar_savg_ahs", "tar_iwahs",
                                   "tar_savg_mfn", "tar_iwmfn"),
                  variable.name = "tariff_name",
                  value.name = "tariff_value")
```

Now we are ready to plot. By now, most of the lines of the following code is well known. Note that we use the function `geom_histogram()`. `bins` specifies the number of bins. The default value is 30. `..density..` plots the histogram with density instead of count on *y*-axis. Finally, we add `guides(fill=guide_legend(nrow = 2, byrow = TRUE))` to break the legend by two rows. The output of this plot is shown in Fig. 3.1.

```
ggplot(TPP_col_l, aes(tariff_value, ..density..,
                      fill = tariff_name)) +
  geom_histogram(bins = 17, position="dodge") +
  theme_classic() +
  xlab("tariffs")  +
  ggtitle("Tariffs Distribution in Colombia") +
  scale_fill_manual(labels = c("simple average of applied tariffs on imports",
                               "weighted average of applied tariffs on imports",
                               "simple average import tariff for most favored
                                  nation MFN",
                               "weighted average tariff rate for MFN"),
                    values = c("red", "blue", "green", "pink")) +
  theme(legend.position = "bottom",
        legend.text = element_text(size = 7.5),
        legend.key.size = unit(0.2, "cm"),
        legend.title = element_blank()) +
  guides(fill=guide_legend(nrow = 2,byrow = TRUE))
```

[3] Note that the plots in this chapter divert from the code in *Practical Guide to Trade Policy Analysis* to show new features of `ggplot()`.

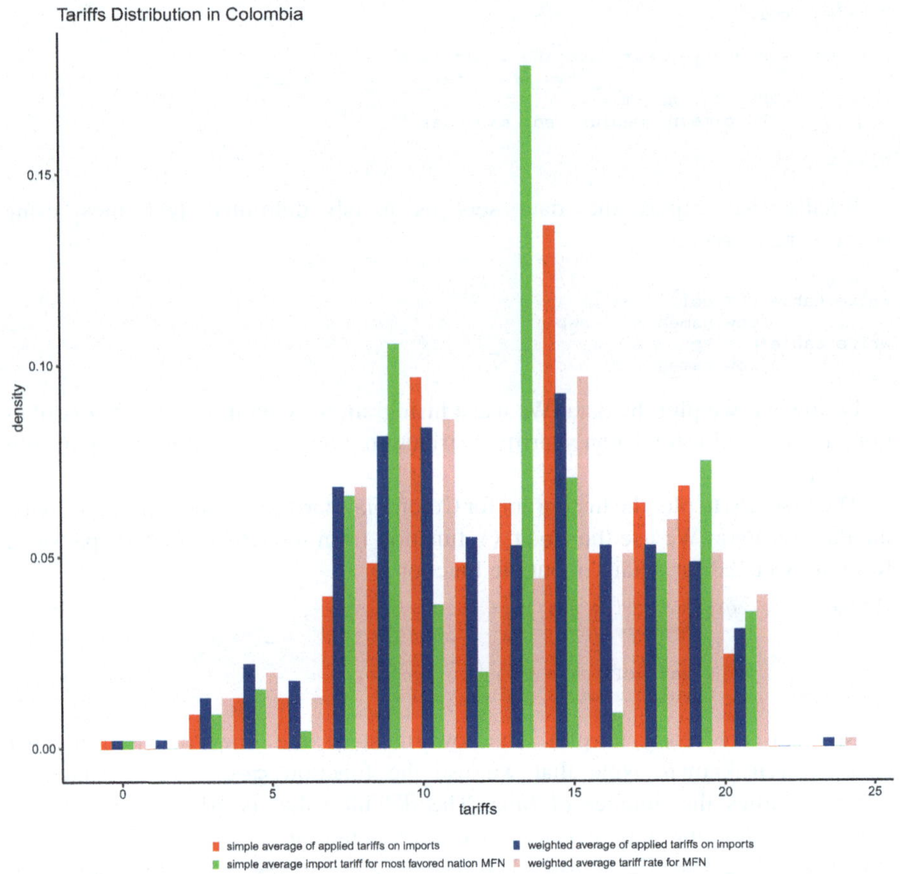

Fig. 3.1 Histogram with `ggplot2`

Next, we plot a density plot for Japan's tariffs. The steps are the same as for the previous plot. First, we reshape the data set.

```
TPP_jpn_l <- melt(setDT(TPP_jpn), id.vars = "sector",
                  measure.vars = c("tar_savg_ahs", "tar_iwahs",
                                   "tar_savg_mfn", "tar_iwmfn"),
                  variable.name = "tariff_name",
                  value.name = "tariff_value")
```

Now we are ready to plot. We use the `geom_density()` function. The rest of the code is the same as the previous figure. However, note that we add `na.rm = T`. If `FALSE`, the default, missing values are removed with a warning. If you replicated the plot for Colombia, you should have received the following warning

```
Warning message:
Removed 2016 rows containing non-finite values (stat\_bin).
```

By setting `TRUE`, missing values are silently removed.

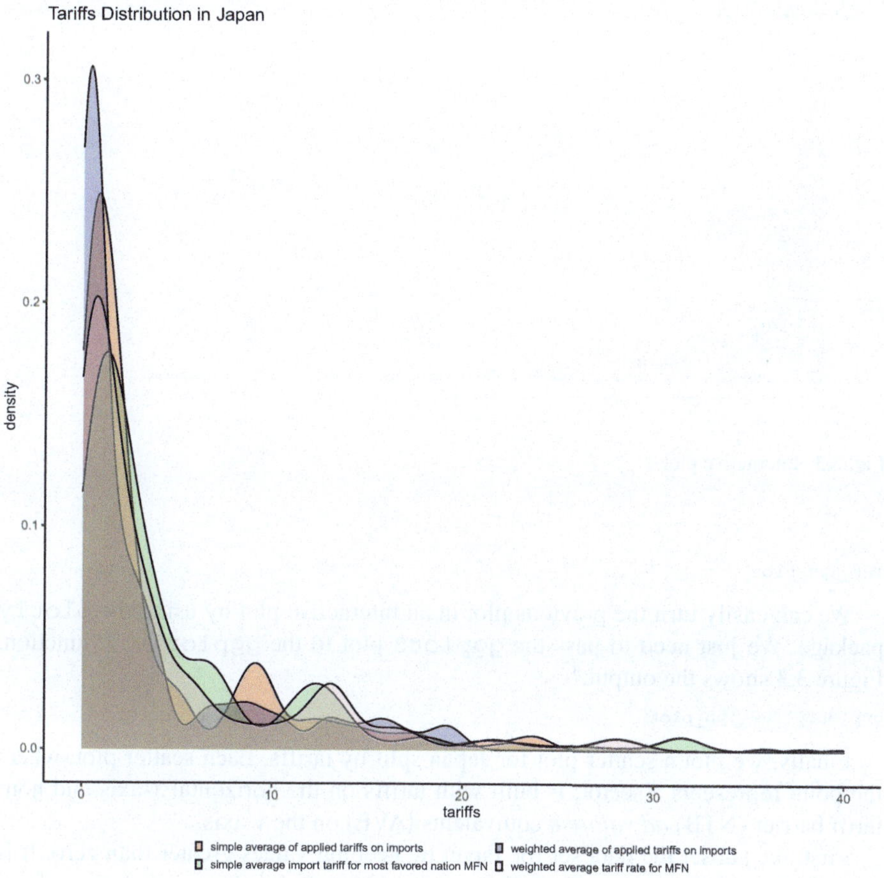

Fig. 3.2 Density plot with `ggplot2`

Finally, note that the value of `alpha` is used to control the level of transparency. The output of this plot is shown in Fig. 3.2.

```
TPP_jpn_plot <- ggplot(TPP_jpn_l, aes(tariff_value,
                                      fill = tariff_name)) +
  geom_density(alpha = .3, na.rm = T) +
  theme_classic() +
  xlab("tariffs")  +
  ggtitle("Tariffs Distribution in Japan") +
  scale_fill_manual(labels = c("simple average of applied tariffs on imports",
                               "weighted average of applied tariffs on imports",
                               "simple average import tariff for most favored
                               nation MFN",
                               "weighted average tariff rate for MFN"),
                    values = c("red", "blue", "green", "pink")) +
  theme(legend.position = "bottom",
        legend.text = element_text(size = 7.5),
        legend.key.size = unit(0.2, "cm"),
        legend.title = element_blank()) +
  guides(fill=guide_legend(nrow = 2,byrow = TRUE))
```

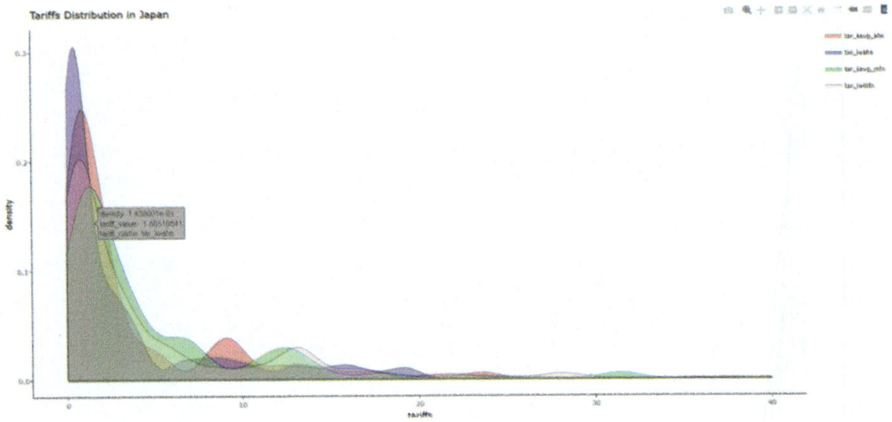

Fig. 3.3 Interactive plot

```
TPP_jpn_plot
```

We can easily turn the previous plot in an interactive plot by using the `plotly` package. We just need to pass the `ggplot2` plot to the `ggplotly()` function. Figure 3.3 shows the output.[4]

```
ggplotly(TPP_jpn_plot)
```

Finally, we plot a scatter plot for Japan split by tariffs. Each scatter plot, where the point represents a sector, is built with tariffs on the horizontal x-axis and non-tariff barrier (NTB) *ad valorem* equivalents (AVE) on the y-axis.

First, we subset the data set for Japan by keeping values greater than zero. It is suggested that when the number of zero values is high, it is best to drop them from the plot to see a clearer picture. We use `filter()` from the `dplyr` package. Note that we name this data set `TPP_jpn` as the previous one. This means that it will be overwritten. If you do not want to overwrite it, just choose a different name. Then, we reshape it long. This time we also keep `year` that will be used to compare the values in the plot.

```
TPP_jpn <- TPP %>%
  filter(ccode == "JPN" & ave_core_sim > 0 & tar_savg_ahs > 0) %>%
  filter(ccode == "JPN" & ave_core_sim > 0 & tar_iwahs > 0) %>%
  filter(ccode == "JPN" & ave_core_sim > 0 & tar_savg_mfn > 0) %>%
  filter(ccode == "JPN" & ave_core_sim > 0 & tar_iwmfn > 0)

TPP_jpn_l <- melt(setDT(TPP_jpn),
                  id.vars = c("sector", "year", "ave_core_sim"),
                  measure.vars = c("tar_savg_ahs", "tar_iwahs",
                                   "tar_savg_mfn", "tar_iwmfn"),
                  variable.name = "tariff_name",
                  value.name = "tariff_value")
View(TPP_jpn_l)
```

[4] Figure 3.3 is a screenshot.

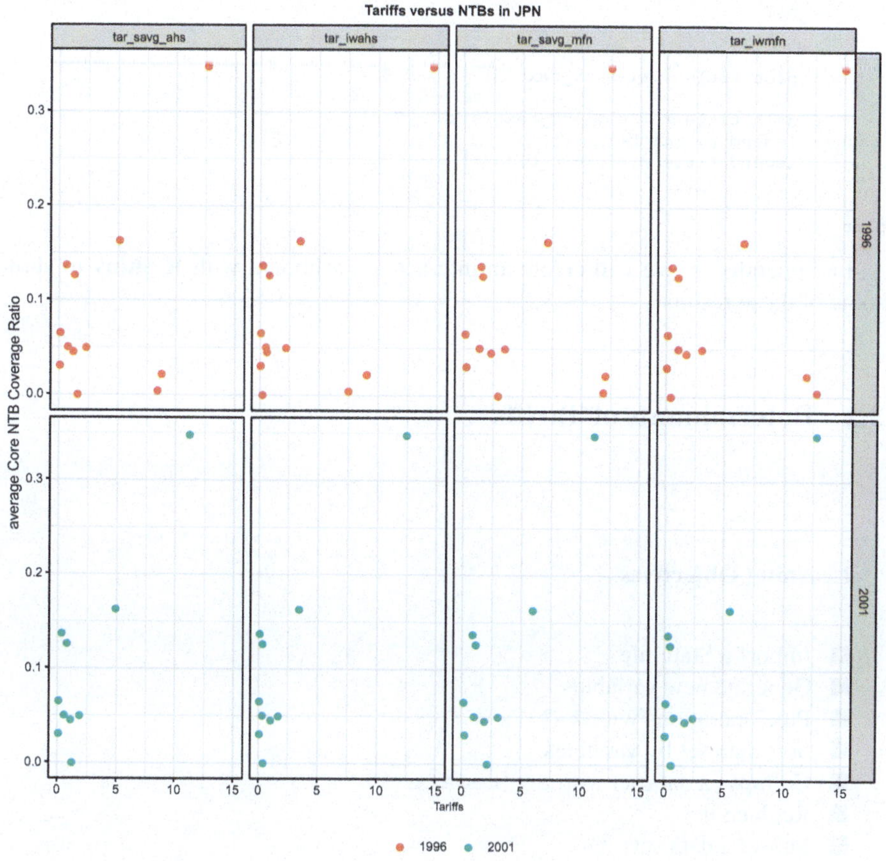

Fig. 3.4 Facets with `ggplot2`

Now we are ready to plot. The main difference with the previous plots is the `facet_grid()` function. `facet_grid()` forms a matrix of panels defined by row and column facetting variables. The first entry is a formula with the rows (of the tabular display) on the LHS and the columns (of the tabular display) on the RHS. If we replace one of the variables in the formula with the dot, we indicate that there should be no faceting on that dimension (either row or column). Refer to Sect. 3.3 and Appendix A for other examples with `facet_grid()`. Additionally, we use a different background for the plot by using `theme_bw()`. The output of this plot is shown in Fig. 3.4.

```
plot_jpn <- ggplot(TPP_jpn_1,
                   aes(x = tariff_value,
                       y = ave_core_sim,
                       colour = as.factor(year))) +
  geom_point(size = 2) +
  facet_grid(year ~ tariff_name) +
```

```
  theme_bw() +
  xlab("Tariffs") + ylab("average Core NTB Coverage Ratio") +
  ggtitle("Tariffs versus NTBs in JPN") +
  theme(plot.title = element_text(hjust = 0.5,
                                  size = 10, face="bold"),
        axis.title.x = element_text(size = 7.5)) +
  theme(legend.position="bottom",
        legend.title = element_blank())

plot_jpn
```

In Appendix A, we will create an interactive dashboard with **R Shiny** to show some of these results.

3.2 Determinants of Tariffs

Learning Objectives

- Import a Stata file
- Generate new variables
- Pipe operations with `%>%`
- Sort data set by variables
- Collapse a data set with `aggregate()`
- Replace if
- Subset a data set
- Generate group id
- Label variables
- Export data set
- Run a regression
- Reproduce Stata robust standard errors
- Export results with `stargazer()`

The aim of this section is to estimate the determinants of tariffs by regressing average tariff on establishment size, proportion of female workers, wage per employee, and import-penetration ratio.[5] First, we generate the covariates and then we estimate the equation.

Open a new script file in **RStudio** and save it as `09_determinants_of_tariffs_2edn`. Let's load the following packages using the `library()` function.

[5] The corresponding Stata code is available in AnalyzingTradePolicy.do.

```
library("haven") # import Stata .dta file
library("Hmisc") # for label
library("dplyr") # combine operations and group id
library("plm") # panel regression
library("sandwich") # replicate Stata robust standard errors
library("lmtest") # replicate Stata robust standard errors
library("stargazer") # export regression results
```

Let's import the UNCTAD & WTO's `TPP.dta` data set in **R**. `TPP` is a data frame with 81,200 observations and 40 variables. Data cover the years 1976–2004.

```
TPP <- read_dta("datWTO/TPP.dta")
class(TPP)
View(TPP)
dim(TPP)
str(TPP)
```

First, we calculate the import-penetration ratios for each sector, defined as

$$mu_{ij} = \frac{M_j}{C_j} \tag{3.1}$$

where

- M_j is imports of good j for a given year;
- C_j is domestic consumption (final demand) of the same good in the same year.

After generating the new variables, we label them and we sort the data set by `ccode` and `isic3d_3dig` with the `order()` function.[6]

```
TPP$M_j <- TPP$imp_tv
TPP$C_j <- TPP$imp_tv + TPP$output
TPP$mu <- TPP$M_j / TPP$C_j

TPP <- upData(TPP,
              labels = c(M_j = "imports of good j",
                         C_j = "domestic consumption of good j",
                         mu = "Import-Penetration"))

TPP <- TPP[order(TPP$ccode, TPP$isic3d_3dig), ]
```

In the next step, we calculate the rate of growth of import-penetration between 1983–1985 and 1998–2000. We need to generate two new variables, `mu_83_85` and `mu_98_00`, which store the average for 1983–1985 and 1998–2000, respectively. We accomplish this task by using the `dplyr` as shown in Sect. 2.4. After generating the new variables, we label them using the `upData()` function from the `Hmisc` package.

```
TPP <- TPP %>%
  group_by(ccode, isic3d_3dig) %>%
  mutate(mu_83_85 = ifelse(year >= 1983 & year <= 1985,
                           mean(mu[year >= 1983 & year <= 1985],
                                na.rm = T), NA),
         mu_98_00 = ifelse(year >= 1998 & year <= 2000,
                           mean(mu[year >= 1998 & year <= 2000],
```

[6] The `isic3d_3dig` is the Sector-Identifier which divides the economic activities into 28 sectors (isic identifier from 311 to 390).

```
                                    na.rm = T), NA))

View(TPP[, c(1, 2, 3, 44, 45)])

TPP <- upData(TPP,
              labels = c(mu_83_85 = "Average Import-Penetration for 1983-1985",
                         mu_98_00 = "Average Import-Penetration for 1998-2000"))
```

Next, we collapse mu_83_85 and mu_98_00 by ccode and isic3d_3dig by using the aggregate() function. Refer to Sects. 2.2 and 2.6 for its use. We assign this operation to a new object, TPP_c.

```
TPP_c <- aggregate(list(mu_83_85 = TPP$mu_83_85,
                        mu_98_00 = TPP$mu_98_00),
                   by = list(ccode = TPP$ccode,
                             isic3d_3dig = TPP$isic3d_3dig),
                   FUN = function(x) mean(x, na.rm = T))
```

Next, we generate the growth rate of import-penetration, mugrate. We replace Inf value with NA and we label it.

```
TPP_c$mugrate <- (TPP_c$mu_98_00 - TPP_c$mu_83_85)/TPP_c$mu_83_85

TPP_c$mugrate[is.infinite(TPP_c$mugrate)] <- NA

TPP_c <- upData(TPP_c,
           labels = c(mugrate = "Growth Rate of Import-Penetration"))
```

Finally, we sort TPP_c by ccode and isic3d_3dig with the order() function. Then, we subset for Colombia and Japan and export the results as a CSV file by using write.csv().

```
TPP_c <- TPP_c[order(TPP_c$ccode, TPP_c$isic3d_3dig), ]

TPP_col <- subset(TPP_c[, c(1, 2, 5)], ccode == "COL")
TPP_jpn <- subset(TPP_c[, c(1, 2, 5)], ccode == "JPN")

# export dataset
write.csv(TPP_col, "TPP_col.csv", row.names = FALSE)
write.csv(TPP_jpn, "TPP_jpn.csv", row.names = FALSE)
```

Next, we generate the other covariates, establishment size as the ratio of employees to establishments, estabsize, the proportion of female workers, femalework, and wages per employee, wagepe, and label them.

We keep only the following variables: ccode, year, isic3d_3dig, tar_savg_ahs, tar_iwahs, tar_savg_mfn, tar_iwmfn, ave_core_sim, ave_core_wgt, estabsize, femalework, wagepe, and mu. We assign this operation to a new object, Ratios.

```
TPP$estabsize <- TPP$n_employees/TPP$n_establ
TPP$femalework <- TPP$n_female_emp/TPP$n_employees
TPP$wagepe <- TPP$wage_bill/TPP$n_employees

TPP <- upData(TPP, labels = c(estabsize = "establishment size",
                              femalework = "proportion of female workers",
                              wagepe = "wage per employee"))

Ratios <- TPP[, c("ccode", "year", "isic3d_3dig", "tar_savg_ahs",
                  "tar_iwahs", "tar_savg_mfn", "tar_iwmfn",
                  "ave_core_sim", "ave_core_wgt", "estabsize",
                  "femalework", "wagepe", "mu")]
```

Next, we generate the panel id, `id`, with the `cur_group_id()` function from the `dplyr` package. Then, we convert the variables into logarithms.

```
Ratios <- Ratios %>%
  group_by(ccode, isic3d_3dig) %>%
  mutate(id = cur_group_id())

Ratios$ln_estabsize <- log(Ratios$estabsize)
Ratios$ln_wagepe <- log(Ratios$wagepe)
Ratios$ln_tar_savg_ahs <- log(Ratios$tar_savg_ahs + 1)
Ratios$ln_femalework <- log(Ratios$femalework + 1)
Ratios$ln_mu <- log(Ratios$mu + 1)
```

Replace the `NaN` values[7] in `ln_tar_savg_ahs`, `ln_wagepe`, and `ln_mu` with `NA`. We use the `is.nan()` function that tests if a numeric value is `NaN`. Do not test equality to `NaN`, or even use identical, since systems typically have many different `NaN` values.

```
Ratios$ln_tar_savg_ahs[is.nan(Ratios$ln_tar_savg_ahs)] <- NA
Ratios$ln_wagepe[is.nan(Ratios$ln_wagepe)] <- NA
Ratios$ln_mu[is.nan(Ratios$ln_mu)] <- NA
```

Now we are ready to estimate the following two equations by using fixed effects with the `plm()` function from the `plm` package:

$$ln\_tar\_savg\_ahs = \beta_0 + \beta_1 ln\_estabsize + \beta_2 ln\_femalework + \beta_3 ln\_wagepe + u \tag{3.2}$$

$$ln\_tar\_savg\_ahs = \beta_0 + \beta_1 ln\_estabsize + \beta_2 ln\_femalework + \beta_3 ln\_wagepe + \beta_4 ln\_mu + u \tag{3.3}$$

The first entry of the `plm()` is a formula. `index =` enables the estimation functions to identify the structure of the data, i.e., the individual and the time period for each observation, `model =` indicates the kind of model to be estimated. In this case, we choose `within` for fixed effects.

Finally, note that to reproduce robust standard errors as in Stata we have to call for another function, `coeftest()` from the `lmtest` package and choose the options `type = "sss"` and `cluster = "group"` in `vcov = vcovHC()`.

```
reg_plm_fe <- plm(ln_tar_savg_ahs ~ ln_estabsize +
                   ln_femalework + ln_wagepe,
                 data = Ratios,
                 index = c("id", "year"),
                 model = "within")

summary(reg_plm_fe)

reg_plm_fe_r <- coeftest(reg_plm_fe,
                         vcov = vcovHC(reg_plm_fe,
                                       type = "sss",
                                       cluster = "group"))
```

[7] `NaN` means "Not a Number".

```
reg_plm_fe_r


reg_plm_fe2 <- plm(ln_tar_savg_ahs ~ ln_estabsize +
                     ln_femalework + ln_wagepe + ln_mu,
                   data = Ratios,
                   index = c("id", "year"),
                   model = "within")
summary(reg_plm_fe2)
reg_plm_fe_r2 <- coeftest(reg_plm_fe2,
                          vcov = vcovHC(reg_plm_fe2,
                                        type = "sss",
                                        cluster = "group"))
reg_plm_fe_r2
```

Here, I print the results of the first model with the conventional standard errors and Stata robust standard errors.

```
> summary(reg_plm_fe)
Oneway (individual) effect Within Model

Call:
plm(formula = ln_tar_savg_ahs ~ ln_estabsize
    + ln_femalework +   ln_wagepe, data = Ratios,
    model = "within", index = c("id",     "year"))

Unbalanced Panel: n = 1170, T = 1-9, N = 3594

Residuals:
     Min.   1st Qu.    Median   3rd Qu.      Max.
-2.569936 -0.090951  0.000000  0.098789  2.670879

Coefficients:
               Estimate Std. Error t-value  Pr(>|t|)
ln_estabsize   0.184586   0.015049 12.2654 < 2.2e-16 ***
ln_femalework  0.536223   0.172928  3.1008  0.001952 **
ln_wagepe     -0.141421   0.026634 -5.3098 1.198e-07 ***
---
Signif. codes:
         0 '***' 0.001 '**' 0.01 '*' 0.05 '.' 0.1 ' ' 1

Total Sum of Squares:    289.73
Residual Sum of Squares: 269.81
R-Squared:       0.06876
Adj. R-Squared: -0.38205
F-statistic:
         59.5863 on 3 and 2421 DF, p-value: < 2.22e-16

> reg_plm_fe_r
```

```
t test of coefficients:

                Estimate Std. Error t value  Pr(>|t|)
ln_estabsize    0.184586   0.017933 10.2932 < 2.2e-16 ***
ln_femalework   0.536223   0.235487  2.2771 0.0228685 *
ln_wagepe      -0.141421   0.038066 -3.7151 0.0002077 ***
---
Signif. codes:
        0 '***' 0.001 '**' 0.01 '*' 0.05 '.' 0.1 ' ' 1
```

However, note that Stata output reports an intercept with fixed effects model.[8] To replicate that result for the intercept with the `plm` package, we need to use the `within_intercept()` function.

```
> within_intercept(reg_plm_fe,
+           vcov = function(x) vcovHC(x, type="sss",
+                                  cluster = "group"))
(overall_intercept)
           1.671349
attr(,"se")
[1] 0.108322
```

After estimating the models, we may want to export the results. We can accomplish this task with the `stargazer` package.

First, note that we store all the regressions results in objects. The first entries of `stargazer()` are one or more model objects (for regression analysis tables) or data frames/vectors/matrices (for summary statistics, or direct output of content). `type` = specifies what type of output the command should produce. The possible values are `latex`, (default) for LaTeX code, `html` for HTML/CSS code, `text` for ASCII text output. `title` = is a character vector with titles for the tables. `digits` = indicates how many decimal places should be used. `column.labels` =, `dep.var.labels` =, and `covariate.labels` = indicate the labels for columns, dependent variable, and independent variables, respectively. `add.lines` = is a list of vectors (one vector per line) containing additional lines to be included in the table. Each element of the listed vectors will be put into a separate column. `out` = contains the path of output files. Depending on the file extension (.tex, .txt, .htm or .html), either a LaTeX/HTML source file or an ASCII text output file will be produced (see Table 3.1).

Note that the code for `stargazer()` differs from the code in the first edition of the book. In the first edition, we used `reg_plm_fe_r` and `reg_plm_fe_r2` as models to get the desired robust standard errors. In this code we use `reg_plm_fe` and `reg_plm_fe2` as models and we modify the standard errors and the p-values

[8] Refer to https://www.stata.com/support/faqs/statistics/intercept-in-fixed-effects-model/.

in the `stargazer()` function by passing a list of numeric vectors to `se =` and `p =`, respectively. The values are matched to covariates by their element names. By doing like this, `stargazer()` automatically will print some statistics such as number of observations, R-squared, Adjusted R-squared, and F statistics.

Refer to Sect. 4.3 for another example with `stargazer`.

```
stargazer(reg_plm_fe, reg_plm_fe2,
          type = "latex",
          title ="Regression output of the determinant of tariffs with
          stargazer",
          digits = 4,
          dep.var.labels = "Log of simple average of applied tariffs on
          imports",
          covariate.labels = c("log of establishment size",
                               "log of proportion of female workers",
                               "log of wage per employee",
                               "log of Import-Penetration"),
          se = list(reg_plm_fe_r[, 2],
                    reg_plm_fe_r2[, 2]),
          p = list(reg_plm_fe_r[, 4],
                   reg_plm_fe_r2[, 4]),
          add.lines = list(c("FE", "YES", "YES")),
          out = "regression_tar.tex")
```

Table 3.1 Regression output of the determinant of tariffs with stargazer

	Dependent variable:	
	Log of simple average of applied tariffs on imports	
	(1)	(2)
log of establishment size	0.1846***	0.1847***
	(0.0179)	(0.0184)
log of proportion of female workers	0.5362**	0.6716***
	(0.2355)	(0.2541)
log of wage per employee	−0.1414***	−0.1210***
	(0.0381)	(0.0406)
log of Import-Penetration		0.1979
		(0.2231)
FE	YES	YES
Observations	3,594	3,295
R^2	0.0688	0.0722
Adjusted R^2	−0.3821	−0.3797
F Statistic	59.5863*** (df = 3; 2421)	43.1112*** (df = 4; 2215)
Note:		*p<0.1; **p<0.05; ***p<0.01

3.3 Analyzing Preferential Market Access

Learning Objectives

- Import a Stata file
- Conversion of objects
- Generate new variables
- Pipe operations with `%>%`
- Drop duplicates
- Label variables
- Reshape the dataset
- Replace if
- Plot with `ggplot()`

In this section we replicate the UNCTAD & WTO's the code to calculate the tariff trade restrictiveness index (TTRI) and the relative preferential margin (RPM) as defined in Fugazza & Nicita (2011).[9]

Fugazza & Nicita (2011) observe that "one consequence of the large number of PTAs is that an increasing share of international trade is not subject to the most favoured nation (MFN) tariff, but enters markets through preferential access. Preferential access affects trade because, by providing some countries with a relative advantage, it is essentially a discriminatory practice".

They provide two indices to measure market access conditions that take into account the complex structure of tariff preferences: the tariff trade restrictiveness index (TTRI) and the relative preferential margin (RPM).

TTRI is defined as

$$TTRI_{jk} = \frac{\sum_{hs} \exp_{jk,hs} \epsilon_{k,hs} \mathrm{T}^{j}_{k,hs}}{\sum_{hs} \exp_{jk,hs} \epsilon_{k,hs}} \tag{3.4}$$

where *exp* are exports, ϵ is the import demand elasticity, T is the tariff, and *hs* are HS six-digit categories.

TTRI index captures direct market access conditions (the overall tariff faced by exports).

RPM is defined as

[9] The corresponding Stata code in available in AnalyzingPreferentialMarketAccess.do.

$$RPM_{jk} = \frac{\sum_{hs} \exp_{jk,hs}\epsilon_{k,hs}\left(\mathrm{T}^{w}_{k,hs} - \mathrm{T}^{j}_{k,hs}\right)}{\sum_{hs} \exp_{jk,hs}\epsilon_{k,hs}}, \quad j \neq k \tag{3.5}$$

with

$$\mathrm{T}^{w}_{k,hs} = \frac{\sum_{v} \exp_{vk,hs}\mathrm{T}^{v}_{k,hs}}{\sum_{v} \exp_{vk,hs}} \tag{3.6}$$

where *exp* are exports, ϵ is the import demand elasticity, T is the tariff, *hs* are HS six-digit categories, v are exporters competing with country j in exporting to country k, and $T^{w}_{k,hs}$ is the trade-weighted average of the tariffs applied by country k to imports originating from each country v (for each HS six-digit product).

RPM index captures relative market access conditions (the overall tariff faced by exports relative to that faced by competitors).

Refer to Fugazza & Nicita (2011) for more details on these indexes and their applicability.

In this section, we calculate the TTRI and RPM for Mexico. We will add a bar plot of the two indexes for year 2000 and 2008 that is not included in *Practical Guide to Trade Policy Analysis*.[10]

Open a new script file in **RStudio** and save it as `10_AnalyzingPreferentialMarketAccess_2edn`.

Let's load the following packages by using the `library()` function.

```
library("haven") # import Stata .dta file
library("Hmisc") # for label
library("dplyr") # combine operations
library("data.table") # reshape the data set
library("ggplot2") # plot with ggplot
library("stargazer") # export results
```

Let's import the UNCTAD & WTO's `PMA_MEX.dta` in **R** by using the `read_dta()` function from the `haven` package. Assign this operation to a new object, `PMA_MEX`. `PMA_MEX` is a data frame with 94,699 observations and 7 variables: year, `year`, importer-reporter, `ccode`, bilateral trade, `exp`, HS-6 code, `hs6`, exporter-partner, `pcode`, applied tariff, `T`, and import demand elasticity, `eps`.

```
PMA_MEX <- read_dta("datWTO/PMA_MEX.dta")
class(PMA_MEX)
View(PMA_MEX)
dim(PMA_MEX)
str(PMA_MEX)
```

First of all, we rename the applied tariff, `T` as `AT` because `T` is short for `TRUE` which is a reserved name in **R**.

```
colnames(PMA_MEX)[6] <- "AT"
```

In the next lines of code we will compute step by step the TTRI and RPM indexes.

[10] The corresponding Stata code in available in AnalyzingPreferentialMarketAccess.do.

```
# COMPUTE THE PREFERENTIAL MARKET ACCESS
## Compute the TTRI measure ----
PMA_MEX <- PMA_MEX %>%
  group_by(ccode, year, pcode) %>%
  mutate(num = sum((exp * AT * eps), na.rm = T))

PMA_MEX <- PMA_MEX[order(PMA_MEX$year, PMA_MEX$pcode), ]

PMA_MEX <- PMA_MEX %>%
  group_by(ccode, year, pcode) %>%
  mutate(den = sum((exp * eps), na.rm = T))

PMA_MEX$TTRI_elas <- PMA_MEX$num/PMA_MEX$den

PMA_MEX <- PMA_MEX %>%
  group_by(ccode, year, pcode) %>%
  mutate(num_ = sum((exp * AT), na.rm = T),
         den_ = sum((exp), na.rm = T))

PMA_MEX$TTRI_noelas <- PMA_MEX$num_/PMA_MEX$den_

# Compute the weighted average tariff for competitors at the hs level (Twc)
PMA_MEX <- PMA_MEX %>%
  group_by(ccode, year, hs6) %>%
  mutate(TotalexpT = sum((exp * AT), na.rm = T),
         Totalexp = sum((exp), na.rm = T))

PMA_MEX$Twc <- ((PMA_MEX$TotalexpT - PMA_MEX$exp * PMA_MEX$AT) /
  (PMA_MEX$Totalexp - PMA_MEX$exp))

# Compute the RPM measure ----
PMA_MEX <- PMA_MEX %>%
  group_by(ccode, year, pcode) %>%
  mutate(num2 = sum((exp * Twc * eps), na.rm = T))

PMA_MEX$TTRI_others_elas <- PMA_MEX$num2 / PMA_MEX$den
PMA_MEX$RPM_elas = PMA_MEX$TTRI_others_elas - PMA_MEX$TTRI_elas

PMA_MEX <- PMA_MEX %>%
  group_by(ccode, year, pcode) %>%
  mutate(num2_ = sum((exp * Twc), na.rm = T))

PMA_MEX$TTRI_others_noelas <- PMA_MEX$num2_ / PMA_MEX$den_
PMA_MEX$RPM_noelas <- PMA_MEX$TTRI_others_noelas - PMA_MEX$TTRI_noelas


# Compute the trade-weighted average for MEX
PMA_MEX <- PMA_MEX %>%
  group_by(ccode, pcode, year) %>%
  mutate(exports = sum((exp), na.rm = T))

PMA_MEX2 <- PMA_MEX[, c(2, 1, 5, 23, 10, 13, 18, 21, 19, 22)]
PMA_MEX2 <- unique(PMA_MEX2)

PMA_MEX2 <- PMA_MEX2 %>%
  group_by(ccode, year) %>%
  mutate(Totalexports = sum((exports), na.rm = T),
         TTRI_elas_bar = mean((TTRI_elas), na.rm = T),
         TTRI_elas_sd = sd((TTRI_elas), na.rm = T),
         TTRI_noelas_bar = mean((TTRI_noelas), na.rm = T),
         TTRI_noelas_sd = sd((TTRI_noelas), na.rm = T),
         TTRI_elas_wbar = sum(((TTRI_elas * exports)/Totalexports),
                              na.rm = T),
         TTRI_elas_wsd = sd(((TTRI_elas * exports)/Totalexports),
                            na.rm = T),
         TTRI_noelas_wbar = sum(((TTRI_noelas * exports)/Totalexports),
                                na.rm = T),
```

```
        TTRI_noelas_wsd = sd(((TTRI_noelas * exports)/Totalexports),
                             na.rm = T),
        RPM_elas_bar = mean(RPM_elas, na.rm = T),
        RPM_elas_sd = sd(RPM_elas, na.rm = T),
        RPM_noelas_bar = mean(RPM_noelas, na.rm = T),
        RPM_noelas_sd = sd(RPM_noelas, na.rm = T),
        RPM_elas_wbar = sum(((RPM_elas * exports) / Totalexports),
                             na.rm = T),
        RPM_elas_wsd = sd(((RPM_elas * exports) / Totalexports),
                          na.rm = T),
        RPM_noelas_wbar = sum(((RPM_noelas * exports) / Totalexports),
                              na.rm = T),
        RPM_noelas_wsd = sd(((RPM_noelas * exports) / Totalexports),
                            na.rm = T))

PMA_MEX2 <- upData(PMA_MEX2,
                   labels =
                   c(TTRI_elas = "Tariff trade restrictiveness index",
                     TTRI_noelas = "Tariff trade restrictiveness index
                           without elasticities as weights",
                     RPM_elas = "Relative preferential margin with
                          elasticities as weights",
                     RPM_noelas = "Relative preferential margin without
                          elasticities as weights",
                     TTRI_elas_bar = "TTRI simple average",
                     TTRI_elas_sd = "TTRI simple standard deviation",
                     TTRI_elas_wbar = "TTRI trade weighted average",
                     TTRI_elas_wsd = "TTRI trade weighted standard
                          deviation",
                     RPM_elas_bar = "RPM simple average",
                     RPM_elas_sd = "RPM simple standard deviation",
                     RPM_elas_wbar = "RPM trade weighted average",
                     RPM_elas_wsd = "RPM trade weighted standard
                           deviation"))

PMA_MEX3 <- PMA_MEX2[, c(1, 2, 12:27)]
PMA_MEX3 <- unique(PMA_MEX3)

RPM <- PMA_MEX3[, c("year", "ccode", "TTRI_elas_bar", "TTRI_elas_wbar",
                   "RPM_elas_bar", "RPM_elas_wbar")]

colnames(RPM) <- c("year", "ccode", "TTRIsimpleavg", "TTRIweightedav",
                   "RPMsimpleavg", "RPMweightedav")

RPM
```

Following, the output of RPM.

```
> RPM
# A tibble: 2 x 6
# Groups:   ccode, year [2]
  year       ccode      TTRIsimpleavg TTRIweightedav RPMsimpleavg RPMweightedav
  <labelled> <labelled> <labelled>    <labelled>     <labelled>   <labelled>
1 2000       MEX        0.12813437    0.01855284     -0.08799973  0.03814564
2 2007       MEX        0.09382693    0.02245499     -0.04912892  0.01055606
```

Now, let's reshape the data set long. We use the pattern in the name of the variables two reshape the data set long with two columns, one for the TTRI index and the other one for the RPM index. We accomplish this operation with the `melt()` function from the `data.table` package. Note that we introduce the `patterns()` argument where we identify the pattern in the name of the variables with ^. The argument `variable.factor = FALSE` prevents the variable column from being converted to factor.

```
RPM2 <- melt(setDT(RPM), id.vars = c("year", "ccode"),
```

```
             measure = patterns("^TTRI", "^RPM"),
             variable.name = "statistics",
             variable.factor = FALSE,
             value.name = c("TTRI", "RPM"))

class(RPM2$statistics)
RPM2$statistics[RPM2$statistics == "1"] <-  "simple average"
RPM2$statistics[RPM2$statistics == "2"] <-  "weighted average"

RPM2
```

```
> RPM2
   year ccode        statistics       TTRI         RPM
1: 2000   MEX   simple average 0.12813437 -0.08799973
2: 2007   MEX   simple average 0.09382693 -0.04912892
3: 2000   MEX weighted average 0.01855284  0.03814564
4: 2007   MEX weighted average 0.02245499  0.01055606
```

Now, let's suppose we want to plot the data as a bar plot. We want to display information of the indexes by statistics and by year. We use `geom_bar()`. The first step is to reshape the data set long because we need our indexes in the same column. We use again the `melt()` function.

```
RPM3 <- melt(setDT(RPM2),
             id.vars = c("year", "ccode", "statistics"),
             measure.vars = c("TTRI", "RPM"))

RPM3
```

As you can see from the printed output, our data set is now long.

```
> RPM3
   year ccode       statistics variable       value
1: 2000   MEX   simple average     TTRI  0.12813437
2: 2007   MEX   simple average     TTRI  0.09382693
3: 2000   MEX weighted average     TTRI  0.01855284
4: 2007   MEX weighted average     TTRI  0.02245499
5: 2000   MEX   simple average      RPM -0.08799973
6: 2007   MEX   simple average      RPM -0.04912892
7: 2000   MEX weighted average      RPM  0.03814564
8: 2007   MEX weighted average      RPM  0.01055606
```

Now we are ready to plot with `ggplot()`. All the arguments of the following plot should be clear (see Fig. 3.5 for the output).

```
ggplot(RPM3, aes(x = variable, y = value,
                 fill = factor(statistics))) +
  geom_bar(stat = "identity", position = "dodge") +
  facet_grid(. ~ year) +
  theme_classic() +
  xlab("") + ylab(" ") +
  ggtitle("TTRI and RPM") +
  theme(plot.title = element_text(hjust = 0.5,
                                  size = 10, face="bold"),
        axis.title.x = element_text(size = 7.5),
        legend.title = element_blank())
```

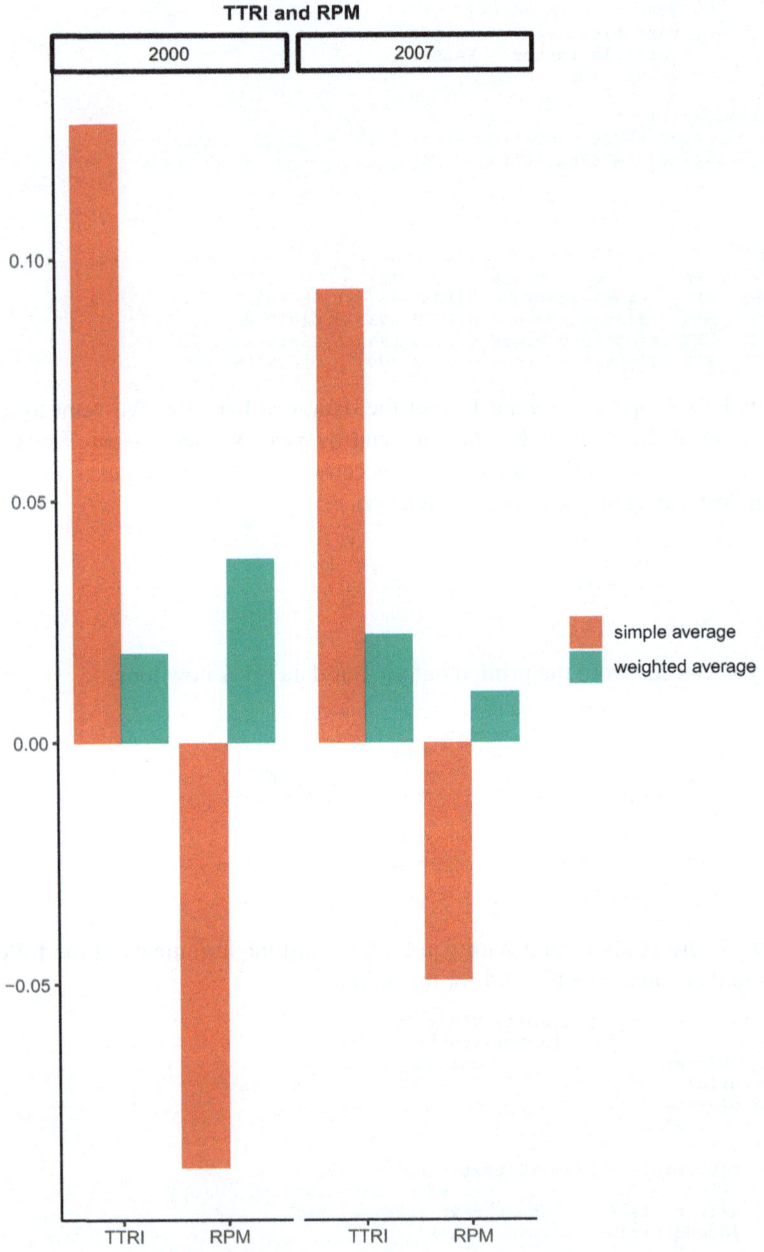

Fig. 3.5 Bar plot and facets with `ggplot2`

Chapter 4
The Gravity Model of Trade

The gravity model for international trade was introduced by Jan Tinbergen in 1962. This model was based on an equation that approximated the theory of gravitation of Newton and therefore it is known as the gravity equation. Basically, the model shows that trade flows between two countries are positively affected by the size of the gross domestic product (GDP) of the two countries and negatively affected by their distance. In its simplest form, the model is represented as follows:

$$X_{ij} = G\frac{GDP_i GDP_j}{Dist_{ij}} \tag{4.1}$$

where:

- X_{ij} denotes exports from country *i* to country *j*;
- G denotes the inverse of world production;
- GDP_i and GDP_j denote the GDP of country *i* and country *j*, respectively;
- $Dist_{ij}$denotes the geographical distance between the two countries that approximates the total trade costs between country *i* and country *j*.

Traditionally, the gravity equation has been estimated through ordinary least-squares (OLS) as the following:

$$lnX_{ij} = \beta_0 + \beta_1 lnGDPi + \beta_2 lnGDP_j + \beta_3 lnDist_{ij} + \varepsilon_{ij} \tag{4.2}$$

where:

- β_0 is a constant;
- ε is the error term;
- the other variables have the meaning explained above but in natural logarithmic form.

© The Author(s), under exclusive license to Springer Nature Switzerland AG 2023
M. Porto, *Using R for Trade Policy Analysis*,
https://doi.org/10.1007/978-3-031-35044-3_4

In order to account for trade costs, a set of dummy variables, denoting whether two countries share a common border, language, religion and colonial ties and whether a country is an island or is landlocked, is generally added to Eq. (4.2).

The gravity equation has been successfully applied to several fields other than trade, such as immigration, investments and tourism. In order to focus on a policy of interest, researchers need to include relevant variables. For example, to estimate the effects of FTAs a dummy variable is added to Eq. (4.2) :

$$lnX_{ij} = \beta_0 + \beta_1 lnGDPi + \beta_2 lnGDP_j + \beta_3 lnDist_{ij} + \beta_4 Z_i + \beta_5 FTA_{ij} + \varepsilon_{ij} \tag{4.3}$$

where:

- Z_i is a vector of the aforementioned dummy variables (common border, language, religion, . . .);
- FTA_{ij} is a dummy variable capturing the presence of a free-trade agreement between partners i and j;
- the other variables have the meaning explained above.

Generally, the "traditional" empirical strategy in estimating (4.3) through OLS consists of estimating it with, firstly, random effect and, secondly, with fixed effect; then test the suitability of the random effect model through the Hausman test.

From its basic version in Eqs. (4.1)–(4.3), the gravity model underwent several developments both in theory and estimation technique. From a theoretical point of view, the gravity equation was initially introduced without any strong theoretical foundations. For this reason, it was criticized by trade economists despite its power to explain bilateral trade flows. Anderson (1979) was the first who tried to fill the gap between the empirical evidence and theory. He derived the gravity model based on constant elasticity of substitution (CES) preferences and goods that are differentiated by country of origin. The gravity model was also derived based on a model of monopolistic competition (Bergstrand, 1989) and on a Ricardian framework (Eaton & Kortum, 2002). Anderson & Van Wincoop (2003), building on Anderson (1979), showed that estimations of gravity equation suffered from omitted variable bias because empirical analysis did not take account of multilateral resistance terms. Anderson & Van Wincoop (2003, p.183) state that "multilateral resistance variables are critical to understanding the impact of border barriers on bilateral trade". Solving the McCallum border puzzle by including the multilateral resistance terms in the estimation of the gravity equation, Anderson & Van Wincoop (2003, p.184) find that "to the extent that border barriers raise average trade barriers faced by an importer and an exporter (multilateral resistance), it dampens the negative impact of the bilateral border barrier on trade between the two countries". The specification of the model due to Anderson & Van Wincoop (2003) is widely recognized and represents a solid basis for further improvements of the gravity model. The gravity model derived by Anderson & Van Wincoop (2003) that includes multilateral resistance terms takes the following form:

$$X_{ij} = \frac{GDP_i GDP_j}{GDP_w}\left(\frac{t_{ij}}{\Pi i P_j}\right)^{1-\sigma} \tag{4.4}$$

where:

- X_{ij} denotes exports from country i to country j;
- GDP_i, GDP_j and GDP_w denote the GDP of country *i*, the GDP of country *j*, and world GDP, respectively;
- t_{ij} denotes the bilateral trade costs between country *i* and country *j* that account for geographical distance, the set of aforementioned dummy variables, bilateral tariffs, whether the countries are parties to an FTA;
- Π_i denotes the outward multilateral resistance and captures the fact that the exports from country *i* to country *j* also depend on the trade costs borne by country *i* towards all possible markets;
- P_j denotes the inward multilateral resistance and captures the fact that the imports of country *i* from country *j* also depend on the trade costs borne by all possible suppliers in country *i*'s market;
- σ denotes the elasticity of substitution.

The contribution of Anderson & Van Wincoop (2003) is not limited to theoretical development. It paved the way for development in the estimation technique because of the issue of how to properly estimate the multilateral resistance terms. Equation (4.4) could be estimated through OLS as follows:

$$lnX_{ij} = \beta_0 + \beta_1 lnGDPi + \beta_2 lnGDP_j + \beta_3 lnt_{ij} + \beta_4 \Pi_i + \beta_5 P_j + \varepsilon_{ij} \tag{4.5}$$

However, it should be noted that the multilateral resistance terms are not directly observable. The empirical literature proposed different ways to estimate them. Anderson & Van Wincoop (2003) estimated them through a nonlinear least-squares (NLS) estimator, which, however, has not been much applied in the empirical literature. An alternative is to include a proxy for the multilateral resistance terms in the form of a "remoteness" index that measures a country's average weighted distance from its trading partners. However, Anderson & Van Wincoop (2003) criticize this "remoteness" index because it does not capture any trade barrier other than distance. The empirical literature mainly estimates the multilateral resistance terms using country fixed effects for importers and exporters in cross-section estimations and using exporter-time and importer-time fixed effects in a dynamic estimation with panel data.[1]

[1] "It should be noted that in addition to accounting for the unobservable multilateral resistance terms, the exporter-time and importer-time fixed effects will also absorb the size variables ($E_{j,t}$ and $Y_{i,t}$) from the structural gravity model as well as all other observable and unobservable country-specific characteristics which vary across these dimensions, including various national policies, institutions, exchange rates, etc." (Piermartini & Yotov, 2016, p. 7).

Recent econometric best practices include the use of country –pair fixed effects to address the problem of endogeneity bias due to unobservable heterogeneity across pairs (Baier & Bergstrand, 2007), estimation in panel data with time interval because "fixed-effects estimation is sometimes criticized when applied to data pooled over consecutive years on the grounds that dependent and independent variables cannot fully adjust in a single year's time" (Cheng & Wall, 2005), and the use of a Poisson Pseudo Maximum Likelihood (PPML) estimator (Santos & Tenreyro, 2006). Santos & Tenreyro (2006) showed the advantages of the PPML estimator compared to OLS. In particular, the PPML estimator accounts for the patterns of heteroskedasticity that plague trade data and performs well even when the proportion of zeros in the sample is very large (Santos Silva & Tenreyro, 2011).

These last developments will be not shown in this book. Refer to *An Advanced Guide to Trade Policy Analysis: The Structural Gravity Model* by the UNCTAD & WTO for practical applications of last best practices in estimating the gravity equations. Furthermore, the book *The gravity model of international trade: a user guide [R version]*, published by the United Nations ESCAP (Shepherd et al., 2019) available at https://www.unescap.org/resources/gravity-model-international-trade-user-guide-r-version, shows several econometric techniques applied to the gravity model of international trade. Therefore, it can be a natural integration to this book. Finally, note that an *ad hoc* package to estimate the gravity equation, `gravity`, has been developed by Woelwer & Burgard (2017). This package provides estimation methods for log-log models and multiplicative models, such as the PPML estimator.

Learning Objectives

- Import csv, txt, and Stata files
- Conversion of objects
- Drop duplicates
- Generate new variables
- Group operations with `ave()`
- Sort data set by variables
- Collapse a data set with `aggregate()`
- Rename column names
- Append data sets
- Use of `complete()`
- Reshape the data set
- Replace if
- Subset a data set
- Generate dummy variables with `ifelse()`
- Generate group id
- Label variables

(continued)

- Export data set
- Run a regression
- Replicates Stata robust standard errors
- Export results with `stargazer()`

In this chapter, we are going to build a database to estimate a gravity equation.[2] We will follow eight steps:

1. import data sets
2. create all possible country-year combinations
3. reshape and merge country-specific data with bilateral trade flows
4. merge with pair-specific data (CEPII, gravity data)
5. generate new country-pair variables
6. compute the log of variables and generate the panel id
7. estimate the model
8. export the results

Open a new script file in **RStudio** and save it as `11_building_database_approach_2edn`.

Let's load the following packages by using the `library()` function.

```
library("readr") # import .csv file
library("haven") # import Stata .dta file
library("Hmisc") # label
library("tidyr") # complete observations
library("data.table") # reshape the dataset
library("plm") # panel regression
library("dplyr") # group id
library("sandwich") # replicate Stata robust standard errors
library("lmtest") # replicate Stata robust standard errors
library("stargazer") # export regression results
```

4.1 Building the Database

In this section we follow the UNCTAD & WTO's good practice to build the data set for the gravity model. First, we import data sets from different sources. We make operations on each of them before importing the next data set. We prepare the data sets to be merged in a single final data set which will contain all the information to run the regression.

Let's start by importing the UNCTAD & WTO's `tradeflows.csv` in **R** by using `read_delim()` from `readr` package. We indicate `;` as delimiter.

[2] The corresponding Stata code is available in BuildingDatabaseApproach.do.

The option `trim_ws = TRUE` trims leading and trailing white space. If the file contains double quotes, the option `escape_double = TRUE` makes the value `"" ""` represent a single quote, `"  "`.

We store the data set as `tf`. `tf` is a data frame with 369,178 observations and 4 variables, `importer`, `exporter`, `year`, and `imports`. Data cover the years 1990–2005.

```
# Step 1: Import data ----
# Import trade flows data (; delimiter)
tf <- read_delim("datWTO/tradeflows.csv",
                             ";", escape_double = FALSE,
                             trim_ws = TRUE)

class(tf)
View(tf)
dim(tf)
str(tf)
```

Next we import the UNCTAD & WTO's dataset for WTO accession data, `joinwto.txt`. This is a text file. We use again `read_delim()`. Note that this time the delimiter is tab, `\t`. We store the data set as `jw`. `jw` is a data frame with 176 observations and 2 variables, `country` and `join`. `join` reports the date of accession to the WTO.

```
# Import WTO accession data (tab delimiter)
jw <- read_delim("datWTO/joinwto.txt",
                          "\t", escape_double = FALSE,
                          trim_ws = TRUE)
class(jw)
View(jw)
dim(jw)
str(jw)
```

We need to correct the data set for Belgium and Luxembourg. If the value of `country` is equal to `BEL` or, `|`, `LUX`, we replace the value with `BLX`. We also replace `COD` with `ZAR`. Drop duplicates with the `unique()` function and sort the data set by `country` with `order()`. For the use of `unique()` refer to Sect. 2.6. For the use of `order()` refer to Sects. 2.2, 2.3 and 2.6. The data set `jw` has 174 observations after dropping duplicates. Note that the imported data set, `joinwto`, reports two values for `COD`.

```
# replace if
jw$country[jw$country == "BEL" | jw$country == "LUX"] <- "BLX"
jw$country[jw$country == "COD"] <- "ZAR"
jw <- unique(jw)
jw <- jw[order(jw$country), ]
dim(jw)
View(jw)
```

Next we import the data set storing GDP data, `GDP.csv`. This is a csv file. This time we use another function to import the data set in **R**, `read_csv()`. We store the data set in `gdp`. `gdp` is a data frame with 228 observations and 54 variables. Variables include `Country Name`, `Country Code`, `Indicator Name`, `Indicator Code` and years from 1960 to 2009.

```
# Import GDP data
gdp <- read_csv("datWTO/GDP.csv")
class(gdp)
```

```
dim(gdp)
View(gdp)
str(gdp)
```

We need to correct for Belgium and Luxembourg also for this data set. We replace the values as we did for the `jw` dataset.

In this case, however, we need to sum the values of the GDP for the two countries. We do this in a few steps.

We subset the `gdp` data set twice. First, we drop from the data set `BLX`. We subset `gdp` if `'Country Code' != "BLX"`, where `!=` is a logical operator that means inequality. We assign this operation to a new object, `gdp_no_blx`.

Second, we keep only `BLX` in the dataset. We subset `gdp` if `'Country Code' == "BLX"`, where `==` is a logical operator that means exact equality. We assign this operation to a new object, `gdp_blx`.

Next, we keep only GDP value per years in `gdp_blx`. Therefore, we keep columns from 5 to 54. We use `[ ]` operator and assign this operation to a new object, `gdp_blx2`. We sum the values in the columns using `colSums()` and append the outcome to `gdp_blx2` by using `rbind()`. We assign this operation to a new object, `gdp_blx3`. Next, we eliminate the first two rows, which correspond to the single values of Belgium and Luxembourg using the `[ ]` operator. We assign this operation to a new object, `gdp_blx4`.

We create a new object from `gdp_blx` which includes `Country Name`, `Country Code`, `Indicator Name`, and `Indicator Code` for `BLX`. We assign this operation to a new object, `gdp_blx_lab`.

Next, we bind by columns, by using `cbind()`, `gdp_blx_lab` and `gdp_blx4`. We assign this operation to a new object, `gdp_blx5`. Now we have the data for `BLX` of the right dimension to be appended to the data set without `BLX`, `gdp_no_blx`. We append these two data sets by using `rbind.data.frame()` in a new object, `gdp2`. We have corrected the data set. We have 227 observations. Finally, we sort the `gdp2` by `'Country Code'` using `order()`.

```
#####################################!
# Adjust for BLX = BEL + LUX
gdp$'Country Code'[gdp$'Country Code' == "BEL" |
                    gdp$'Country Code' == "LUX"] <- "BLX"
gdp$'Country Name'[gdp$'Country Name' == "Belgium" |
                    gdp$'Country Name' == "Luxembourg"] <- "BENELUX"

# subset eliminating BLX
gdp_no_blx <- subset(gdp, gdp$'Country Code' != "BLX")
dim(gdp_no_blx)

# subset only BLX
gdp_blx <- subset(gdp, gdp$'Country Code' == "BLX")
dim(gdp_blx)
View(gdp_blx)

# keep only value in gdp_blx for sum
gdp_blx2 <- gdp_blx[, 5:54]
View(gdp_blx2)
gdp_blx3 <- rbind(gdp_blx2, colSums(gdp_blx2))
gdp_blx4 <- gdp_blx3[-c(1,2),]
View(gdp_blx4)
```

```
gdp_blx_lab <- gdp_blx[1, c(1:4)]
View(gdp_blx_lab)

gdp_blx5 <- cbind(gdp_blx_lab, gdp_blx4)
View(gdp_blx5)

# rbind gdp with and without BLX
gdp2 <- rbind.data.frame(gdp_no_blx, gdp_blx5)
dim(gdp2)
gdp2 <- gdp2[order(gdp2$'Country Code'), ]
View(gdp2)
#######################################################!
```

Next, we import the data set `dist_cepii224.dta` as `dist_cepii`. This data set contains gravity variables such as distance between two countries in km `dist`, contiguity (dummy variable which takes value 1 if two countries share same borders, 0 otherwise), `contig`, language (dummy variable which takes value 1 if two countries share the same language, 0 otherwise), `comlang_off`, landlocked (dummy variable which takes value 1 if a reporter, `REPlandlocked`, or a partner, `PARTlandlocked`, have no access to the sea, and so on. The source of this data set is the French Centre d'Etudes Prospectives et d'Informations Internationales (CEPII). In total, the data set contains 50,176 observations and 30 variables.

```
# Import dataset with gravity variables
dist_cepii <- read_dta("datWTO/dist_cepii224.dta")
class(dist_cepii)
View(dist_cepii)
dim(dist_cepii)
str(dist_cepii)
```

We rename `country`, `partner`, `repnum`, and `partnum` as shown in the next block of code. Then, we adjust for Belgium and Luxembourg.

```
# Open gravity variables and correct for BLX = BEL + LUX
## rename
colnames(dist_cepii)[1] <- "exporter"
colnames(dist_cepii)[2] <- "importer"
colnames(dist_cepii)[15] <- "exporternum"
colnames(dist_cepii)[23] <- "importernum"

dist_cepii$exporter[dist_cepii$exporter == "BEL" |
                      dist_cepii$exporter == "LUX"] <- "BLX"
dist_cepii$importer[dist_cepii$importer == "BEL" |
                      dist_cepii$importer == "LUX"] <- "BLX"
```

Next, we use `aggregate()` to collapse the variables `exporternum`, `importernum`, `contig`, `comlang_off`, `colony`, `dist`, `REPlandlocked`, and `PARTlandlocked` by `exporter` and `importer`. Refer to Sect. 2.6 for details about `aggregate()`. Note that we nest `aggregate()` in `with()`. Refer to Sect. 2.1 for the use of `with()`. We assign this operation to a new object, `dist_cepii2`.

Finally, we keep the observations if exporter is different from importer, `exporternum != importernum`, by using `subset()`. We assign this operation to a new object, `dist_cepii3`. Then, we sort the data set by `exporter` and `importer`. We assign this operation to a new object, `cepii`.

```
dist_cepii2 <- with(dist_cepii,
                    aggregate(list(exporternum = exporternum,
```

```
                                importernum = importernum,
                                contig = contig,
                                comlang_off = comlang_off,
                                colony = colony,
                                dist = dist,
                                REPlandlocked = REPlandlocked,
                                PARTlandlocked = PARTlandlocked),
                           by = list(exporter = exporter,
                                     importer = importer),
                           FUN = function(x) mean(x, na.rm = T)))

View(dist_cepii2)
dist_cepii3 <- subset(dist_cepii2, exporternum != importernum)
dim(dist_cepii3)
View(dist_cepii3)
cepii <- with(dist_cepii3, dist_cepii3[order(exporter, importer),])
```

In Step 2 of the gravity database building approach, we create all possible country-pairs-year combinations. We use the `complete()` function. The `complete()` function turns implicit missing values into explicit missing values. The first entry of the function is a data frame. To find all unique combinations of `importer`, `exporter`, and `year`, including those not found in the data, we supply each variable as a separate argument. The argument `fill` allows to supply a value per variable instead of `NA`. In this case, we supply 0 to `imports`. We assign this operation to a new object, `tf2`.

Finally, we keep the observations if exporter is different from importer, `exporter != importer`, using `subset()`. We assign this operation to a new object, `gvty_t1`. `gvty_t1` has 996,000 observations and 4 variables.

```
#  Step 2: Create all possible country-pairs-year combinations ----
tf2 <- complete(tf, importer, exporter, year, fill = list(imports = 0))
View(tf2)
dim(tf2)
gvty_t1 <- subset(tf2, exporter != importer)
dim(gvty_t1)
```

We start Step 3 by keeping only `` `Country Code` `` and years in `gdp2`. We assign this operation to a new object, `gdp3`. Then, we reshape the data set long with the `melt()` function. We assign this operation to a new object, `gdp4`. Refer to Sect. 2.3 for details about `melt()`. We rename the columns of `gdp4` with `colnames()`.

Finally, we copy `gdp4` in two new objects, `gdp_exporter` and `gdp_importer` and rename `countrycode` as `exporter` and `importer`, respectively, and rename `gdp` as `gdp_exporter` and `gdp_importer`, respectively.

```
# Step 3: Reshape and Merge country-specific data with bilateral trade flows ----
gdp3 <- gdp2[, c(2, 5:54)]
View(gdp3)
gdp4 <- melt(setDT(gdp3), id.vars = 1, measure.vars = c(2:51))
colnames(gdp4) <- c("countrycode", "year", "gdp")
View(gdp4)

gdp_exporter <- gdp4
colnames(gdp_exporter)[which(
  colnames(gdp_exporter) == "countrycode")] <- "exporter"
```

```
colnames(gdp_exporter)[which(
  colnames(gdp_exporter) == "gdp")] <- "gdp_exporter"

gdp_importer <- gdp4
colnames(gdp_importer)[which(
  colnames(gdp_importer) == "countrycode")] <- "importer"
colnames(gdp_importer)[which(
  colnames(gdp_importer) == "gdp")] <- "gdp_importer"
```

Now we are ready to start to merge the data sets. We add the information with gdp per exporter, `gdp_exporter`, and importer, `gdp_importer`, to the data set with bilateral data, `gvty_t1`. by using the `merge()` function. First, we merge `gvty_t1` and `gdp_exporter`. We merge the two data sets only with observations which appear in both data sets. We assign this operation to a new object, `gvty_t1m`. Next, we merge `gdp_importer` to `gvty_t1m`. We assign this operation to a new object, `gvty_t2`. Then, we sort it by `exporter`, `importer`, and `year`.

```
# Merge the country-specific data with bilateral trade
gvty_t1 <- gvty_t1[order(gvty_t1$exporter,
                         gvty_t1$year), ]

gvty_t1m <- merge(gvty_t1, gdp_exporter,
                  by = c("exporter", "year"))


gvty_t1m <- gvty_t1m[order(gvty_t1m$importer, gvty_t1m$year), ]

gvty_t2 <- merge(gvty_t1m, gdp_importer,
                 by = c("importer", "year"))


gvty_t2 <- gvty_t2[order(gvty_t2$exporter,
                         gvty_t2$importer,
                         gvty_t2$year), ]
dim(gvty_t2)
View(gvty_t2)
```

We repeat the same operation for the WTO accession data, `jw`. This data set reports the year of accession to the WTO. Therefore, contrary to the previous operation, we need to choose the option `all.x = TRUE` in the `merge()` function. This option adds extra rows to the output, one for each row in `x` that has no matching row in `y`. These rows will have `NAs` in those columns that are usually filled with values from `y`. The final data set after these operations will be `gvty_t3`.

```
jw_exp <- jw
colnames(jw_exp)[which(colnames(jw_exp) == "country")] <- "exporter"
colnames(jw_exp)[which(colnames(jw_exp) == "join")] <- "join_exporter"

jw_imp <- jw
colnames(jw_imp)[which(colnames(jw_imp) == "country")] <- "importer"
colnames(jw_imp)[which(colnames(jw_imp) == "join")] <- "join_importer"

gvty_t2 <- gvty_t2[order(gvty_t2$exporter, gvty_t2$year), ]
gvty_t2m <- merge(gvty_t2, jw_exp,
                  by = c("exporter"), all.x = TRUE)
dim(gvty_t2m)
gvty_t2m <- gvty_t2m[order(gvty_t2m$importer,gvty_t2m$year), ]

gvty_t3 <- merge(gvty_t2m, jw_imp,
                 by = c("importer"), all.x = TRUE)
```

```
dim(gvty_t3)
View(gvty_t3)
```

In Step 4, we start by merging gvty_t3 with the gravity data from CEPII, cepii. We keep the data in the new object, gvty_t3m if they appear in both data sets.

```
# Step 4: Merge with pair-specific data (CEPII Gravity data) ----
gvty_t3 <- gvty_t3[order(gvty_t3$exporter,
                         gvty_t3$importer,
                         gvty_t3$year), ]

gvty_t3m <- merge(gvty_t3, cepii,
                  by = c("exporter", "importer"))
```

Next, we import the data set Religion.dta as rel with read_dta(). rel has 41,820 observations and 3 variables, exporter, importer, and religion. relion takes value 1 if exporter and importer share the same religion, 0 otherwise.

Then, we merge rel with gvty_t3m in a new object, gvty_t4. We also replace NA values in religion with 0

```
rel <- read_dta("datWTO/Religion.dta")
class(rel)
View(rel)
dim(rel)
str(rel)

gvty_t4 <- merge(gvty_t3m, rel,
                 by = c("exporter", "importer"),
          all.x  = T)

gvty_t4 <- gvty_t4[order(gvty_t4$exporter,
                         gvty_t4$importer,
                         gvty_t4$year), ]

any(is.na(gvty_t4$religion))
gvty_t4$religion[which(is.na(gvty_t4$religion))] <- 0
dim(gvty_t4)
```

In Step 5, we generate dummy variables for the WTO membership with ifelse(). First, replace NA in join_exporter and join_importer with a random number, 9999, which is functional to building the WTO membership.

We generate the following dummy variables:

- onein equal 1 if one of the country pair is member of the WTO, 0 otherwise;
- bothin equal 1 if both countries are members of the WTO, 0 otherwise;
- nonein equal 1 if none of the country pair is member of the WTO, 0 otherwise.

After generating the dummy variables for the WTO membership, we drop join_exporter and join_importer from the data set. We assign this operation to a new object, gvty_def. Now the data set is complete with all the data for the gravity model.

```
# Step 5: Generate new country-pair variables ----

gvty_t5 <- gvty_t4
```

```
gvty_t5$join_exporter[which(is.na(gvty_t5$join_exporter))] <- 9999
gvty_t5$join_importer[which(is.na(gvty_t5$join_importer))] <- 9999
View(gvty_t5)
dim(gvty_t5)

# dummy variables
gvty_t5$onein <- with(gvty_t5, ifelse(
  join_exporter <= year & join_importer > year |
  join_importer <= year & join_exporter > year,
  1, 0))
gvty_t5$bothin <- with(gvty_t5, ifelse(
  join_exporter <= year & join_importer <= year,
  1, 0))
gvty_t5$nonein <- with(gvty_t5, ifelse(
  join_exporter > year & join_importer > year,
  1, 0))

# drop the columns with join_exporter join_importer
gvty_def <- gvty_t5[, -c(7, 8)]
dim(gvty_def)
View(gvty_def)
```

In Step 6, we compute the log of the variables imports, `imports`, GDP for exporter, `gdp_exporter`, GDP for importer, `gdp_importer`, and distance, `dist`.

We replace `-Inf` in the log of imports, `limports`, with `NA`.

We generate the panel id, `pairid`, by exporter and importer by using the `cur_group_id()` function from the `dplyr` package.

Then, we label the variables by using `upData()`.

The data set is now complete. We can export it by using the `write.csv()` function. The argument `file = " "` write the file to your working directory. The argument `row.names = FALSE` omit the row names.

```
# Step 6: Compute the log of the variables imports, GDPs and distance ----
gvty_def$limports <- log(gvty_def$imports)
gvty_def$lgdp_exporter <- log(gvty_def$gdp_exporter)
gvty_def$lgdp_importer <- log(gvty_def$gdp_importer)
gvty_def$ldist <- log(gvty_def$dist)

# susbstitute -inf in imports with NA
gvty_def$limports[gvty_def$limports == -Inf] <- NA

# generate panel id
gvty_def <- gvty_def %>%
  group_by(exporter, importer) %>%
  mutate(pairid = cur_group_id())

# label
gvty_def <- upData(
  gvty_def,
  labels = c(importer = "reporter",
             exporter = "partner",
             imports  = "Imports value in thousand",
             gdp_exporter = "GDP in current USD",
             gdp_importer = "GDP in current USD",
             exporternum = "IFS code exporter",
             importernum = "IFS code importer",
             contig = "1 for contiguity",
             comlang_off = "1 for common official language",
             colony = "1 for pairs ever in colonial relationship",
             dist = "simple distance",
             REPlandlocked = "1 if exporter landlocked",
```

```
            PARTlandlocked = "1 if importer landlocked",
            religion = "1 if common main religion for both countries",
            onein = "one of the country pair is member of the WTO",
            bothin = "both countries is member of the WTO",
            nonein = "none of the country pair is member of the WTO",
            limports = "Log of imports value",
            lgdp_exporter = "log of exporter's GDP",
            lgdp_importer = "log of importer's GDP",
            ldist = "log of distance",
            pairid = "panel id"))

label(gvty_def)

View(gvty_def)

### export dataset as csv
write.csv(gvty_def, file = "gvty_def.csv",
          row.names = FALSE)
# Note that the file is written to your working directory.
# row.names = FALSE -> omit the row names
```

Finally, we copy the data set to be used in Appendix B

```
## make a copy of the data set

df <- gvty_def
```

4.2 Estimating the Gravity Model

The data set `gvty_def` contains all the information needed for the estimation of the following equation:

$$
\begin{aligned}
limports = {} & \beta_0 + \beta_1 lgdp\_exporter + \beta_2 lgdp\_importer + \beta_3 ldist + \beta_4 colony \\
& + \beta_5 contig + \beta_6 comlang\_off + \beta_7 onein + \beta_8 bothin \\
& + \beta_9 nonein + u \qquad (4.6)
\end{aligned}
$$

First, we estimate Eq. (4.6) with OLS with country and year fixed effects. We use the `lm()` function that specifies a linear regression of `limports` on the regressors and an implicitly defined constant. $\sim$ is the regressor operator. To add dummy variables for year, exporter and importer, we simply add these values as factor. We can use the `factor()` function inside `lm()`. Finally, `data` = refers to the data frame which contains the variables in the model.

Note that to reproduce robust standard errors as in Stata we have to call for another function, `coeftest()` in `lmtest` package and choose the option `vcov = vcovHC(x, "HC1")`, where x represents a fitted model object.

```
# Step 7: estimating the gravity model ----

## ols with country fixed effects
reg_lm <- lm(limports ~ lgdp_exporter + lgdp_importer +
               ldist + colony +
               contig + comlang_off + onein + bothin +
               factor(year) +
```

```
              factor(exporter) + factor(importer),
            data = gvty_def)
summary(reg_lm)
reg_lm_r <- coeftest(reg_lm, vcov = vcovHC(reg_lm, "HC1"))
reg_lm_r
```

Second, we estimate the model with fixed effects using the `plm()` function for estimating linear model for panel data. The first entry of the `plm()` is a formula. `index` enables the estimation functions to identify the structure of the data, i.e., the individual and the time period for each observation. `model` indicates the kind of model to be estimated: `within` for fixed effects and `random` for random effects.[3]

Note that to reproduce robust standard errors as in Stata we have to call for another function, `coeftest()` in `lmtest` package and choose the options `type = "sss"` and `cluster = "group"` in `vcov = vcovHC()`.

```
## fixed effects
reg_plm_fe <- plm(limports ~ lgdp_exporter + lgdp_importer +
                    onein + bothin +
                    factor(year),
                  data = gvty_def,
                  index = c("pairid", "year"),
                  model = "within")
summary(reg_plm_fe)
reg_plm_fe_r <- coeftest(reg_plm_fe,
                         vcov = vcovHC(reg_plm_fe,
                                       type = "sss",
                                       cluster = "group"))
reg_plm_fe_r
```

Finally, we estimate a random effects model. Note we change the kind of model to `random`.[4]

```
## random effects
reg_plm_re <- plm(limports ~ lgdp_exporter + lgdp_importer +
                    ldist + colony +
                    contig + comlang_off + onein + bothin +
                    factor(year),
                  data = gvty_def,
                  index = c("pairid", "year"),
                  model = "random")
summary(reg_plm_re)
reg_plm_re_r <- coeftest(reg_plm_re,
                         vcov = vcovHC(reg_plm_re,
                                       type = "sss",
                                       cluster = "group"))
reg_plm_re_r
```

[3] Please note that the effects are introduced in the model by the `plm()` function by setting `effect` = one of `"individual"`, `"time"`, `"twoways"`, or `"nested"`. The approached followed here is to replicate the same R-squared computed by Stata for the fixed effects model.

[4] In random model, we find slightly different results between `plm()` and Stata because they use different procedures. Refer to https://cran.r-project.org/web/packages/plm/vignettes/B_plmFunction.html for more info regarding the estimation with the `plm` function. To get closer results, you may want to use the Swamy-Aurora version of the random effects model in Stata. I took this suggestion from https://rlhick.people.wm.edu/stories/econ_407_notes_panel_companion.html.

4.3 Exporting Regression Output

Finally, we may want to export our results. We can accomplish this task with the `stargazer` package.

First, note that we stored all the regression in objects. The first entries of `stargazer()` are one or more model objects (for regression analysis tables) or data frames/vectors/matrices (for summary statistics, or direct output of content). `type` = specifies what type of output the command should produce. The possible values are `latex`, (default) for LaTeX code, `html` for HTML/CSS code, `text` for ASCII text output. `title` = is a character vector with titles for the tables. `digits` = indicates how many decimal places should be used. `column.labels` =, `dep.var.labels` =, and `covariate.labels` = indicate the labels for columns, dependent variable, and independent variables, respectively. `omit` = specifies which of the explanatory variables should be omitted from presentation in the table. For `se` = and `p` = refer to the code to generate Table 3.1. `add.lines` = is a list of vectors (one vector per line) containing additional lines to be included in the table. Each element of the listed vectors will be put into a separate column. `keep.stat` = specifies which of the statistics should be printed. `out` = contains the path of output files. Depending on the file extension (.tex, .txt, .htm or .html), either a LaTeX/HTML source file or an ASCII text output file will be produced (see Table 4.1 for the output).

```
## Step 8: export results ----
stargazer(reg_lm, reg_plm_fe, reg_plm_re,
          type = "latex",
          title ="Regression output with Stargazer",
          digits = 4,
          column.labels = c("OLS", "FE", "RE"),
          dep.var.labels = "Log of imports value",
          covariate.labels = c("log of exporter's GDP",
                               "log of importer's GDP",
                               "log of distance",
                               "1 for pairs ever in colonial relationship",
                               "1 for contiguity",
                               "1 for common official language",
                               "one of the country pair is member of the WTO",
                               "both countries is member of the WTO"),
          omit = c("factor"),
          se = list(reg_lm_r[, 2], reg_plm_fe_r[, 2], reg_plm_re_r[, 2]),
          p = list(reg_lm_r[, 4], reg_plm_fe_r[, 4], reg_plm_re_r[, 4]),
          add.lines = list(c("Year FE", "YES", "YES", "YES"),
                           c("Country FE", "YES", "NO", "NO")),
          keep.stat = c("n", "rsq", "adj.rsq"),
          out = "regression.tex")
```

Table 4.1 Regression output with Stargazer

	Dependent variable:		
	Log of imports value		
	OLS	*panel linear*	
	OLS	FE	RE
	(1)	(2)	(3)
log of exporter's GDP	0.3290***	0.3450***	1.0046***
	(0.0216)	(0.0237)	(0.0050)
log of importer's GDP	0.5966***	0.6860***	0.8386***
	(0.0201)	(0.0211)	(0.0052)
log of distance	−1.5007***		−1.1940***
	(0.0060)		(0.0157)
1 for pairs ever in colonial relationship	1.0812***		1.5722***
	(0.0258)		(0.0854)
1 for contiguity	0.6540***		1.0844***
	(0.0291)		(0.0934)
1 for common official language	0.8206***		0.8893***
	(0.0130)		(0.0335)
one of the country pair is member of the WTO	−0.2772***	0.0574	−0.0092
	(0.0264)	(0.0421)	(0.0365)
both countries is member of the WTO	−0.0589	0.1462***	0.1055***
	(0.0359)	(0.0456)	(0.0383)
Constant	−5.1910***		−26.7828***
	(0.6323)		(0.2398)
Year FE	YES	YES	YES
Country FE	YES	NO	NO
Observations	291,859	291,859	291,859
R^2	0.7194	0.0681	0.1554
Adjusted R^2	0.7191	−0.0352	0.1553
Note:	*p<0.1; **p<0.05; ***p<0.01		

Appendix A
Interactive Dashboard with R Shiny

In this appendix, we create a simple **R Shiny** interactive dashboard to allow the reader to interact with the results of the tariff analysis from Sect. 3.1.

The code to build an interactive dashboard in **R Shiny** has some peculiarities that make it different from the code we have written until now. Here, we will cover the essential elements to build our dashboard. The reader is referred to the following resources to learn more about **R Shiny**:

- Shiny, Shiny Tutorial, https://shiny.rstudio.com/tutorial/written-tutorial/lesson1/
- *Mastering Shiny* (Wickham, 2021) that is also made free available online at the following address: https://mastering-shiny.org/index.html

Let's start!

First, we need to open and save the `app.R` file where we code our dashboard. Refer to Fig. A.1 to open the file and to Fig. A.2 to save it. Save it as `08b_tariff_statistics_2edn`. This will generate a folder with that name that will contain the `app.R` file. Copy the `TPP` data set we used in Sect. 3.1 in this folder (Fig. A.3)

The beginning of the file starts by loading the packages we need to run our code with the `library()` function. We need the same packages we used in Sect. 3.1 with the addition of `shiny`.

Then, we import the `TPP` data set with the `read_dta()` function and convert `sector` and `year` in factors. We convert `sector` and `year` in factors because we will make a slight modification to the plot.

From now on, the code starts to differ from the code we are used to. First, we need to understand the structure of the **R Shiny** app.

The file to build the app is structured in three parts:

1. definition of user interface for application, `ui`
2. definition of the server logic, `server`
3. run of the application, `shinyApp()`

© The Author(s), under exclusive license to Springer Nature Switzerland AG 2023

M. Porto, *Using R for Trade Policy Analysis*,
https://doi.org/10.1007/978-3-031-35044-3

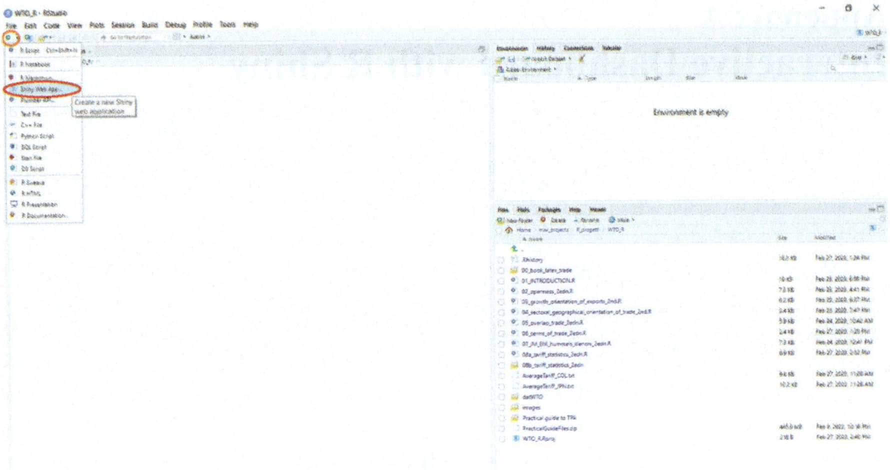

Fig. A.1 Create a new Shiny web dashboard (1)

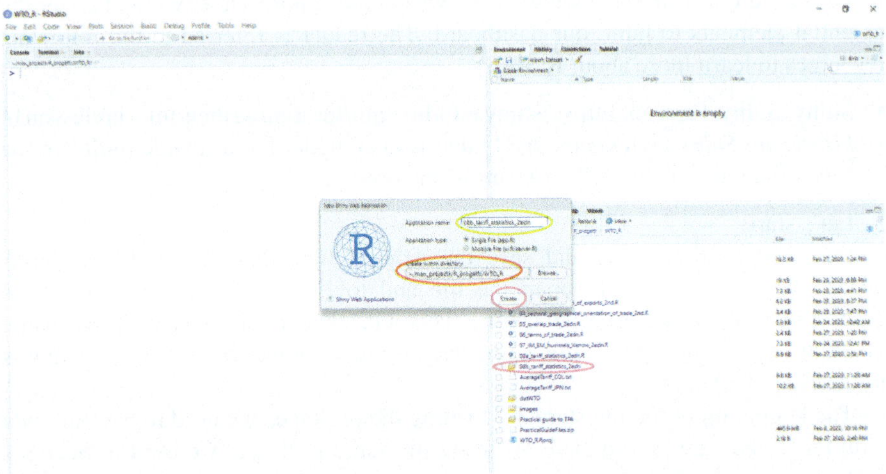

Fig. A.2 Create a new Shiny web dashboard (2)

A.1 User Interface

We create the page layout with `fluidPage()`. The horizontal space is divided in 12-unit wide grid. We will return to this number shortly. All the remaining code for the user interface will be inside `fluidPage()`.

The first line of code is `shinyFeedback::useShinyFeedback()`. We need this line of code to give feedback to the users of our dashboard. Since it is a two step process, we will cover it in Sect. A.2.

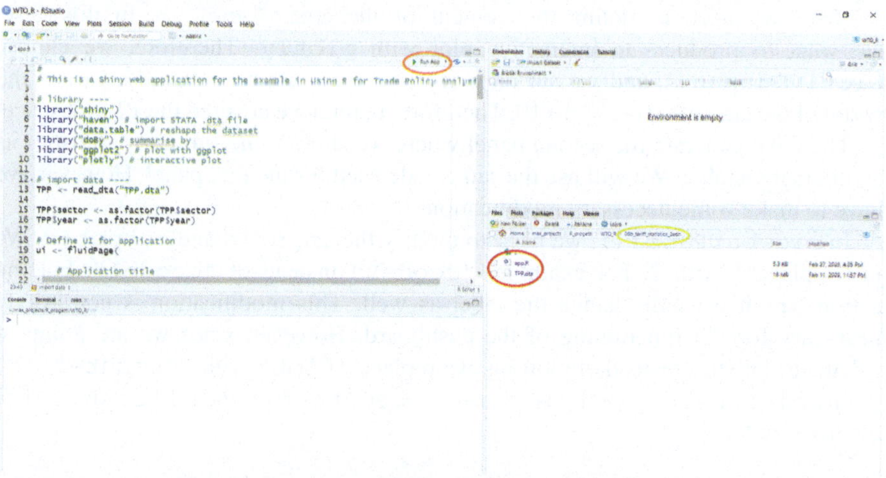

Fig. A.3 Create a new Shiny web dashboard (3)

We create a panel containing the application title with `titlePanel()`. Below we write additional information about our app by using `h3()` and `p()`.

Our dashboard will have two viewable sections. One will show the plot as output and the other one will show a table with tariff statistics. We generate multiple viewable sections with `tabsetPanel()`. The first panel is built with `tabPanel()`. We set a title for it `"Data visualization"` and then we organize it in two panels: a `sidebarLayout()` and a `mainPanel()`.

In `sidebarLayout()` we create the input controls to control for the output. `selectInput()` creates a select list that can be used to choose a single or multiple items from a list of values. In our case, we create the list from the unique values of `ccode` in `TPP` and we do not allow for multiple selections (`multiple = FALSE`, default value), and we set the width to 100%. The first two entries are the `inputId` and the `label`. The `inputId` needs to be unique. We set it as `"ccode1"`. The `label` is the label that will describe the input control. We choose `"Select country: "`.

We also create two buttons. The first button is an action button, `actionButton()`. Again, the first entry is the `inputId` and the second entry is the `label`. We set `"button1"` as `inputId` and `"Plot"` as label. We also choose a CSS `class` to apply to the tag for the button. Briefly, this is the button that the user will have to push to generate the plot in the dashboard.

The second button is a `downloadButton()`. By pushing this button, the user can download on her/his computer the data used for the plot. We just set the `outputId` as `"download1"`. We keep the default value for the `label` that is `"Download"`.

Finally, we set the width of the `sidebarLayout()` to 2.

Next, we need to define the content of the `mainPanel()`. In this case, we want to produce an interactive plot with `plotly`. Therefore, we choose `plotlyOutput()` and we set its `outputId` as `"Plot"`. Finally, we set the width of the `mainPanel()` to 10. Therefore, in total we covered the 12-unit space.

Then, we generate the second panel where we show some summary statistics as an interactive table. We will use the same code used for the first panel. However, we have to make some necessary modifications.

In `sidebarPanel()`, we need to modify the `inputId` and `outputId`. We just replace 1 with 2. For example, `"ccode2"` instead of `"ccode1"`. For the action button we will change the label as well. This modification is not strictly necessary for the functioning of the dashboard. However, since we are going to calculate statistics instead of plotting, we replace `"Plot"` with `"Compute"`.

In `mainPanel()`, we choose `dataTableOutput()` and set `"statistics"` as `outputId`.

A.2 Server Logic

In Sect. A.1, we set up the user interface. Next step consists in defining the underlying logic to make our dashboard work. We write the `server` as a function of two inputs `function(input, output)`. If now we jumped directly to Sect. A.3 and run the app, we would create the dashboard. However, if we pushed the buttons nothing would happen. Because the app does not know what to do. Therefore, we write the steps the app needs to implement inside the function.

First, we need to prepare the data for the plot and generate the plot with `ggplot()`. In `temp1`, first we subset the data set `TPP`, then we reshape it and finally we pass it to `ggplot()` to make the plot. In this plot, we also group by `sector`. Note three key elements:

- `eventReactive()`: in this case the subset is triggered when the user click the button. Note that the first argument of `eventReactive()` is the id that we set for the button that we call with `input$button1`;
- `req()`: ensure that the values are available. In this case, we make sure that the user selected a country (`input$ccode1`) to plot;
- in the `subset()` function, the country to subset for is associated with `input$ccode1`. That is, the user will select the name of the country among the options provided by `unique(TPP$ccode)` and by clicking the action button will trigger the subset. We also use `input$ccode1` for the title of the plot in `ggtitle()`

Another key aspect of the code in **R Shiny** is that `temp1`, that has been generated with `eventReactive()`, is treated as a function. In fact, it is passed to `ggplotly()` as `temp1()`. The interactive plot with `ggplotly()` is rendered by `renderPlotly()`. This is our output in the first panel and it is assigned to `output$Plot` because `Plot` is the id that we chose in `plotlyOutput()` in `mainPanel()` defined in the user interface.

Another output of the first panel is generated by the download button. In `output$download1`, with `downloadHandler()` we return a csv file, that takes the name of the selected country, containing the data used to plot. Note that in `write.csv()` we retrieve the data set from the `ggplot2` object `temp1()`.

Next, we move to define the output for the second panel. Here we have an interactive table that is rendered by `renderDataTable()` and a csv file to download containing the summary statistics showed in the table.

Finally, let's discuss about `shinyFeedback`. When a user uses an app, some commands or requests may cause the app to crash. In our case, for example, the main problem is related to the subset of the data set to produce the plot in the first panel because the conditions for subsetting can not be hold true for all countries. This implies that a data set with no rows could be returned. If this is the case, the plot will fail and the error message from the console pane will be printed.

There are two issues related to it:

1. the printed error message does not explain what the issue is to the user. Therefore, we want to generate our own message to communicate what the problem is with the selection of the user;
2. the crash of the app is not aesthetically pleasing. Consequently, if the error is generated, we want to prevent the app from updating and printing the error message from the console pane.

For these tasks we use the functions from the `shinyFeedback` package. As we said, this is two step process. First, we add `useShinyFeedback` to the `ui` to set up "the needed HTML and JavaScript for attractive error message display" (Wickham, 2021). Second, in the `server()` function we add `feedbackWarning()`. The first argument is the `inputId` that takes the same id of the input where the feedback should be placed. In our case, `"ccode1"`. The second argument is the condition to be checked. In our case that number of rows of the subsetted data set is zero. The third argument is the message we want to print in case of error. In our case, `"No subset data for this country"`. The fourth argument sets the color of the message as red. We can also omit because the color has a default value.

With these modifications we took care of the issue 1, i.e. we generate our error message to communicate the issue to the user. However, only with these modifications the app will continue to work and definitely crash, i.e. it will not produce the plot but it will print the error message from the console pane. To prevent the app from running after we identified the cause of error, we add another `req()`. This time the condition is that the number of rows of the data set is greater than zero. In other words, if the data set after being subsetted has no rows the app has to stop running.

A.3 Run the Application

Now we are ready to run the app with `shinyApp()` where the two arguments are `ui` and `server`. We can run it as shown in Fig. A.3 or by using the keyboard shortcut **CTRL + SHIFT + ENTER** on Windows (**CMD + SHIFT + ENTER** on Mac). Figures A.4, A.5, and A.6 show the output of our dashboard.

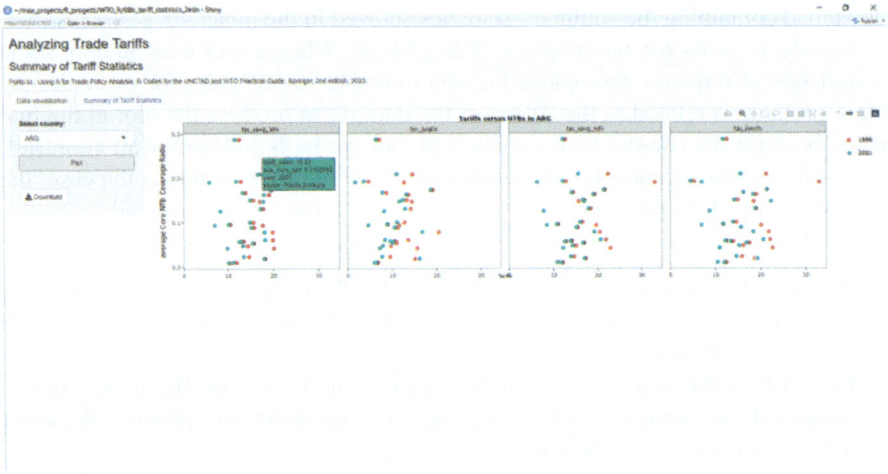

Fig. A.4 Our R Shiny dashboard—panel 1

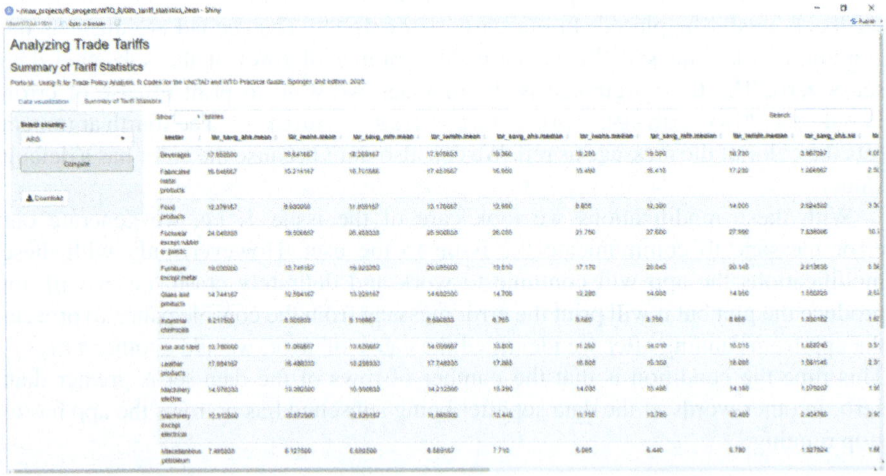

Fig. A.5 Our R Shiny dashboard—panel 2

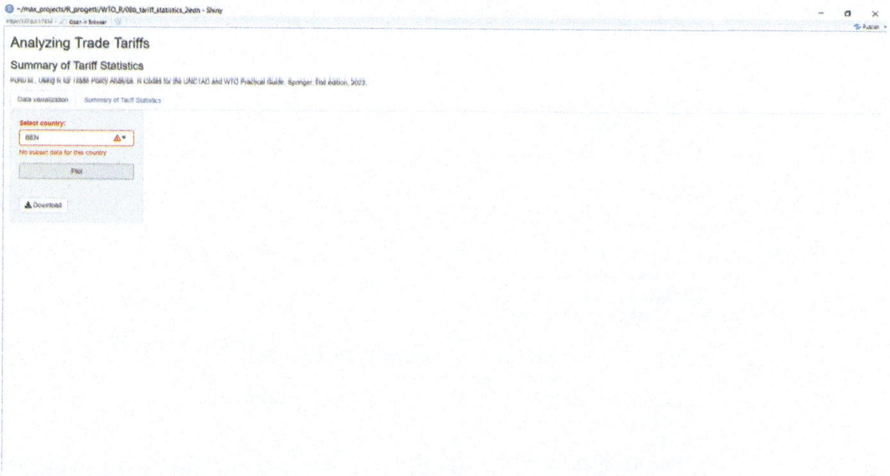

Fig. A.6 Our R Shiny dashboard—error message

```
# library ----
library("shiny")
library("haven") # import STATA .dta file
library("data.table") # reshape the data set
library("dplyr") # combine operations
library("doBy") # summarise by
library("ggplot2") # plot with ggplot
library("plotly") # interactive plot

# import data ----
TPP <- read_dta("TPP.dta")

TPP$sector <- as.factor(TPP$sector)
TPP$year <- as.factor(TPP$year)

# Define UI for application
ui <- fluidPage(

  shinyFeedback::useShinyFeedback(),

  # Application title
  titlePanel("Analyzing Trade Tariffs"),
  h3("Summary of Tariff Statistics"),
  p("Porto M., Using R for Trade Policy Analysis.
      R Codes for the UNCTAD and WTO Practical Guide,
      Springer, 2nd edition, 2023."),

  # Panels
  tabsetPanel(# Panel 1
    tabPanel("Data visualization",
             sidebarLayout(
               sidebarPanel(
                 selectInput("ccode1",
                             "Select country:",
                             choices =  unique(TPP$ccode),
                             width = "100%"),
                 actionButton("button1", "Plot", class = "btn-block"),
                 br(),
                 br(),
```

```
              downloadButton("download1"),
              width = 2
            ),

            mainPanel(
              plotlyOutput("Plot"),
              width = 10
            )
          )
  ),
  # Panel 2
  tabPanel("Summary of Tariff Statistics",
           sidebarLayout(
             sidebarPanel(
               selectInput("ccode2",
                           "Select country:",
                           choices =  unique(TPP$ccode),
                           width = "100%"),
               actionButton("button2", "Compute", class = "btn-block"),
               br(),
               br(),
               downloadButton("download2"),
               width = 2
             ),

             mainPanel(
               dataTableOutput("statistics"),
               width = 10
             )
           ))
 )
)

# Define server logic
server <- function(input, output) {

  # plot
  temp1 <- eventReactive(input$button1, {
    req(input$ccode1)

    TPP_s <- TPP %>%
      filter(ccode == input$ccode1 & ave_core_sim > 0 & tar_savg_ahs > 0) %>%
      filter(ccode == input$ccode1 & ave_core_sim > 0 & tar_iwahs > 0) %>%
      filter(ccode == input$ccode1 & ave_core_sim > 0 & tar_savg_mfn > 0) %>%
      filter(ccode == input$ccode1 & ave_core_sim > 0 & tar_iwmfn > 0)

    # check subset data set
    shinyFeedback::feedbackWarning("ccode1", isTRUE(nrow(TPP_s) == 0),
                                   "No subset data for this country",
                                   color = "red")

    req(nrow(TPP_s) > 0)

    TPP_s_1 <- melt(setDT(TPP_s),
                    id.vars = c("sector", "year", "ave_core_sim"),
                    measure.vars = c("tar_savg_ahs", "tar_iwahs",
                                     "tar_savg_mfn", "tar_iwmfn"),
                    variable.name = "tariff_name",
                    value.name = "tariff_value")


    plot_s <- ggplot(TPP_s_1,
                     aes(x = tariff_value,
                         y = ave_core_sim,
                         colour = year,
                         group = sector)) +
      geom_point(size = 2) +
```

```
      facet_grid(. ~ tariff_name) +
      theme_bw() +
      xlab("Tariffs") + ylab("average Core NTB Coverage Ratio") +
      ggtitle(paste0("Tariffs versus NTBs in ", input$ccode1)) +
      theme(plot.title = element_text(hjust = 0.5,
                                      size = 10, face="bold"),
            axis.title.x = element_text(size = 7.5)) +
      theme(legend.title = element_blank())


  })


  output$Plot <- renderPlotly({
    ggplotly(temp1())
  })

  # download
  output$download1 <- downloadHandler(
    filename = function() {
      paste0(input$ccode1, ".csv") # create the name of the file
    },
    content = function(file) {
      write.csv(temp1()$data, file,
                row.names = FALSE)
    }
  )

  # table
  temp2 <- eventReactive(input$button2, {
    req(input$ccode2)

    TPP_s2 <- subset(TPP, ccode == input$ccode2)

    tar <- summaryBy(tar_savg_ahs + tar_iwahs +
                       tar_savg_mfn + tar_iwmfn ~ sector,
                     TPP_s2, na.rm = T,
                     FUN=c(mean, median, sd, min, max))


  })


  output$statistics <- renderDataTable(
    temp2(), options = list(pageLength = 16)
  )

  # download
  output$download2 <- downloadHandler(
    filename = function() {
      paste0(input$ccode2, "_tariff_statistics.csv")
    },
    content = function(file) {
      write.csv(temp2(), file,
                row.names = FALSE)
    }
  )

}

# Run the application
shinyApp(ui = ui, server = server)
```

Now we have created the dashboard but this is only available on our computer. When we build a dashboard with **R Shiny** in most cases it is because we want to share it. I will not cover how to deploy the app. You can refer to "Lesson 7" of the Shiny Tutorial I indicated at the beginning of this section to learn several ways to share your app that may meet your needs.

In my case, I use `shinyapps.io`, **RStudio**'s hosting service for **Shiny** apps. You can visit the dashboard we created at the following address:

https://mporto.shinyapps.io/example_using_r_trade_policy/

For an example of a more elaborated dashboard that uses the same framework, you may visit

https://mporto.shinyapps.io/japanese-affiliates-italy

that is an interactive dashboard I built to narrate the evolution of the network of Japanese affiliates in Italy.

Appendix B
Additional Code for Chap. 4: Conditional Replacement with Nested Loop

In Chap. 4, we built a database to estimate a gravity model by following the approach shown in the the Stata do file BuildingDatabaseApproach.do.

At Step 6 in that file, the author mentions a limitation in computing country-time dummies for Stata/IC users, since they will not be able to increase the number of variables to create all the dummies. To address this issue, the author proposes three solutions. Here, I am interested in the solution number 2 that consists in computing country-period dummies.

To accomplish this task, the author use a conditional replacement with a nested for loop. I think it is a good exercise for us because this is a kind of code that we did not implement in the book. Additionally, I think the code may be useful in other cases.

Therefore, in this section we implement that part of code that leads us to generate country-period id.

The main part of the code consists in a nested loop generate with `for()` and a conditional replacement inside the inner loop.

First, we subset `df`, that we created at the end of Step 6 in Sect. 4.1, if `year > 1995`. We assign this operation to `dfs`. Then, we initialize a column `time` in `dfs`. Before setting the loop, we generate `step` that defines the steps of the sequence in the loop. We set equal to 3. It corresponds to the number of years for a period. Additionally, we coerce the tibble data frame to a data frame with `as.data.frame()`.

Second, we implement the nested `for()` loop. We have an external loop and an internal loop. In the external loop, the loop runs over a sequence from the minimum year to the maximum year in the data frame. The increment of the sequence is controlled by `by =`. In this case the increment corresponds to the number stored in `step`. Then we have the internal loop that runs over a sequence from 0 to the number stored in `step`.

© The Author(s), under exclusive license to Springer Nature Switzerland AG 2023
M. Porto, *Using R for Trade Policy Analysis*,
https://doi.org/10.1007/978-3-031-35044-3

Third, we write the conditional statement inside the loop. That is, if `year` is equal to the sum of `i` and `j`, we replace the value that currently is `NA` with that of the formula.

```
## subset the dataset if year > 1995

dfs <- subset(df, year > 1995)
View(dfs)

# initialize column
dfs$time <- NA

# conditional replacement with for loop
step <- 3

dfs <- as.data.frame(dfs)

for(i in seq(min(dfs$year), max(dfs$year), by = step)){

  for(j in 0:step){

    dfs[dfs$year == (i+j), "time"] <- (i - min(dfs$year))/step

  }

}

head(dfs[, c("year", "time")], 20)
```

Following, I print a section of the output

```
> head(dfs[, c("year", "time")], 20)
   year time
1  1996    0
2  1997    0
3  1998    0
4  1999    1
5  2000    1
6  2001    1
7  2002    2
8  2003    2
9  2004    2
10 2005    3
11 1996    0
12 1997    0
13 1998    0
14 1999    1
15 2000    1
16 2001    1
17 2002    2
18 2003    2
19 2004    2
20 2005    3
```

Finally, we generate the country-period id.

```
dfs <- dfs %>%
  group_by(exporter, time) %>%
  mutate(exportertime = cur_group_id())

dfs <- dfs %>%
  group_by(importer, time) %>%
  mutate(importertime = cur_group_id())
```

Bibliography

Anderson, J. (1979). A theoretical foundation for the gravity equation. *The American Economic Review, 69*(1), 106–116.

Anderson, J. E., & Van Wincoop, E. (2003). Gravity with gravitas: A solution to the border puzzle. *American Economic Review, 93*(1), 170–192.

Baier, S. L., & Bergstrand, J. H. (2007). Do free trade agreements actually increase members' international trade? *Journal of International Economics, 71*(1), 72–95.

Bergstrand, J. H. (1989). The generalized gravity equation, monopolistic competition, and the factor-proportions theory in international trade. *The Review of Economics and Statistics, 71*(1), 143–153.

Blair, G., Cooper, J., Coppock, A., Humphreys, M., & Sonnet, L. (2021). *estimatr: Fast estimators for design-based inference*. R package version 0.30.4. https://CRAN.R-project.org/package=estimatr.

Burns, P. (2012). *The R Inferno*. https://www.burns-stat.com/documents/books/the-r-inferno/. ISBN 9781471046520

Chang, W., Cheng, J., Allaire, J., Sievert, C., Schloerke, B., Xie, Y., Allen, J., McPherson, J., Dipert, A., & Borges, B. (2021). *shiny: Web application framework for R*. R package version 1.6.0. https://CRAN.R-project.org/package=shiny.

Cheng, I.-H., & Wall, H. J. (2005). Controlling for heterogeneity in gravity models of trade and integration. *Federal Reserve Bank of St. Louis Review, 87*(1), 49–63.

Croissant, Y., & Millo, G. (2008). Panel data econometrics in R: The plm package. *Journal of Statistical Software, 27*(2). http://www.jstatsoft.org/v27/i02/.

Dowle, M., & Srinivasan, A. (2017). *data.table: Extension of 'data.frame'*. R package version 1.10.4. https://CRAN.R-project.org/package=data.table.

Eaton, J., & Kortum, S. (2002). Technology, geography, and trade. *Econometrica, 70*(5), 1741–1779.

Fugazza, M., & Nicita, A. (2011). On the importance of market access for trade. *United Nations Conference on Trade and Development (UNCTAD)*. Blue series (No. 51).

Gagolewski, M. (2020). *R package stringi: Character string processing facilities*. http://www.gagolewski.com/software/stringi/.

Georgakopoulos, H. (2015). *Quantitative trading with R*. Palgrave Macmillan.

Grossman, G. (2016). The purpose of trade agreements. In K. Bagwell, & R. Staiger (Eds.), Handbook of Commercial Policy (Chap. 7, pp. 379–434). North-Holland.

Harrell, F. E., Jr., with contributions from Charles Dupont & many others. (2021). *Hmisc: Harrell Miscellaneous*. R package version 4.5-0. https://CRAN.R-project.org/package=Hmisc.

© The Author(s), under exclusive license to Springer Nature Switzerland AG 2023

M. Porto, *Using R for Trade Policy Analysis*,
https://doi.org/10.1007/978-3-031-35044-3

Helpman, E. (1987). Imperfect competition and international trade: Evidence from fourteen industrial countries. *Journal of the Japanese and International Economies, 1*(1), 62–81.

Højsgaard, S., & Halekoh, U. (2023). *doBy: Groupwise statistics, LSmeans, linear estimates, utilities*. R package version 4.6.16. https://CRAN.R-project.org/package=doBy.

Hlavac, M. (2018). *Stargazer: Well-formatted regression and summary statistics tables*. Central European Labour Studies Institute (CELSI), Bratislava, Slovakia. R package version 5.2.2. https://CRAN.R-project.org/package=stargazer.

Kassambara, A. (2019). *ggpubr: 'ggplot2' based publication ready plots*. R package version 0.2.1. https://CRAN.R-project.org/package=ggpubr.

Merlino, A., & Howard, P. (2021). *shinyFeedback: Display user feedback in shiny apps*. R package version 0.4.0. https://CRAN.R-project.org/package=shinyFeedback.

Monahan, J. F. (2011). *Numerical methods of statistics*. Cambridge University Press.

Ooms, J. (2018). *gifski: Highest quality GIF encoder*. R package version 0.8.6. https://CRAN.R-project.org/package=gifski.

Pedersen, T. L., & Robinson, D. (2020). *gganimate: A grammar of animated graphics*. R package version 1.0.5. https://CRAN.R-project.org/package=gganimate.

Piermartini, R. & Yotov, Y. V. (2016), Estimating trade policy effects with structural gravity. *WTO Staff Working Paper, No. ERSD-2016-10* .

Porto, M. (2022). *Introduction to mathematics for economics with R*. Springer Nature.

R Core Team. (2020). *R: A language and environment for statistical computing*. R Foundation for Statistical Computing, Vienna, Austria. https://www.R-project.org/.

RStudio Team. (2020). *RStudio: Integrated development environment for R*. RStudio, PBC, Boston, MA. http://www.rstudio.com/.

Santos, S., & Tenreyro, S. (2006). The log of gravity. *The Review of Economics and Statistics, 88*(4), 641–658.

Santos Silva, J. M., & Tenreyro, S. (2011). Further simulation evidence on the performance of the Poisson pseudo-maximum likelihood estimator. *Economics Letters, 112*(2), 220–222. http://dx.doi.org/10.1016/j.econlet.2011.05.008.

Shepherd, B., Doytchinova, H., & Kravchenko, A. (2019). The gravity model of international trade: A user guide [R version].

Sievert, C. (2020). *Interactive web-based data visualization with R, plotly, and shiny*. Chapman and Hall/CRC. https://plotly-r.com.

Terry, M. T., & Patricia, M. G. (2000). *Modeling survival data: Extending the cox model*. Springer.

UNCTAD, & WTO. (2012). *A practical guide to trade policy analysis*. Geneva.

Urbanek, S. (2013). *png: Read and write PNG images*. R package version 0.1-7. https://CRAN.R-project.org/package=png.

Wickham, H. (2009). *ggplot2: Elegant graphics for data analysis*. Springer-Verlag. http://ggplot2.org.

Wickham, H. (2018). *scales: Scale functions for visualization*. R package version 1.0.0. https://CRAN.R-project.org/package=scales.

Wickham, H. (2019a). *Advanced R*. The R Series (2nd ed.). CRC Press/Taylor & Francis Group.

Wickham, H. (2019b). *stringr: Simple, consistent wrappers for common string operations*. R package version 1.4.0. https://CRAN.R-project.org/package=stringr.

Wickham, H. (2021). *Mastering shiny*. O'Reilly Media.

Wickham, H., & Henry, L. (2019). *tidyr: Easily tidy data with 'spread()' and 'gather()' functions*. R package version 0.8.3. https://CRAN.R-project.org/package=tidyr.

Wickham, H., & Miller, E. (2020). *haven: Import and export 'SPSS', 'Stata' and 'SAS' files*. R package version 2.3.1. https://CRAN.R-project.org/package=haven.

Wickham, H., François, R., Henry, L., & Müller, K. (2019). *dplyr: A grammar of data manipulation*. R package version 0.8.3. https://CRAN.R-project.org/package=dplyr.

Woelwer, A.-L., & Burgard, J. P. (2017). *gravity: Estimation methods for gravity models*. R package version 0.6. https://CRAN.R-project.org/package=gravity.

Wooldridge, J. M. (2012). *Introductory econometrics: A modern approach* (5th ed.). South-Western.

Zeileis, A. (2004). Econometric computing with HC and HAC covariance matrix estimators. *Journal of Statistical Software*, *11*(10), 1–17. http://www.jstatsoft.org/v11/i10/.

Zeileis, A., & Grothendieck, G. (2005). zoo: S3 infrastructure for regular and irregular time series. *Journal of Statistical Software*, *14*(6), 1–27.

Zeileis, A., & Hothorn, T. (2002). Diagnostic checking in regression relationships. *R News*, *2*(3), 7–10. https://CRAN.R-project.org/doc/Rnews/.

Index

© The Editor(s) (if applicable) and The Author(s), under exclusive license to Springer Nature Switzerland AG 2023
M. Porto, *Using R for Trade Policy Analysis*,
https://doi.org/10.1007/978-3-031-35044-3

The manufacturer's authorised representative in the EU is Springer Nature Customer Service Centre GmbH, Europaplatz 3, 69115 Heidelberg, Germany. If you have any concerns regarding our products, please contact ProductSafety@springernature.com

Printed and bound by CPI Group (UK) Ltd, Croydon, CR0 4YY
01/10/2026
02225875-0015